THE NEW GILDED AGE

THE NEW GILDED AGE

The Critical Inequality Debates of Our Time

Edited by David B. Grusky and Tamar Kricheli-Katz

STANFORD UNIVERSITY PRESS
STANFORD, CALIFORNIA

Stanford University Press
Stanford, California

Printed in the United States of America on acid-free,
archival-quality paper

Library of Congress Cataloging-in-Publication Data

The new gilded age : the critical inequality debates of our
time / edited by David B. Grusky and Tamar Kricheli-Katz.
        pages cm
    Includes bibliographical references and index.
    ISBN 978-0-8047-5935-9 (alk. paper) —
    ISBN 978-0-8047-5936-6 (pbk. : alk. paper)
    1. Equality—United States.   2. Poverty—United States.
3. Discrimination—United States.   4. Equality.   5. Poverty.
I. Grusky, David B., editor of compilation.   II. Kricheli-Katz,
Tamar, editor of compilation.
HN90.S6N447 2012
3050973—dc23
                                                  2011040726

Typeset by Newgen in 10/14 Sabon

To Michelle Jackson

CONTENTS

THE NEW GILDED AGE

Introduction

Poverty and Inequality in a New World

David B. Grusky and Tamar Kricheli-Katz

The idea that inequality is a major social problem in the United States was once a small-niche belief limited to hard-core leftists, socialists, and Marxists. There was much hand-wringing within this crowd about the false consciousness (to use an old term!) of the general public: Why, it was asked, is the U.S. public so tolerant, even unaware, of the spectacular takeoff in income inequality, a takeoff that's generated levels of inequality approaching those of the First Gilded Age? When, just when, would the middle-class voter come to her or his senses, recognize the takeoff for what it is, and stop backing the political party that was causing it?

David B. Grusky is a professor of sociology at Stanford University, director of the Stanford Center on Poverty and Inequality, coeditor of *Pathways Magazine*, and coeditor of the Stanford University Press Social Inequality Series. He is a fellow of the American Association for the Advancement of Science, recipient of the 2004 Max Weber Award, founder of the Cornell University Center for the Study of Inequality, and a former Presidential Young Investigator. His recent and forthcoming books are *Social Stratification* (with Manwai C. Ku and Szonja Szelényi), *Poverty and Inequality* (with Ravi Kanbur), *Mobility and Inequality* (with Stephen Morgan and Gary Fields), *Occupational Ghettos* (with Maria Charles), *The Declining Significance of Gender?* (with Francine Blau and Mary Brinton), *Inequality: Classic Readings in Race, Class, and Gender* (with Szonja Szelényi), *The Inequality Reader* (with Szonja Szelényi), *The Inequality Puzzle* (with Roland Berger, Tobias Raffel, Geoffrey Samuels, and Christopher Wimer), and *The Great Recession* (with Bruce Western and Christopher Wimer).

Tamar Kricheli-Katz is a doctoral candidate in the Department of Sociology at Stanford University and a JSD candidate at Stanford Law School. Her research explores the relationships among choice, responsibility, moral judgment, and discrimination.

But that was then. We now live in a new world in which the public increasingly knows about the takeoff and is questioning whether extreme inequality can be justified by simply assuming, as Americans once did, that those at the top are distinguished by their unusually hard work, talent, and marginal product. There is instead growing sentiment that poverty and inequality are major social problems that may be generated as much from corruption and other market imperfections as more narrowly competitive forces. The percentage of Americans who now agree that it's the government's responsibility to "reduce income differences between the rich and poor" stands at 52 percent (up from 39 percent in 1985), while the percentage who agree that "large differences in income are necessary for America's prosperity" has fallen to 24 percent (as compared to 34 percent in 1987).[1] We're just not buying anymore the conventional liberal story that our particular constellation of quasi-market institutions will, when left to their own devices, automatically bring about affluence, let alone increasingly diffused affluence.

What accounts for the sea change? The sources of such radicalization haven't yet been definitively teased out,[2] but it's not likely the result of some gradual diffusion and dissemination of information about the takeoff. The main cause may instead be recent highly publicized news events (e.g., the financial crisis, the Great Recession, Hurricane Katrina) that have exposed troubling inequalities and fed the presumption that we should care about them. The effect of any one of these events might have been quite minor or transitory,[3] yet the rare confluence of so many system-challenging events seems to have worn down our commitment to the conventional liberal justification of inequality. The backbreaking event in this regard may well prove to be the ongoing economic crisis. This crisis registers in a very direct way: indeed, instead of merely reading or hearing *stories* on the news about the experiences of others, a large proportion of Americans have been directly affected through unemployment, the loss of a house, and declining retirement accounts or housing values.[4] Although the recession's effects on public opinion haven't as yet been profound,[5] they may become so insofar as the labor and housing markets fail to recover in the coming years or insofar as Occupy Wall Street continues to develop and grow.

The key assumption behind this conjecture—and indeed it's just that— is that the financial crisis and subsequent recession will make some people less willing to justify inequality as the outcome of hard work and talent. This very American justification might be undermined in two ways. First and most obviously, insofar as a great many talented and hardworking workers remain unemployed or underemployed during a prolonged recession, it becomes more difficult for them (and perhaps others) to embrace the simple premise that hard work and talent straightforwardly make for success. Second, such widespread duress at the bottom of the class structure, in itself challenging to a conventional legitimation of inequality, has developed in the context of highly public revelations that at least some top executives have reaped extraordinary riches despite their firm's poor performance. The common view that merit earns rewards may therefore come under challenge in light of concerns that neither the unemployed poor nor amply compensated rich fully deserve their fate.

We are, then, in the midst of a historic moment in which many forces have come together and have quite suddenly raised the prominence of debates about poverty and inequality. If the long view of history is taken, issues of inequality appear to have regularly cycled in and out of fashion, with the last period of high concern occurring in the 1960s and 1970s and yielding a renewed commitment to civil rights (e.g., voting rights), equal opportunity (e.g., antidiscrimination law), and even equal outcomes (e.g., affirmative action). We're suggesting here that a new period of heightened concern about poverty and inequality appears to be upon us.

The rationale behind this book, therefore, is to bring together leading scholars in such fields as philosophy, sociology, economics, and political science and ask them to develop and prosecute these increasingly prominent debates about inequality in a rigorous yet readable way. If public debate about poverty and inequality is on the rise, that's not to suggest that such debate is always carried out with full access to the relevant empirical evidence or to the sometimes complicated normative issues at stake. We thus hope to enrich the public debates at a time when it becomes increasingly important to do so.

Although the debates presented here take on weighty topics, we have sought to engage with them in a highly readable way and thereby avoid the academic's tendency to wring any bit of interest out of a topic through pedantic or obscure prose. If the typical academic book focuses on topics that only an academic can love, this is hopefully anything but such a book. But how does one present weighty topics in an engaging way? We have settled here on the format of delivering an explicit debate between top scholars on five core questions about the sources, future, or legitimacy of inequality. We will be exploring (a) whether those who are relatively well off should feel a pressing personal obligation to share their wealth with others who are less fortunate, (b) whether economic inequality creates incentives to get ahead and therefore raises total economic output, (c) whether the U.S. takeoff in income inequality was driven by political decisions rather than nonpolitical "market forces," (d) whether the pay gap between women and men may be attributed to discrimination by employers, and (e) whether racial divides will continue to be fundamental in the future. For all five topics, two leading scholars were asked to weigh in, with each being given instructions to focus on the core empirical or normative issues of interest in that debate.

There are, alas, two sins of omission to which we must confess. The careful reader will note, firstly, that most of our selected debates are playing out *within* a given discipline, even though their implications always reach far beyond that particular discipline. Although we could have easily manufactured any number of cross-discipline debates, our objective here was to expose to the wider public such debates as are presently underway. For better or worse, the pressing debates of our time mainly take a within-discipline form, hardly a surprising state of affairs given that contemporary scholarship is, even now, largely practiced within the disciplines. However fashionable interdisciplinarity may be, it would be hard to deny the importance of the within-discipline debates upon which we've focused; and hence our first sin is, we hope, a forgivable one.

The second sin: We have commissioned debates that focus disproportionately but not exclusively on the U.S. case. The characteristic tendency is, of course, to treat poverty and inequality as problems of other countries, especially those of the Southern Hemisphere. The rising engagement with poverty issues in the United States does, in part, take the form of worrying more about poverty in other countries. Although our first debate is relevant to this type of outward-looking worry, most of our debates are more relevant to inward-looking worries about poverty or inequality within the United States and other similarly rich countries. It's precisely the rise of such inward-looking worries that makes the current period so special and hence worthy of our attention. If it's typically a matter of some embarrassment to focus on the United States and other rich countries, in the present case it thus seems especially appropriate to suspend those usual rules.

DO WE HAVE AN OBLIGATION TO ELIMINATE OR REDUCE POVERTY?

The first debate takes on the simple question of whether and under what circumstances rich people should feel obliged to contribute money for the purpose of reducing poverty. Is it, for example, tantamount to murder when we opt to buy a luxury car rather than donate that same money to a relief organization that could then use it to save someone from starvation? Should there be a special obligation to help those in need when they are family or community members? Or is there instead a generic obligation to assist regardless of such special ties? We have asked two leading philosophers, Peter Singer and Richard Miller, to weigh in on these questions.

It bears emphasizing that Singer and Miller agree that U.S. citizens don't engage in nearly enough charitable giving. The debate between them turns not on the importance of ratcheting up giving but on whether we should feel just as obliged to help strangers in other countries as to assist our own family, community, or society members. For Singer, the dying stranger is just as deserving as the dying family member, and we can't shirk our responsibility to assist simply because those in need often live far away. Although Miller argues, by contrast, that it's distinctively human to honor those particularistic relations of family or community, he also recognizes that our responsibilities to strangers, while less profound, are still important enough to trigger substantial charitable giving, certainly far more than we currently practice.

How do students and others exposed to the Singer-Miller debate react to this conclusion? In our own experience, it is not uncommon for students to be shocked and moved, but typically not so shocked and moved as to increase substantially their own giving, a result that leads us to wonder why such a compelling argument doesn't always register at the level of behavior. There is of course much evidence suggesting that in general we don't necessarily act in line with our beliefs. In this particular case, we suspect that inaction is an especially common response because consumption is deeply embedded in our everyday behavior and is not easily shed, even when it's appreciated that it's ethically problematic. Despite the best of intentions, it becomes difficult to honor them given that consumption is organically interwoven into our lives, rendering it more a style of life than some unit act, such as abortion, that could conceivably be surgically removed through ethical argument. The twin forces of the Great Recession and climate change may be calling our high-consumption lifestyle into question, but it remains to be seen whether such forces will bring about purely marginal changes in behavior (e.g., a preference for hybrid cars) rather than more fundamental and revolutionary ones (e.g., forgoing driving altogether).

The deep embedding of consumption in everyday life thus makes it difficult for all of us, even those persuaded by Singer, to scale back our high-consumption lifestyles. It's also problematic, of course, that a pro-charity argument does not resonate well with everyone, as it comes into direct conflict with the cherished principle that our earnings are a reflection of our marginal product and hence justly spent by ourselves (and on ourselves). We believe, in other words, that we are entitled to the money we make because it reflects how much value we create in the economy, a principle that makes us balk whenever we are told that our money should instead be handed over to others. The commitment to this principle is so strong that it allows us to ignore the brute consequences of our actions (e.g., the death of a starving child) and insist instead on our right to spend on ourselves. However persuasive the case for charitable giving may be, one accordingly has to wonder whether it can overcome at once our entrenched high-consumption lifestyle, and our equally entrenched view that our earnings are justly earned and thus properly spent on our own needs.

This is all to suggest that poverty is not likely to be greatly reduced in the near term through some sudden bottom-up recommitment to charity. There are, however, a great many examples of successful top-down antipoverty initiatives, perhaps most obviously the *Bolsa Família* program in Brazil, the *Oportunidades* program in Mexico, and the *New Labour* program in the U.K. (which is now being dismantled). Although a sudden increase in charitable giving doesn't seem likely in the current economic downturn,[6] it's always possible to recast labor market and economic institutions from the top down in ways that lead to a profound reduction in poverty or inequality (e.g., via union law, minimum wage increases, tax policy, incarceration policy). The second debate, to which we now turn, examines our "tastes" for such top-down reforms.

IS THERE A POLITICAL SOLUTION TO RISING INEQUALITY?

It hasn't been adequately appreciated in U.S. politics that a country must *choose* its level of poverty and inequality in just the same way that it chooses its abortion policy, education policy, or gun policy. Rather, the tendency in the United States has been to view poverty and inequality as a natural and inevitable consequence of market forces, almost as if there's only one type of market that then generates some inalterable amount of poverty or inequality. The cross-national record reveals, very much to the contrary, that different types of markets can yield widely varying amounts of poverty and inequality.

We might therefore ask whether the recent run-up in U.S. inequality, which has been spectacular,[7] may be understood as the consequence of political tinkering with tax policy and labor market institutions. The second debate takes on just this question. The two contributors to this debate, John Ferejohn and Jeffrey Manza, agree that political forces are very much behind the run-up, yet they choose to emphasize different types of political forces. For Ferejohn, the run-up must be understood as a distinctively "Republican outcome," as Republicans almost invariably push tax policy that favors the rich, even if such policy is adroitly marketed as across-the-board. Although Manza agrees with Ferejohn that inequality is a Republican outcome, he also points out that it's not very satisfying to simply end the analysis there. Indeed, a complete analysis would have to further explain why Republicans have (until recently) reliably posted electoral victories, especially given that they push policies that would appear to appeal only to narrow (i.e., rich) constituencies. As Manza views it, this electoral success may be attributed not just to unusually savvy campaigns, as is conventionally argued, but also to a host of Republican-advantaging electoral institutions. These institutions include campaign finance laws that allow the rich to provide financial support to their candidates as well as the tendency for the rich to register and vote more frequently than the poor (a difference that is partly generated by high incarceration rates and the disenfranchisement of felons). The complete story behind the run-up therefore requires a twofold argument to the effect that (a) campaign finance law, voter registration law, and other electoral institutions serve the interests of Republicans and thus raise their chances of electoral success (i.e., the Manza argument), and (b) once elected

Republicans will favor tax and employment policy that privileges those at the top of the income distribution (i.e., the Ferejohn argument).

It does not follow, however, that a Democratic president, such as Barack Obama, will instantly change distributional politics in the United States.[8] With tongue partly in cheek, Ferejohn does suggest that those wishing for less inequality need only elect a Democrat, although he additionally appreciates that Democrats have traditionally lacked the spine to put forward a strong and coherent anti-inequality narrative. If we took this caveat seriously, we might conclude that only rarely does that special politician, the one replete with spine, come along and bring about fundamental change. Why, then, are spines in such short supply? The short answer, as Manza points out, is that we live in an institutional and cultural environment that doesn't select for candidates with spines. The very Republican-advantaging institutions that make it difficult for Democrats to be elected make it equally unlikely, whenever a Democrat *is* elected, that she or he will be able to successfully push a serious anti-inequality platform. The upshot is that wide-reaching institutional reforms of the sort that reduced inequality in the Depression period are less likely to be pushed for and adopted now. Although the base probability of some fundamental reform may be unlikely, that's not to gainsay the equally important point that it is probably higher now than it's been for some time, as the success of Occupy Wall Street suggests.

HOW MUCH INEQUALITY DO WE NEED?

We shouldn't conclude that the run-up in inequality is problematic simply because political forces were behind it. Indeed, the overt ideology behind the Republican love affair with inequality is that it incentivizes effort and initiative, thereby increasing total economic output and yielding benefits (in the form of higher income) even among those at the bottom of the income distribution. The famous trade-off thesis thus implies that a taste for equality is exercised at the cost of reducing total output and potentially rendering all worse off. We can't, as Arthur Okun so cleverly put it, "have our cake of market efficiency and share it equally."[9]

The trade-off thesis is treated by ideologues as an article of faith, but it can be rendered testable by simply asking whether groups or societies with higher inequality are indeed more productive. The third debate, which features contributions by Richard Freeman and Jonas Pontusson, approaches the debate from precisely this empirical stance. In Freeman's piece, the trade-off thesis is laid out very clearly, albeit now with the revision that extreme forms of inequality may in fact be counterproductive and serve to reduce output. The relevant thought experiment here is that of the golf tournament in which all prize money is allocated exclusively to the winner. In this winner-take-all setup, the mediocre golfers who have no chance of winning lack any incentive to exert themselves, with the implication that total output in the form of pooled golf strokes will diminish. It follows that we do well to set up more graduated payoff schedules that incentivize participants of all ability levels. There are, in other words, certain forms of extreme inequality (e.g., winner-take-all forms) that don't succeed in creating the incentives that the trade-off thesis presumes.

Although Freeman provides compelling experimental evidence in support of this modified thesis, Pontusson points out that actual cross-national data on inequality and economic growth don't reveal the presumed curvilinear relationship. We don't find that countries with low inequality have low growth, those with medium inequality have high growth, and those with high inequality then revert back to low growth. The results suggest, to the contrary, that the relationship between inequality and growth is weak and follows neither a linear nor curvilinear form. The simple conclusion proffered by Pontusson: The available data cannot support a trade-off thesis either in its original or Freeman-modified version.

It's less difficult than one might think to reconcile this conclusion with that of Freeman. It has to be borne in mind, after all, that those high-redistribution countries that "soak" the rich (e.g., Sweden) are hardly burning the resulting tax receipts. Rather, they use these receipts to undertake other initiatives (e.g., Social Security, health care), and the economic growth that obtains within such countries therefore reflects whatever additional productivity such initiatives may generate. If, for example, the receipts are used to open up educational opportunities for the poor and thereby allow new talent to be discovered, it's altogether possible that the resulting growth swamps any negative incentive effects of the sort featured in a trade-off thesis. The truly compelling test of the thesis requires, then, that we find a country that introduced a progressive tax structure without at the same time undertaking potentially confounding changes in its institutions. Although such a critical test would speak to the net effect of incentives and thus interest academics, there's also pragmatic value in assessing the total effects of progressivity (i.e., the incentive effects combined with the associated institutional investments) insofar as such effects speak to the real trade-offs that countries face. That is, a country considering whether to raise tax rates at the top has to take into account not just the incentive effects of such a change, but also the institutional investments that become possible with the new tax revenues. The decision that in practice must be made is whether these two presumably countervailing forces will, when taken together, work to increase or decrease GNP and other outcomes of interest.

WHY IS THERE A GENDER GAP IN PAY?

The foregoing debates refer in turn to the responsibility of rich individuals to address poverty by ratcheting up their charitable giving, the effects of political forces in generating recent increases in inequality, and the extent to which inequality incentivizes workers and thereby increases effort, initiative, and ultimately total output. The focus in all these debates is thus on the overall amount of inequality rather than which groups tend to benefit most from it. In our final two debates, we turn explicitly to gender and racial gaps in income and other valued goods, a shift in focus that allows us to consider how different groups are faring under the rapid overall growth in inequality.

It is striking in this regard that, despite the recent takeoff in overall inequality, the pay gap between women and men has been growing progressively smaller. Because the earnings distribution has been "stretching out" over the last 30–40 years, the baseline expectation has to be that those who earn less (e.g., women) will, on average, fare poorly relative to those who earn more (e.g., men). The data happily belie this expectation: the ratio of women's earnings to men's earnings (for full-time workers) has in fact increased from .59 in the 1970s to .78 in 2007.[10] It must be concluded that the forces making for gender equality are so profound as to overcome the various generic inequality-increasing forces.

The main question taken on in our fourth debate is whether employer discrimination plays an important role in explaining the wage gap that nonetheless remains even after this historic equalization. Do employers still have a "taste" for hiring men for the best-paying jobs even when female candidates are equally qualified? Or is the residual gap principally explained in terms of the different qualifications and credentials that women and men bring into the labor market? The gender difference in qualifications arises in part because the traditional division of labor has men primarily responsible for earning income and women primarily responsible for homemaking and child care. Moreover, because women anticipate shorter and discontinuous work lives (by virtue of childrearing), their incentive to invest in on-the-job training is less than that of men. It follows that women tend to accumulate less training than men and will accordingly earn less as well. The matter at hand is whether this gender difference in qualifications, which arises out of the traditional division of labor, accounts for rather more of the contemporary wage gap than outright employer discrimination.

Although our two participants in this debate, Solomon Polachek and Francine Blau, agree that both employer discrimination and differential qualifications account for some of the gap, they attach different weights to these two sources, with Blau emphasizing discrimination rather more than Polachek does. As with the last debate, here again it's a matter of weighing the implications of quite complicated statistical analyses, and Polachek and Blau alike are masterful in presenting the evidence that each side must take into account. We won't attempt to review that evidence here. Rather, we would simply stress that such evidence has more than purely academic implications, as it speaks directly to the types of policies that are likely to be successful in reducing the wage gap. Perversely, we might well root for Blau's position that employer discrimination is a prominent source of the residual gap, given that there are quite straightforward policy measures that could successfully take this discrimination on. We might, for example, work to toughen up enforcement of discrimination law, although even here the policy response is complicated by the role that subtle and subconscious forms of employer discrimination may well play.[11]

It's arguably more difficult to take on that portion of the wage gap that is generated by the traditional division of labor and the resulting gender gap in qualifications. We now know that the gender revolution has been a profoundly asymmetric one, a revolution in which females have increasingly moved into the labor force and assumed male-typed jobs, while males have proven reluctant to take on child care and domestic duties or assume female-typed jobs. Moreover, even though the diffusion of egalitarian ideologies might appear to challenge the traditional division of labor, these ideologies require only a purely formal commitment to "equal opportunity" and can readily coexist with the essentialist view that women and men remain fundamentally different, have very distinctive skills and abilities (e.g., the "nurturant" women, the "technical" man), and will therefore avail themselves of formally equal opportunities in very different ways.[12] The persistence of such essentialist views of women and men make it challenging to take on the traditional division of labor (even as the pejorative tag "traditional" suggests some amount of ongoing delegitimation).

THE FUTURE OF RACE AND ETHNICITY

The final debate addresses similar questions about trends in racial and ethnic inequality. As with gender inequality, here again we find dramatic change over the last half century, but at the same time real concern that the forces for change may have stalled or that such changes as have occurred are more shallow than most of us appreciate. By some accounts, we find ourselves poised at a crossroads in which two very plausible futures appear before us, a pessimistic scenario that treats the civil rights revolution as unfulfilled and emphasizes that racism is deeply entrenched, and an optimistic scenario that assumes that racial and ethnic inequalities will continue to erode away, if only very gradually. With the election of Obama, the latter position instantly became more fashionable in some circles, with many commentators even going so far as to suggest that a new "post-racial order" has taken hold. Although the debate between pessimists and optimists is classic and long-standing, the election of Obama makes it especially important to revisit, and we have accordingly selected two scholars who are formidable representatives of these different views on the likely trajectory of change.

The essay by Mary Waters lays out the historic changes underway that serve to blur the boundaries between conventionally recognized racial groups and to reduce the homogeneity of life chances and experiences within these groups. The boundary-blurring effect of intermarriage is prominently featured in her account. In the last thirty years, the proportion of all couples from different races rose from 1 to 5 percent, with smaller groups tending to have higher out-marriage rates than larger ones. The out-marriage rate for American Indians, Asians, blacks, and whites is 57 percent, 16 percent, 7 percent, and 3 percent respectively. As intermarriage becomes more common, a new multiracial population has emerged that often refuses to self-identify in monoracial or monoethnic terms, a development that the census recognized in 2000 by allowing respondents to check more than one race (a choice that approximately 2.4 percent of the population took up). The rise of intermarriage and the resulting growth of the multiracial population mean that boundaries between groups are becoming "more permeable and harder to define" (Waters, p. 241). Moreover, just as the boundaries *between* racial groups are growing more amorphous, one finds new divides based on immigration status emerging *within* them. Most notably, black immigrants often outperform their native counterparts on standard indicators, including schooling or income. This development again renders any conventional racial classification less meaningful in terms of the information about life chances that it conveys.

How does Howard Winant, our other contributor to this debate, respond to such arguments? Although he's well aware of ongoing trends in racial intermarriage and identification, he suggests they bespeak a decline in particular types of racial boundaries rather than some more global decline in our collective tendency to racialize. This tendency to racialize runs deep in U.S. culture. Indeed, even as some racial boundaries are weakened by intermarriage, others are emerging or strengthening in response to perceived cultural, economic, or military threats (e.g., emergent "Islamophobia," emergent antipathy to Chinese-Americans). The extreme racialization of U.S. life is further revealed in the ongoing use of racial profiling, the continuing need to resort to racial politics to win elections, and the well-documented role of racial discrimination in labor markets.[13] Although life in the United States remains profoundly racialized in all these ways, the great irony of our times, Winant suggests, is that many U.S. citizens or residents don't see such racialization, with the result being that "color-blind policies" (e.g., dismantling affirmative action) have become increasingly attractive to many.

It is clear that Waters agrees with Winant that U.S. life is deeply racialized and that such racialization is not always fully understood or appreciated. This omnipresent racialization of everyday life and life chances is surely one of the exceptional features of the United States, although it's present to some degree in all countries. If Waters breaks with Winant's account, it's only because she stresses that there are also forces at work that are weakening at least some racial boundaries, forces that may work slowly and fitfully but even so are hardly a trivial side story.

CONCLUSION

We have chosen a debate-based format that perhaps lends itself to the conclusion that current scholarship on poverty and inequality is rife with discord and disagreement. If this is indeed the impression conveyed, it would be a partial and potentially misleading one. Although there is much healthy debate in the field, it's also striking that our contributors and the field at large appear to be settling into a new shared orientation toward inequality, a new zeitgeist of sorts that challenges the more benign narratives about inequality that were once fashionable. We will conclude by speculating briefly about the sources of this new orientation, the various ways in which our contributors and the larger inequality field appear to be moving toward it, and how it differs from past views of inequality and its legitimation. This discussion of the changing views of scholars will complement our earlier introductory comments on how the wider public is likewise changing their views of inequality as the New Gilded Age unfolds.

It's useful to set the stage by first describing how inequality (and its legitimacy) has been approached over the last quarter century or so. Obviously, there's always been a diversity of scholarly views about the conditions under which inequality is acceptable, but a prominent feature of the closing decades of the twentieth century was the rise of a neoconservative orientation. This orientation featured such claims as (a) some amount of inequality is necessary to create incentives and maximize total output, (b) inequality can and should be justified as the consequence of individual-level choice (e.g., differential effort, investments in education, training), and (c) all poverty interventions will inevitably create perverse incentives that make poverty more attractive and thereby increase the total amount of poverty. These views, all of which represent inequality or poverty as a necessary evil, were commonplace not just among populist neoconservative commentators but among more academic scholars of inequality as well, especially within economics. We don't mean to overstate the diffusion of such views. Throughout this period, the dominant orientation toward inequality among social scientists remained a disapproving one (at least outside the discipline of economics), yet the neoconservative position was also legitimate and influential and put conventional liberals frequently on the defensive, all the more so given that economics emerged during this period as the definitively high-status social science.

But the pendulum seems now to have swung against such broad and comprehensive justifications for inequality. In part, this new approach to inequality has been informed by a broadened conception of *rights*, the claim being that all citizens should be guaranteed the right to participate in economic life and to avoid the most extreme forms of social and economic exclusion (see esp. Winant's essay). It would nonetheless be a mistake to understand the rising concern with poverty and inequality as exclusively or even principally fueled by some sudden realization that social inclusion is a fundamental right. Although a rights formulation appeals to some philosophers and sociologists, it is simple *consequentialism* that seemingly underwrites the quite rapid shift in the orientation of some economists (and political scientists) toward inequality. In recent years, economists and political scientists have been much affected by the mounting evidence that extreme forms of inequality can in fact lower total output, an effect that may partly arise from the dynamics that Freeman identifies. Also, insofar as much inequality is generated by discrimination (see Blau's essay), it implies an economy rife with inefficiencies that lower overall output.

The negative consequences of extreme inequality may not be exclusively economic. There is additionally a growing tendency to emphasize the more generic threat that inequality poses for the world community as a whole. The rhetoric of "sustainability," although more frequently featured in discussions of environmental problems, is increasingly taken as relevant to discussions of inequality as well. In adopting this rhetoric, the claim is that extreme inequality is counterproductive not just because it reduces total economic output but also because other very legitimate objectives, such as reducing mortality rates or the threat of terrorism, might be compromised if inequality remains so extreme. This "externalities" orientation appears most prominently in our two essays examining the effects of extreme inequality on political participation.

The legitimacy of inequality has also increasingly been called into question within the context of micro-level models of decision-making. If in the past the characteristic trope was to justify poverty as the result of freely made decisions to forgo education in favor of immediate gratification, it has proven increasingly difficult to sustain that position in light of the constraints within which such decisions are now understood to be made. The behavioralist fashion is of course to focus on various cognitive constraints (or "deficits") that, because they are built into our physiology, preclude us from fairly blaming the decision-maker for her or his decisions. Although many economists are attracted to the behavioralist approach, others additionally appreciate the constraints that are built into social structure (not just individual physiology). The standard argument here, and indeed one that Polachek takes up, is that inequality is reproduced because those at the bottom of the distribution are induced, by virtue of their position, to make decisions that further mire them. The woman who "chooses," in other words, to invest less in workplace training does so because of the societal presumption (and hence constraint) that she is principally responsible for child care and domestic duties. This type of rational-action account is widely applicable: the child born into a poor neighborhood and thereby consigned to poor schooling may, for example, rationally decide that attempting to attend college would be highly risky and yield low expected payoff, no matter how much talent she or he has. These types of rational-action accounts differ fundamentally from those that justify inequality as the outcome of randomly distributed proclivities to defer gratification.

This is all to suggest, then, that a confluence of factors have come together to induce all academics, even economists, to increasingly view inequality and poverty as important social problems. To be sure, this view has long been the dominant one within academia, but the "right tail" of the distribution of beliefs (i.e., the pro-inequality tail) has now shrunk in size and been put very much on the defensive. The present book is ample testimony to such shrinkage. It nonetheless remains unclear whether this is mere academic fad or instead presages a renewed commitment to take on poverty and inequality.

Part I

DO WE HAVE AN OBLIGATION TO ELIMINATE POVERTY?

Rich and Poor in the World Community[1]

Peter Singer

SAVING A LIFE

Bob is close to retirement. His proudest possession is a very rare vintage car, a Bugatti, worth two hundred thousand dollars. Its rising market value means that he will be able to sell it and live comfortably after retirement. It also is something that he puts a lot of time into maintaining, polishing, and taking out for drives in the country. Unfortunately, it is so expensive that no one will insure it for him. He takes a risk every time he drives it, but he thinks it's worth doing; he doesn't like the idea of the car just being a museum piece.

One afternoon Bob takes the Bugatti out and drives it to a place where he often likes to park. It is a good spot for going for a walk, along a disused railway siding. He parks his Bugatti, and walks up the siding, normally a pleasant, quiet stroll. But today, as he comes to the point where the disused siding meets a major line, he looks up and he notices, to his surprise, that there is a train coming down the line. He is surprised because no trains are

---

Peter Singer is the Ira W. DeCamp Professor of Bioethics in the University Center for Human Values at Princeton University. His books include *Animal Liberation*, *Democracy and Disobedience*, *Practical Ethics*, *The Expanding Circle*, *Marx*, *Hegel*, *Animal Factories* (with Jim Mason), *The Reproduction Revolution* (with Deane Wells), *Should the Baby Live?* (with Helga Kuhse), *How Are We to Live?*, *Rethinking Life and Death*, *Ethics into Action*, *A Darwinian Left*, *One World*, *Pushing Time Away*, *The President of Good and Evil*, *How Ethical Is Australia?* (with Tom Gregg), *The Way We Eat* (with Jim Mason), and *The Life You Can Save*. He was the founding president of the International Association of Bioethics, and with Helga Kuhse, founding coeditor of the journal *Bioethics*. He is the cofounder and honorary chair of The Great Ape Project, an international effort to obtain basic rights for chimpanzees, gorillas, and orangutans.

due at this time. When he looks more closely he sees that, in fact, this is a runaway train; there is no one in it. And he looks further down the main line, and there he sees, to his horror, a small girl playing just inside the tunnel that the train is heading towards.

The child is too far away to warn of the danger. It seems very likely that she is going to be killed by the runaway train. What can Bob do? He looks down and sees a switch near him. If he throws it (though it's a little rusty, he can throw it with some effort), it will divert the train down the disused siding, thus saving the child's life. But, if the train goes down the disused siding, given the speed at which it's traveling, it will almost certainly crash through the rotten old barrier at the end of the siding. And what will it do? It will pile straight into his precious, uninsured Bugatti and, undoubtedly, destroy it.[2]

Peter Unger tells this story in his book *Living High and Letting Die.* He forces us to face the question: What should Bob do? Should Bob throw the switch, saving the child's life and destroying his Bugatti? Or, should he not throw the switch, almost certainly condemning the child to death, but saving his Bugatti?

When I tell this story and ask this question, almost everyone immediately responds that Bob should throw the switch and save the child's life. If it comes to a choice between the almost certain loss of a child's life and the loss of your most precious possession (something worth two hundred thousand dollars and a significant part of your net assets), almost everyone thinks you should choose to save the child's life. And I think that's right. The question I want to explore is, what does that say about what we ought to do in other situations where we can save children's lives?

Unger's story of Bob's Bugatti is a modified version of a story that I told many years ago in an article, "Famine, Affluence and Morality," first published in 1972. My story involved noticing that a small child had fallen into a shallow pond and was in danger of drowning. You realize that you could walk into the pond and save the child's life. No one else seems to be around to save the child. The cost to you, since the pond is a shallow one, is simply that you are going to ruin your shoes and the nice two-hundred-dollar suit that you are wearing and be late for a meeting. In this Drowning Child case, as in the case of Bob's Bugatti, almost everyone says, "Obviously you should save the child's life." In both of these cases the child was close enough to us for us to be able to see her and save her. In terms of closeness, the drowning child in the shallow pond is somewhat closer, because you actually wade in and fetch out the child with your bare hands. But note that Bob's greater distance does not lessen his duty to rescue the child from the train. In general, greater distance as such would be an arbitrary basis for denying that a child whose life is in danger ought to be rescued.

Now suppose that the child in danger is in some remote part of the world in a developing country. Every day, according to UNICEF, about 21,000 children die from poverty-related causes.[3] Among these causes of child death are starvation and malnutrition (getting enough in terms of calories, but not a balanced healthy diet). Not eating enough, or not eating the right food, might contribute to being at higher risk of having certain diseases, which a healthy child could resist. The risk is further magnified by an unsafe water supply, which can convey diseases again and again. While growing up in these conditions, many millions of children lack even the most minimal health care. They cannot even obtain oral rehydration therapy, which essentially consists of some salts that you give to a child suffering from diarrhea so that the child can better survive. Other children die from measles, because they were not immunized against that disease, or from malaria, because they did not have bed nets to sleep under. These are just some of the causes that lead to those thousands of deaths daily of children from poverty-related causes. Just as much as the pool and the train in my earlier stories, they are threats to children's lives.

I focus on children, but this is just a way to simplify the argument. If I were to talk about adults, people would say such things as "Why couldn't they have gotten a job?" In fact, often that's not a realistic solution, but talking about children eliminates that argument. Clearly, children are not responsible for the poverty that they are in.

How much does it really cost to save a child's life in the third world? It's very hard to put a figure on this. In oral rehydration therapy, for example, the actual ingredients cost less than a dollar, but that's not the true cost of getting adequately trained people to bring the medicine to the children who need them. In my book *The Life You Can Save*, I cite several estimates, ranging from $300 to $1,000.[4] If you were to donate that amount to an NGO that is working to save lives and reduce poverty in the third world, you could expect to save the life of one of the thousands of children who are dying every day. (You can find suggested organizations in the book I just mentioned or on the website www.thelifeyoucansave.com.) If that's so, and if you thought that Bob ought to sacrifice his Bugatti to save a child's life, shouldn't you give what is needed to save the life of a child endangered in the third world?

What is the morally relevant difference between those situations? I want to argue that there is none, or, in any case, none that is remotely strong enough to justify those who can comfortably afford it in not giving five hundred or a thousand dollars to Oxfam America, Partners in Health, or one of the other NGOs that are out there helping to relieve poverty in the poor nations. After all, the sacrifice made by that donation is not remotely as great as the sacrifice that, as almost everyone thinks, Bob should make of his Bugatti—not remotely as great in terms of impact on lifestyle, nor in terms of loss of a cherished possession.

What are some of the differences that people might think exist between the two situations? In response to the pond example, someone might say, "You are certainly saving a child who is going to drown. But if you give to an aid agency, you can't really know for sure that you are going to save a child." That is one of the advantages of the Bob and Bugatti example over my pond case. You don't know for sure that the train is going to kill the child. Maybe the child will look up and see the train hurtling toward her and just in the nick of time dash out of the tunnel and escape. Or, miraculously, she may find room between the side of the tunnel and the train. That's why I said the child would "very likely," but not certainly, be killed. Equally, it is very likely, but not certain, that if you give a substantial donation to one of the more effective NGOs working to save children in developing countries, your donation will save at least one life.

At this point, people may say, "Don't I have a special duty to those who in some way are part of my community?" Let's assume that the child in the pond and the child in the railroad tunnel are in some sense part of my community. We might even assume that I know that the child is a compatriot, say, a fellow American. We may have some obligations to people who are closer to us. Parents have special obligations to their children. Maybe we can expand that into obligations to other close relatives and friends, and then to those with whom we are in some sort of reciprocal relationship where we owe favors or owe a debt of gratitude. All of those things make some difference. But how big a difference should they make? Maybe, if you can save your compatriot or someone who is not a compatriot, but not both, there is some sort of obligation to save the one to whom you are more closely related. But if we are not saving anyone at all—if we are comfortably enjoying our relatively luxurious lives without giving substantial sums to people in the third world to save their lives—I don't see the relevance of the special obligation to our compatriots.

ETHICS AND IMPARTIALITY

How can we decide whether we have special obligations to "our own kind," and if so, who is "our own kind" in the relevant sense? The twentieth-century Oxford philosopher R. M. Hare argued that for judgments to count as moral judgments they must be universalizable, that is, the speaker must be prepared to prescribe that they be carried out in all real and hypothetical situations, not only those in which she benefits from them but also those in which she is among those who lose.[5] Consistently with Hare's approach, one way of deciding whether there are special duties to "our own kind" is to ask whether accepting the idea of having these special duties can itself be justified from an impartial perspective.

In proposing that special duties need justification from an impartial perspective, I am reviving a debate that goes back two hundred years to William Godwin, whose book *Political Justice* shocked British society at the time of the French Revolution. In the book's most famous passage, Godwin imagined a situation in which a palace is on fire, and two people are trapped inside. One of them is a great benefactor of humanity—Godwin chose as his example a celebrated and edifying writer of his day, Archbishop Fénelon, "at the moment when he was conceiving the project of his immortal *Telemachus.*" The other person trapped is the Archbishop's chambermaid. The choice of Fénelon seems odd today, since his "immortal" work is now unread except by scholars, but let's suppose we share Godwin's high opinion of the good Archbishop. Whom should we save? Godwin answers that we should save Fénelon, because by doing so, we would be helping thousands, those who have been cured of "error, vice and consequent unhappiness" by reading *Telemachus.* Then he goes on to make his most controversial claim:

> Supposing I had been myself the chambermaid, I ought to have chosen to die rather than that Fénelon should have died. The life of Fénelon was really preferable to that of the chambermaid. But understanding is the faculty that perceives the truth of this and similar propositions; and justice is the principle that regulates my conduct accordingly. It would have been just in the chambermaid to have preferred the archbishop to herself. To have done otherwise would have been a breach of justice. Supposing the chambermaid had been my wife, my mother or my benefactor. That would not alter the truth of the proposition. The life of Fénelon would still be more valuable than that of the chambermaid; and justice—pure, unadulterated justice—would still have preferred that which was most valuable. Justice would have taught me to save the life of Fénelon at the expense of the other. What magic is there in the

pronoun "my" to overturn the decisions of everlasting truth? My wife or my mother may be a fool or a prostitute, malicious, lying or dishonest. If they be, of what consequence is it that they are mine?[6]

In Godwin's time and in ours, most readers have found his impartiality excessive. Samuel Parr, a well-known liberal clergyman of the time, preached and subsequently published a sermon that was a sustained critique of Godwin's "universal philanthropy." As the text for his sermon, Parr takes an injunction from Paul's epistle to the Galatians, in which Paul offers yet another variant on who is of our own kind: "As we have, therefore, opportunity, let us do good unto all men, especially unto them who are of the household of faith." In Paul's words, Parr finds a Christian text that rejects equal concern for all, instead urging greater concern for those to whom we have a special connection. Parr defends Paul by arguing that to urge us to show impartial concern for all is to demand something that human beings cannot, in general and most of the time, give. "The moral obligations of men," he writes, "cannot be stretched beyond their physical powers."[7] Our real desires, our lasting and strongest passions, are not for the good of our species as a whole, but, at best, for the good of those who are close to us.

Modern critics of impartialism argue that an advocate of an impartial ethic would make a poor parent, lover, spouse, or friend, because the very idea of such personal relationships involves being partial toward the other person with whom one is in the relationship. This means giving more consideration to the interests of your child, lover, spouse, or friend than you give to a stranger, and from the standpoint of an impartial ethic this seems wrong. Feminist philosophers, in particular, tend to stress the importance of personal relationships, which they accuse male moral philosophers of neglecting. Nel Noddings, author of a book called *Caring*, limits our obligation to care to those with whom we can be in some kind of relationship. Hence, she states, we are "not obliged to care for starving children in Africa."[8]

Those who favor an impartial ethic have responded to these objections by denying that they are required to hold that we should be impartial in every aspect of our lives. Godwin himself wrote (in a memoir of his wife Mary Wollstonecraft after her death following the birth of their first child):

A sound morality requires that nothing human should be regarded by us as indifferent; but it is impossible we should not feel the strongest interest for those persons whom we know most intimately, and whose welfare and sympathies are united to our own. True wisdom will recommend to us individual attachments; for with them our minds are more thoroughly maintained in activity and life than they can be under the privation of them, and it is better that man should be a living being, than a stock or a stone. True virtue will sanction this recommendation; since it is the object of virtue to produce happiness; and since the man who lives in the midst of domestic relations will have many opportunities of conferring pleasure, minute in the detail, yet not trivial in the amount, without interfering with the purposes of general benevolence. Nay, by kindling his sensibility, and harmonizing his soul, they may be expected, if he is endowed with a liberal and manly spirit, to render him more prompt in the service of strangers and the public.[9]

In the wake of his own grief for his beloved wife from whom he had been so tragically parted, Godwin found an impartial justification for partial affections. In our own times, Hare's two-level version of utilitarianism leads to the same conclusion. Hare argues that in everyday life it will often be too difficult to work out the consequences of every decision we make, and if we were to try to do so, we would risk getting it wrong because of our personal involvement and the pressures of the situation. To guide our everyday conduct we need a set of principles of which we are aware without a lot of reflection. These principles form the intuitive, or everyday, level of morality. In a calmer or more philosophical moment, on the other hand, we can reflect on the nature of our moral intuitions, and ask whether we have developed the right ones, that is, the ones that will lead to the greatest good, impartially considered. When we engage in this reflection, we are moving to the critical level of morality that informs our thinking about what principles we should follow at the everyday level. Thus the critical level serves as a testing ground for moral intuitions.

Henry Sidgwick, the author of *The Methods of Ethics*, one of finest books of moral philosophy ever written, described the common moral sense of Victorian England by saying that it recognized special obligations to, in descending order of priority, parents, spouse, children, other kin, those who have rendered services to you, friends, neighbors, fellow-countrymen, to "those of our own race . . . and generally to human beings in proportion to their affinity to ourselves."[10] Do any of these preferences survive the demand for impartial justification, and if so, which ones?

The first set of preferences mentioned by Sidgwick—family, friends, and those who have rendered services to us—stands up quite well. The love of parents for their children and the desire of parents to give preference to their children over the children of strangers go very deep. It may be rooted in our nature as social mammals with offspring who need our help during a long period of dependence when they are not capable of fending for themselves. We can speculate that the children of parents who did not care for them would have been less likely to survive, and thus uncaring parents did not pass their genes on to future generations as frequently as caring parents did. Bonds between parents and children (and especially between mothers and children, for in earlier periods a baby not breast-fed by its mother was very unlikely to survive) are therefore found in all human cultures. To say that a certain kind of behavior is universal and has its roots in our evolutionary history does not necessarily mean that it cannot be changed, nor does it mean that it should not be changed. Nevertheless, in this particular case the experience of utopian social experiments has shown that the desire of parents to care for their children is highly resistant to change. In the early days of the Israeli kibbutzim, the more radical of these socialist agricultural collectives sought to equalize the upbringing of children by having all children born to members of the kibbutz brought up communally, in a special children's house. For parents to show particular love and affection for their own child was frowned upon. Nevertheless, mothers used to sneak into the communal nursery at night to kiss and hold their sleeping children. Presumably, if they shared the ideals of the kibbutz, they felt guilty for doing so.

So even if, like the founders of these idealistic collective settlements, we were to decide that it is undesirable for parents to favor their own children, we would find such favoritism very difficult to eradicate. Any attempt to do so would have high costs and would require constant supervision or coercion. Unless we are so intent on suppressing parental bias that we are willing to engage in an all-out campaign of intense moral pressure backed up with coercive measures and draconian sanctions, we are bound to find that most parents constantly favor their children in ways that cannot be directly justified on the basis of equal consideration of interests. If we were to engage in such a campaign, we may well bring about guilt and anxiety in parents who want to do things for their children that society now regards as wrong. Such guilt will itself be a source of much unhappiness. Will the gains arising from diminished partiality for one's own children outweigh this? That seems unlikely, because for the children themselves, the care of loving and partial parents is likely to be better than the care of impartial parents or impartial community-employed caregivers. There is evidence, too, that children are more likely to be abused when brought up by people who are not their biological parents. Given the unavoidable constraints of human nature and the importance of bringing children up in loving homes, there is an impartial justification for approving of social practices that presuppose that parents will show some degree of partiality toward their own children.

It is even easier to find an impartial reason for accepting love and friendship. If loving relationships, and relationships of friendship, are necessarily partial, they are also, for most people, at the core of anything that can approximate to a good life. Very few human beings can live happy and fulfilled lives without being attached to particular other human beings. To suppress these partial affections would destroy something of great value, and therefore cannot be justified from an impartial perspective. Bernard Williams has claimed that this defense of love and friendship demands "one thought too many." We should, he says, visit our sick friend in hospital because he is our friend and is in hospital, not because we have calculated that visiting sick friends is a more efficient way of maximizing utility than anything else we could do with our time.[11] This objection may have some force if pressed against those who claim that we should be thinking about the impartial justification of love or friendship at the time when we are deciding whether to visit our sick friend; but it is precisely the point of two-level utilitarianism to explain why we *should* have an extra thought when we are thinking at the critical level, but not at the level of everyday moral decision-making.

Consider the idea, supported to some degree in the passage I quoted from Sidgwick, that whites should care more for, and give priority to, the interests of other whites. That idea had, in its time, an intuitive appeal very similar to the intuitive appeal of the idea that we have obligations to favor family and friends. But racist views have contributed to many of the worst crimes of our century, and it is not easy to see that they have done much good, certainly not good that can compensate for the misery to which they have led. Moreover, although the suppression of racism is difficult, it is not impossible, as the existence of genuinely multiracial societies, and even the history of desegregation in the American South, shows. White people in the South no longer think twice about sharing a bus seat with an African American, and even those who fought to defend segregation have, by and large, come to accept that they were wrong. Taking an impartial perspective shows that partialism along racial lines is something that we can and should oppose, because our opposition can be effective in preventing great harm to innocent people.

Thus we can turn Williams's aphorism against him: philosophers who take his view have one thought too few. To be sure, to think *always* as a philosopher would mean that, in our roles as parent, spouse, lover, and friend, we would indeed have one thought too many. But if we *are* philosophers, there should be times when we reflect critically on our intuitions—indeed, not only philosophers, but all thoughtful people, should do so. If we were all simply to accept our feelings without the kind of extra reflection we have just been engaged in, we would not be able to decide which of our intuitive inclinations to endorse and support and which to oppose. The fact that intuitive responses are widely held is not evidence that they are justified. They are not rational insights into a realm of moral truth. Some of them—roughly, those that we share with others of our species, irrespective of their cultural background—are responses that, for most of our evolutionary history, have been well suited to the survival and reproduction of beings like us. Other intuitive responses—roughly, those that we do not share with humans from different cultures—we have because of our particular cultural history. Neither the biological nor the cultural basis of our intuitive responses provides us with a sound reason for taking them as the basis of morality.

Let us return to the issue of partiality for family, lovers, and friends. We have seen that there are impartial reasons for accepting some degree of partiality here. But how much? In broad terms, as much as is necessary to promote the goods mentioned earlier, but no more. Thus the partiality of parents for their children must extend to providing them with the necessities of life, and also their more important wants, and must allow them to feel loved and protected; but there is no requirement to satisfy every desire a child expresses, and many reasons why we should not do so. In a society like America, we should bring up our children to know that others are in much greater need, and to be aware of the possibility of helping them, if unnecessary spending is reduced. Our children should also learn to think critically about the forces that lead to high levels of consumption, and to be aware of the environmental costs of this way of living. With lovers and friends, something similar applies: the relationships require partiality, but they are stronger where there are shared values, or at least respect for the values that each holds. Where the values shared include concern for the welfare of others, irrespective of whether they are friends or strangers, then the partiality demanded by friendship or love will not be so great as to interfere in a serious way with the capacity for helping those in great need.

What of the other categories on Sidgwick's list of those to whom we are under a special obligation to show kindness: parents, kin, "those who have rendered services," "neighbors," and "fellow-countrymen"? Can all of these categories be justified from an impartial perspective? The inclusion of "those who have rendered services" is seen by ethicists who rely on intuition to be a straightforward case of the obligation of gratitude. From a two-level perspective, however, the intuition that we have a duty of gratitude is not an insight into some independent moral truth, but something desirable because it helps to encourage reciprocity, which makes cooperation, and all its benefits, possible. Here too, evolutionary theory can help us to see why reciprocity, and with it the sense of gratitude, should have evolved and why it is, in some form or other, a universal norm in all human societies. To give such an evolutionary explanation, however, says nothing about the motives people have when they engage in cooperative behavior, any more than explaining sexual behavior in terms of reproduction suggests that people are motivated to have sex because they wish to have children.

Once a duty of gratitude is recognized, it is impossible to exclude parents from the circle of those to whom a special duty of kindness is owed. Because parents have generally rendered countless services to their children, we can hardly subscribe to a general principle of gratitude without recognizing a duty of children toward their parents. The exception here would be children who have been maltreated or abandoned by their parents—and it is the exception that proves the rule, in the sense that it shows that the obligation is one of gratitude, not one based on blood relationships.

Another of Sidgwick's categories, that of our neighbors, can be handled in the same way. Geographical proximity is not in itself of any moral significance, but it may give us more opportunities to enter into relationships of friendship and mutually beneficial reciprocity. Increasing mobility and communication have, over the course of the past century, eroded the extent to which neighbors are important to us. We walk past our neighbors, barely nodding at them, as we talk on our cell phones to friends in other cities. When we run out of sugar, we don't go next door to borrow some, because the supermarket down the street has plenty. In these circumstances it becomes doubtful if we have special duties of kindness to our neighbors at all, apart from, perhaps, a duty to do the things that neighbors are best placed to do, such as feeding the cat when they go on vacation.

"Kin," the next on Sidgwick's list, is an expression that ranges from the sibling with whom you played as a child and with whom you may later share the task of caring for your parents, to the distant cousin you have not heard from for decades. The extent to which we have a special obligation to our kin should vary accordingly. Kin networks can be important sources of love, friendship, and mutual support, and then they will generate impartially justifiable reasons for promoting these goods. But if that distant cousin you have not heard from for decades suddenly asks for a loan because she wants to buy a new house, is there an impartially defensible ground for believing that you are under a greater obligation to help her than you would be to help an unrelated equally distant acquaintance? At first glance, no, but perhaps a better answer is that it depends on whether there is a recognized system of cooperation among relatives. In rural areas of India, for example, such relationships between relatives can play an important role in providing assistance when needed, and thus in reducing harm when something goes awry. Under these circumstances, there is an impartial reason for recognizing and supporting this practice. In the absence of any such system, there is not. (In different cultures, the more impersonal insurance policy plays the same harm reduction role, and thus reduces the need for a system of special obligations to kin, no doubt with both good and bad effects.)

THE ETHICAL SIGNIFICANCE OF THE NATION-STATE

Finally, then, what impartial reasons can there be for favoring one's compatriots over foreigners? Several classes of such reasons are considered here.

Compatriots as Extended Kin

On some views of nationality, to be a member of the same nation is like an extended version of being kin. Michael Walzer expresses this view when, in discussing immigration policy, he writes:

> Clearly, citizens often believe themselves morally bound to open the doors of their country—not to anyone who wants to come in, perhaps, but to a particular group of outsiders, recognized as national or ethnic "relatives." In this sense, states are like families rather than clubs, for it is a feature of families that their members are morally connected to people they have not chosen, who live outside the household.[12]

Until quite recently, Germany had a citizenship law that embodied the sense of nationality that Walzer has in mind. Descendants of German farmers and craft workers who settled in Eastern Europe in the eighteenth century are recognized in the German Constitution as having the right to "return" to Germany and become citizens, although most of them do not speak German and come from families none of whom have set foot in the country for generations. On the other hand, before new citizenship laws came into effect in 2000, foreign guest workers could live in Germany for decades without becoming eligible for citizenship, and the same was true of their children, even though they were born in Germany, educated in German schools, and had never lived anywhere else. Although Germany's pre-2000 laws were an extreme case of racial or ethnic preference, most other nations have, for much of their history, used racist criteria to select immigrants, and thus citizens. As late as 1970, when immigrants of European descent were being actively encouraged to become Australian citizens, the "White Australia" policy prevented non-European immigrants from settling in Australia. If we reject the idea that we should give preference to members of one's own race, or those "of our blood," it is difficult to defend the intuition that we should favor our fellow citizens, in the sense in which citizenship is seen as a kind of extended kinship, because all citizens are of the same ethnicity or race. The two are simply too close.

A Community of Reciprocity

What if we empty all racist elements from the idea of who our fellow citizens are? We might hold that we have a special obligation to our fellow citizens because we are all taking part in a collective enterprise of some sort. Eamonn Callan has suggested that to be a citizen in a state is to be engaged in a community of reciprocity:

> So far as citizens come to think of justice as integral to a particular political community they care about, in which their own fulfillment and that of their fellow citizens are entwined in a common fate, the sacrifices and compromises that justice requires cannot be sheer loss in the pursuit of one's own.[13]

Walter Feinberg takes a similar view: "The source of national identity is . . . connected to a web of mutual aid that extends back in time and creates future obligations and expectation."[14] The outpouring of help from Americans for the families of the victims of the terrorist attacks of

September 11, 2001, was a striking instance of this web of mutual aid, based on the sense that Americans will help each other in times of crisis. In more normal times, Americans can still feel that by their taxes they are contributing to the provision of services that benefit their fellow Americans by providing Social Security and medical care when they retire or become disabled, fight crime, defend the nation from attack, protect the environment, maintain national parks, educate their children, and come to the rescue in case of floods, earthquakes, or other natural disasters. If they are male, and old enough, they may have served in the armed forces in wartime, and if they are younger, they might have to do so in the future.

It is therefore possible to see the obligation to assist one's fellow citizens ahead of citizens of other countries as an obligation of reciprocity, though one that is attenuated by the size of the community and the lack of direct contact between, or even bare knowledge of, other members of the community. But is this sufficient reason for favoring one's fellow citizens ahead of citizens of other countries whose needs are far more pressing? Most citizens are born into the nation, and many of them care little for the nation's values and traditions. Some may reject them. Beyond the borders of the rich nations are millions of refugees desperate for the opportunity to become part of those national communities. There is no reason to think that, if we admitted them, they would be any less ready than native-born citizens to reciprocate whatever benefits they receive from the community. If we deny admission to these refugees, it hardly seems fair to then turn around and discriminate against them when we make decisions about whom we will aid, on the grounds that they are not members of our community and have no reciprocal relationships with us.

The Efficiency of Nations

Robert Goodin defends a system of special obligations to our compatriots "as an administrative device for discharging our general duties more efficiently."[15] If you are sick and in hospital, Goodin argues, it is best to have a particular doctor made responsible for your care, rather than leaving it up to all the hospital doctors in general; so too, he says, it is best to have one state that is clearly responsible for protecting and promoting the interests of every individual within its territory. There is no doubt something in this, but it is an argument with very limited application in the real world. In any case, efficiency in administration within units is one thing, and the distribution of resources between units is another. Goodin recognizes this, saying: "If there has been a misallocation of some sort, so that some states have been assigned care of many more people than they have been assigned resources to care for them, then a reallocation is called for."[16]

While it may, other things being equal, be more efficient for states to look after their own citizens, this is not the case if wealth is so unequally distributed that a typical affluent couple in one country spends more on going to the theater than many in other countries have to live on for a full year. In these circumstances the argument from efficiency, understood in terms of gaining the maximum utility for each available dollar, far from being a defense of special duties toward our compatriots, provides grounds for holding that any such duties are overwhelmed by the much greater good that we can do abroad.

Justice Within States and Between States

Christopher Wellman has suggested three further impartial reasons for thinking that it may be particularly important to prevent economic inequality from becoming too great *within* a society, rather than *between* societies. The first is that political equality within a society may be adversely affected by economic inequality within a society, but is not adversely affected by economic inequality between societies. The second is that inequality is not something that is bad in itself, but rather something that is bad in so far as it leads to oppressive relationships, and hence we are right to be more concerned about inequality among people living in the same nation than we are about inequality between people living in different countries who are not in a meaningful relationship with each other.[17]

These two points are at least partly answered by the phenomenon that underlies so much of the argument of this book: increasingly, we are facing issues that affect the entire planet. Whatever it is we value about political equality, including the opportunity to participate in the decisions that affect us, globalization means that we should value equality between societies, and at the global level, at least as much as we value political equality within one society. Globalization also means that there can be oppressive relationships at the global scale, as well as within a society.

The third point that Wellman makes is about the comparative nature of wealth and poverty. Marx provided the classic formulation of this third point:

A house may be large or small; as long as the surrounding houses are equally small it satisfies all social demands for a dwelling. But let a palace arise beside the little house, and it shrinks from a little house to a hut. . . .
However high it may shoot up in the course of civilization, if the neighboring palace grows to an equal or even greater extent, the occupant of the relatively small house will feel more and more uncomfortable, dissatisfied and cramped with its four walls.[18]

But today it is a mistake to think that people compare themselves only with their fellow citizens (or with all their fellow citizens). Inhabitants of rural Mississippi, for example, probably do not often compare themselves with New Yorkers, or at least not in regard to income. Their lifestyle is so different that income is merely one element in a whole package. On the other hand, many Mexicans obviously do look longingly north of the border, and think how much better off they would be financially if they could live in the United States. They reveal their thoughts by trying to get across the border. And the same can be true of people who are not in close geographical proximity, as we can see from the desperate attempts of Chinese to travel illegally to the United States, Europe, and Australia, not because they are being politically persecuted, but because they already have enough of an idea about life in those faraway countries to want to live there.

Despite the different picture that globalization gives, let us grant that there are some reasons for thinking that we should place a higher priority on avoiding marked economic inequality within a given society than across the entire range of the planet's inhabitants. Wellman's three points can be given some weight when they are brought against the strong claim that it is less desirable to eliminate marked economic inequality between any of the world's inhabitants than it is to eliminate it within a single society. But the weight we should give them is limited, and subject to particular circumstances. In particular, the question of whether to seek greater equality within societies or between societies only arises if we cannot do both. Sometimes we can. We can increase taxes on people in rich nations who have higher incomes or leave large sums to their heirs, and use the revenue to increase aid to those people in the world's poorest nations who have incomes well below average even for the nation in which they are living. That would reduce inequality both in the poor nations and between nations.

Granted, if we live in a rich nation, we could reduce equality within our own society even further if we used the revenue generated by taxes on the wealthiest people within our own society to help the worst-off within our own society. But even if we accept Wellman's arguments, that would be the wrong choice. For then we would be choosing to reduce inequality within our own nation rather than reducing both inequality within poor nations, and inequality between nations. Wellman has offered reasons why it may be more important to focus on inequality within a nation than on inequality between nations, but that is not the same as finding reasons for giving greater priority to overcoming inequality within one's own society than in any other society. If I, living in America, can do more to reduce inequality in, say, Bangladesh than I can do to reduce inequality my own country, then Wellman has not given me any grounds for preferring to reduce inequality in America—and if giving money to those near the bottom of the economic ladder in Bangladesh will both reduce inequality there and reduce inequality between nations, that seems the best thing to do. Wellman has failed to find any magic in the pronoun "my."

In any case, in the present situation we have duties to foreigners that override duties to our fellow citizens, for even if inequality is often relative, the state of absolute poverty that has already been described is a state of poverty that is not relative to someone else's wealth. Reducing the number of human beings living in absolute poverty is surely a more urgent priority than reducing the relative poverty caused by some people living in palaces while others live in houses that are merely adequate. Here Sidgwick's account of the common moral consciousness of his time is in agreement. After giving the list of special obligations I quoted earlier, he continues: "And to all men with whom we may be brought into relation we are held to owe slight services, and such as may be rendered without inconvenience: but those who are in distress or urgent need have a claim on us for special kindness."[19]

AN ETHICAL CHALLENGE

When subjected to the test of impartial assessment, there are few strong grounds for giving preference to the interests of one's fellow citizens, and none that can override the obligation that arises whenever we can, at little cost to ourselves, make an absolutely crucial difference to the well-being of another person in real need. So the duty to help people in developing countries that I derived from the cases of the Drowning Child and Bob's Bugatti cannot be evaded by appealing to a prior duty to help one's own.

Still, there is a genuinely important difference between current circumstances of world poverty and the situation of the children in Unger's and my examples. Ironically, it makes the duty of foreign aid more, not less demanding. When you read that for three hundred or a thousand dollars you can save a child's life, you might think, "Okay, good. What I will do now is to start saving that thousand dollars. And then, when I have saved that money and donated it, I'll be okay. I'll be ethically in the clear because I've saved a child's life." But of course, in contrast to the situation of the Drowning Child or Bob's Bugatti, you don't have just one opportunity to save the life of a child starving in the third world. There are thousands who are dying everyday, many of whom we could reach if we had more resources. So, after you have written that check for a thousand dollars, there is still another child that you ought to be helping. And after you have written the second check for a thousand dollars, there's still another, and so on. So, one significant difference is that this obligation is practically limitless from your point of view.

Looking at your situation in another way, you might find this judgment too extreme. Assume that you are an average middle-class citizen of the developed world. You're not Warren Buffett or Bill Gates, but you do have a lot more than you need to meet your basic needs. If everyone at least as well-off were to contribute to relieve world poverty, then the obligation would not be at all limitless. We could, for a relatively small amount of our income, according to some estimates as little as 2 percent, produce a world in which almost everyone had safe drinking water, minimal health care, adequate diet, and so on. And that would not be a huge sacrifice.

Unfortunately, the reality of aid is very different, and this makes a big difference to your obligations. If you were farther from the drowning child than someone in a better position to wade in and save her, yet you could see that this callous person could not be expected to do his part, then it would not be all right for you to refuse to do what is needed. And, unfortunately, most people and their governments are not remotely doing their part to produce a world in which almost everyone has the basic necessities.

Many years ago, the United Nations set a target for development aid of 0.7 percent of Gross National Income (GNI). A handful of developed nations—Denmark, Luxembourg, the Netherlands, Norway, and Sweden— meet or surpass this very modest target of giving $0.70 of every $100 that their economy produces to the developing nations. Most of them fail to reach it. On average, among the affluent nations, official development assistance is at around 0.42 percent of GNI. But of all the affluent nations, none fails so miserably to meet the United Nations target as the United States, which in 2010, the last year for which figures are available, gave 0.21 percent of its GNI, or just 21 cents for every $100 its economy produces, less than a third of the United Nations target. And even that miserly sum exaggerates the U.S. aid to the most needy, for much of it is strategically targeted for political purposes. In 2009, the most recent year for which a country-by-country breakdown of U.S. aid is available, the two largest single recipients of U.S. official development assistance were Afghanistan and Iraq, each of which received more than twice as much aid as the third-placed country, Sudan.[20]

When I make these points to audiences in the United States, some object that to focus on official aid is misleading. The United States, they say, is a country that does not believe in leaving everything to the government, as some other nations do. If private aid sources were also included, the United States would turn out to be exceptionally generous in its aid to other nations. But non-government aid everywhere is dwarfed by government aid, and that is true in the United States too, where on the best estimates, adding in non-government aid does not take the United States' aid above 0.33 percent of GNI. This is still less than a quarter of the modest United Nations target.[21]

CONCLUSION

With respect to the many millions of people who are threatened by hunger and disease in developing countries, we are in the same situation as the person who, at small cost, can save a child's life. The vast majority of us living in the developed nations of the world have disposable income that we spend on frivolities and luxuries, things of no more importance to us than avoiding getting our shoes and trousers muddy. If we do this when people are in danger of dying of starvation and when there are agencies that can, with reasonable efficiency, turn our modest donations of money into lifesaving food and basic medicines, how can we consider ourselves any better than the person who sees the child fall in the pond and walks on?

As individuals, we can do two things about this situation. First, we can give substantially to organizations working to help the world's poorest people. Second, we can encourage others to do the same. Psychological studies have shown that people are more likely to give if they believe that others are giving too. So it is important to overcome our natural modesty and tell others that we are giving. You can also go to a website I have set up, and pledge to give in accordance with a scale I suggest there. In that way you will make it easier for others to give. The website, www.thelifeyou cansave.com, also contains information about organizations that will make effective use of your donation.

Global Needs and Special Relationships

Richard W. Miller

The question that Peter Singer and I address gnaws at the conscience of relatively affluent people in the per-capita richest countries, on account of the staggering scale of global inequality: "To what extent am I morally obliged to make sacrifices in order to help needy people, who mostly live abroad in countries with meager resources for relieving their burdens?" An argument that Singer first presented in 1973, in "Famine, Affluence and Morality," which he has vigorously defended in the decades since, remains at the vital center of the search for a principled answer. Singer claims that nearly all of us would be forced by adequate reflection on our own deep moral convictions to impose a huge demand in response to the gnawing question, an obligation to give that is so demanding that, for example, it prohibits spending money on clothing "not to keep ourselves warm but to look 'well-dressed.'"[1] Radical though his answer is, Singer says that it follows from uncontroversial empirical claims about global poverty together with a general principle of beneficence that most people find to be "undeniable"[2] if they adequately reflect on their secure convictions about moral equality and duties of rescue, as in his famous story about rescuing a drowning toddler.

I think that Singer's project of deriving the radical from the obvious depends on misinterpretations of ordinary morality. If your deepest convictions are like most people's, you have grounds for rejecting the huge duty to

Richard W. Miller is the Wyn and William Y. Hutchinson Professor in Ethics and Public Life in the Department of Philosophy at Cornell University. His many writings in political philosophy, ethics, and the philosophy of science include *Analyzing Marx*, *Fact and Method*, *Moral Differences*, and *Globalizing Justice: The Ethics of Poverty and Power*.

donate that he would impose. Adequate reflection will lead you to embrace a more moderate principle of general beneficence, as an expression of the equal respect you owe to all: one's underlying responsiveness to neediness ought to be sufficiently demanding that greater concern would impose a significant risk of worsening one's life. Although this duty does require most relatively affluent people (American professors very much included) to give more than we do, it does not dictate giving up all luxuries and frills. For this would worsen the lives of people who are attached to worthwhile, expensive personal goals. Other duties of aid add further requirements to give up advantages in the interests of needy people in developing countries, but these further demands depend on specific relationships and circumstances.

Of course, reflection on ordinary moral convictions is not the only basis for deriving duties to help the needy. Another possible starting point is utilitarianism, the doctrine that one has a duty always to make a choice that creates as much overall well-being as one can. Singer himself is drawn to this doctrine, so my concentration on ordinary moral convictions might seem unfair. But in fact, this emphasis is a tribute to what is powerful and innovative in his discussions of aid. Utilitarianism does, obviously, require someone to give up luxuries and frills to help the needy, and more besides: it requires a person to contribute funds to help the needy until giving more would create as much suffering on her part as she relieves. But this isn't the end of the remarkable dictates that seem to follow from utilitarianism. Others are outlandish, even appalling. If I know that I can save someone from death by buzz saw but only at a sacrifice of both my arms, those arms must go, or I do wrong. If four young people can be saved from imminent death but only by transplants requiring the harvesting of my vital organs, surgeons operating on my gall bladder who could harvest me without serious adverse consequences beyond my mysterious death in gall bladder surgery are wrong not to seize the opportunity and cut out my organs. This is just a sample of the appalling apparent consequences that have led most philosophers to reject utilitarianism. Singer's writings on aid to the world's needy have been profoundly influential and enriching, over the course of more than thirty years, precisely because he does *not* appeal to this embattled, extraordinary doctrine, but starts within the circle of ordinary morality and seeks to derive a conclusion about aid to the world's needy that is quite radical (if less radical than utilitarianism's). His innovative work is a challenge to people with ordinary moral convictions to see if we can remain faithful to our own deepest moral beliefs while spending money to enjoy stylish clothes, more than basic stereo equipment, and nice meals in restaurants.

In my response to this challenge, I will begin by comparing my principle of general beneficence with Singer's in more detail, showing why I take my principle to express the dictates of equal respect for all. Here, a disagreement about the moral status of special relationships, such as parental nurturance or friendship, will turn out to be crucial, producing different construals of the most fundamental principles of moral equality. Then, I will consider Singer's extremely powerful argument from ordinary judgments of the duty to rescue imperilled people close at hand to his radical demand for contributions to help needy people worldwide, arguing that special attention to those nearby is not, as he supposes, morally arbitrary. Finally, against the background of the limits to what we must do to help others apart from special relationships and circumstances, I will describe why current relationships between people in rich countries and people in poor ones dictate duties of aid to the foreign poor that are quite demanding, even if not as demanding as Singer requires. Despite large disagreements concerning the nature of moral equality, the demands of neediness, and the moral importance of special relationships, Singer and I both think that the current level of transnational help to needy people in poor countries is grossly inadequate. Anyone who is at all satisfied with its extent should be disturbed by this convergence on sharp criticism of current practice from such different general perspectives.

TWO PRINCIPLES

Singer has claimed that the following principle, which I will call "the Principle of Sacrifice," is "virtually undeniable":

> [I]f it is in our power to prevent something very bad from happening, without thereby sacrificing anything else morally significant, we ought, morally, to do so.[3]

Supplemented by a few further premises, which virtually all informed decent people would, on reflection, accept, this principle entails what I will call "the radical conclusion":

> Everyone has a duty to give up all luxuries and frills and donate the savings to help those in dire need (unless the purchase of a luxury or frill is part of a strategy that makes him or her more effective in relieving dire need).

The parenthetical proviso permits someone to work as a lawyer for a Wall Street firm, dressing in the elegant suits that the firm requires, so long as this is part of a strategy of making and then donating big bucks that is a more effective way for her to help the needy than any less luxurious alternative. I will follow Singer in largely ignoring this proviso from now on, since it does not create a large loophole for most of us. A luxury or frill is an item of the sort that a person might be unable to afford without being poor. So (apart from the proviso), the radical conclusion tells us that we have a duty to donate until donating more would impoverish ourselves or our dependents.

Two further premises connect the Principle of Sacrifice with the radical conclusion. First, on any particular occasion, or any small bunch of particular occasions, on which one has the opportunity to buy a luxury or frill, the choice, instead, to spend no more than what is needed to buy a plain, functional alternative is not a morally significant sacrifice. If my sweater wardrobe is threadbare and I discover a stunning designer-label sweater on sale for $39.99, I may prefer buying it to buying a plain warm department store–label sweater selling for $22.95, but surely making the less expensive purchase is not a morally significant sacrifice. Second, because of the availability of international aid agencies, forgoing the choice of a luxury or frill and donating the money saved (perhaps combined with money saved on other similar occasions in a small bunch) is always a way of preventing something very bad from happening. For example, I can buy the less expensive sweater instead (or decide not to upgrade my stereo or decide to eat a cheap nutritious meal at home rather than a more interesting meal at a restaurant) and donate the savings to UNICEF, who will use the donation to immunize a child (or many children, in the case of the stereo) who will otherwise be in serious peril of death or crippling by readily preventable infection.

People find this argument frightening, and rightly so. It makes a shopping mall seem a site of grave moral danger. If you are drawn to buying that stylish designer-label sweater and realize that you could save a child's life through donating money saved by not purchasing it, Singer's argument makes it seem quite wrong to go ahead and buy it. Given the moral importance of the peril that could be ended by the donation, a valid justification of going ahead and spending will not rest on the moral importance of that particular opportunity to have a designer-label sweater. Rather, the justification must be more indirect, an argument that a more moderate rival to Singer's principle, permitting the purchase, is the relevant principle of aid.

I will call my rival principle, used, like Singer's, to describe our duty to help others when no special relationship, circumstance, or past history is in play, "the Principle of Sympathy":

> One's underlying disposition to respond to neediness as such ought to be sufficiently demanding that giving that expresses greater underlying concern would impose a significant risk of worsening one's life, if one fulfilled one's other responsibilities.

Someone's choices or a pattern of choices on his part violate this principle if and only if they could not express the attitude of responsiveness it dictates if he is relevantly well informed.

This principle looks at the impact of basic concern for neediness on how well someone is apt to fare in her life as a whole, an impact that depends, in part, on the worthwhile goals to which she is actually attached and from which she could not readily detach, the goals that give point and value to her particular choices. Its central question is, "Would an underlying attitude of greater concern create a significant risk that I could not pursue worthwhile goals with which I identify enjoyably and well?" Most of us do identify with goals requiring some purchases of luxuries and frills. For example, most of us identify with the goal of displaying one's aesthetic sensibility and engaging in the fun of mutual aesthetic recognition through the way one dresses, which requires some purchases of clothing more expensive than the functional and plain. This goal, like other common, somewhat luxurious personal goals, is worthwhile. If no one had an interest in connecting dress with aesthetic fun, not just with covering up and keeping warm, and everything else were the same, the world would be worse. (In contrast, if no one cared about such silly competitions as the best-dressed lists, the world would be better.) In general, if the Principle of Sympathy puts the right ceiling on our duty to make sacrifices in response to neediness as such, it is not wrong sometimes to buy luxuries and frills, just as a means of enjoyed consumption. The crucial reason is one of legitimate self-interest: observing a sterner prohibition would worsen your life.

Within the circle of ordinary morality, which is the starting point of Singer's argument about aid as well as mine, the fact that a change would impose a significant risk of worsening someone's life certainly counts as morally significant. The sensitivity to neediness that the Principle of Sympathy regulates includes a concern to prevent very bad things from happening.

So the difference in the demands imposed by the two principles depends on what is scrutinized in order to determine whether neglect of neediness has an appropriately serious justification: the impact of particular choices on particular occasions or the impact of an underlying attitude on a life as a whole. The Principle of Sacrifice scrutinizes particular occasions of choice for relevant moral significance, and only permits the choice not to prevent something very bad from happening when abstention from spending on luxuries or frills on those particular occasions would be morally significant. There is no occasion or small bunch of occasions on which my declining an opportunity to buy a stylish, more expensive article of clothing, buying a plain, cheap one instead, constitutes a morally significant loss. After all, such a choice never makes my life worse; at most it involves a minor episode of frustration.[4] So, because of the opportunity presented by aid agencies, abstention is dictated by Singer's principle. But by prohibiting luxurious purchases on all particular occasions, it prohibits them, period (with the usual proviso about strategic use of luxuries). This would make it impossible for a typical, relatively affluent person to pursue, enjoyably and well, goals that are worthwhile objects of secure attachment, such as the sartorial goal that I described. So observance of the principle would have an impact on someone's life as a whole in virtue of which it is to be rejected, as too demanding, if the Principle of Sympathy is right. No purchase prohibited by Singer's principle is morally significant, but the loss imposed by commitment to the principle is, i.e., it is the sort of loss that can make it all right to embrace a less demanding commitment, which would otherwise be morally inadequate.

Still, even though the Principle of Sympathy does not support Singer's radical conclusion, it does have a moderately demanding outcome:

> Most of us ought to give more than we actually do to help the needy, even though we are not obliged to give up all luxuries and frills.

Most people who identify with worthwhile, relatively expensive goals could devote far fewer resources to them and still pursue them enjoyably and well. We are constantly tempted to exaggerate what is really just a matter of frustration into a harm that worsens our lives. Moreover, our choices tend to be distorted by excessive anxiety that leads us to treat insignificant possibilities that more altruism will worsen our lives as significant risks of self-worsening. The Principle of Sympathy contributes to my agreement about the moral necessity of doing more for the world's poor.

EQUAL CONCERN AND EQUAL RESPECT

The Principle of Sympathy stands in need of some sort of grounding in something more general. This is not just a philosopher's demand imposed from outside the circle of ordinary morality. For ordinary morality is not a mere collection of relatively specific principles governing particular spheres of conduct, such as responsiveness to neediness. Most reflective, decent people are committed to comprehensive precepts linking moral duty to a perspective of moral equality. They think that a choice is wrong if and only if it could not be made, under the circumstances, by someone displaying equal respect for all persons; if and only if it is incompatible with the ascription of equal worth to every person's life; if and only if, under the circumstances, it violates every moral code that no one could reasonably reject. These (and, no doubt other) coextensive, mutually supportive principles are different ways of describing the perspective of moral equality from which choices should be scrutinized. Each sometimes requires interpretation in light of further, particularly compelling moral judgments, in much the same way as a general phrase in the U.S. Constitution such as "equal protection of the law" is clarified in hard cases by finding interpretations that fit obvious applications and established findings. Still, the dictates of these comprehensive precepts (again, like the sentences in a constitution) are, on reflection, sufficiently clear that they can guide and organize our scrutiny of more specific norms.

The Principle of Sympathy, I would claim, is an adequate expression of this fundamental perspective of moral equality. On the one hand, a person who would not display greater basic concern for neediness even if this imposed no significant risk of worsening his life and did not detract from his other responsibilities does attribute less value to others' lives than to his own. Someone who is unresponsive to another's deprivation does not treat her life as equally important unless his lack of responsiveness is supported by adequate reasons, which the person who violates the Principle of Sympathy lacks. On the other hand, someone whose responsiveness to neediness as such is as limited as the Principle of Sympathy permits can appreciate the equal worth of everyone's life, express equal respect for all, and reject self-governance by a more stringent principle as unreasonably demanding. "I show appreciation of the equal worth of everyone's life through sensitivity to others' neediness as such, but stop short of a sensitivity that would impose a significant risk of worsening my own life if I live up to my other responsibilities" is not an internally inconsistent self-portrayal.

No doubt, a more demanding principle, at least as demanding as the Principle of Sacrifice, would be endorsed from a perspective of equal *concern* for all. But equal respect does not entail equal concern. I am, for example, more concerned for my daughter than for the daughter in the family that lives across the street, but I do not regard her life as more valuable. When my wife and I pay for our daughter's education at an excellent college, to avoid a significant risk of worsening her life, we do not express the view that her life is more valuable than the lives of several children in poor countries—yet we know that several children are apt to die at an early age because we do not insist that she go to a much cheaper college, not so good, in order to make a very big contribution to Oxfam. This unequal concern expresses a proper valuing of the history of nurturance and dependence that we share, not the appalling assessment of the lives of five children in Mali as worth less than the life of my daughter. If one can respond to another's intimate dependence through such favoritism while equally respecting all, one can also equally respect all in spite of special concern for one's most intimate dependent, oneself.

In defending a moderate principle of aid, I have just touched on a disagreement concerning the nature of moral equality. Although Singer and I agree that our duties reflect a comprehensive imperative of equal respect, we disagree as to whether attitudes compatible with equal respect must be certified from some further, authoritative perspective of equal concern. In his resourceful discussion of special relationships in his book *One World*, Singer seems to take the view that an attachment such as my parental tie is only legitimate to the extent that it makes the person who is so attached more productive of overall well-being, so that the partiality would be approved from a fundamental perspective of impartial concern.[5] This seems wrong to me. If my daughter became a salesperson and I were in the horrible situation of having time to save only one person from a burning building, her or a brain surgeon with special lifesaving skills, I would not do wrong or show unequal respect for persons if I saved my daughter. A skillful doctor working in a chronically understaffed inner city emergency room, routinely tired, emotionally frayed and preoccupied, but functioning well enough to enormously benefit humanity, does not show that she regards the lives of people in the hospital's neighborhood as less valuable than lives in her family if she quits and sets up a much less beneficent suburban practice when she sees that she is becoming detached from her family through the wear and tear of her beneficent work.

The point is not merely that certain relationships entailing special concern are inherently valuable—an assessment that might also be affirmed by a utilitarian who insists that one always act so as to maximize total value. The failure to shift spending from tuition to Oxfam leads to the early deaths of people who would otherwise become nurturant parents themselves. The medical shortfalls due to the doctor's leaving would, similarly, reduce the prevalence of nurturance by increasing mortality among the medically deprived. Rather, the point is that the proper appreciation of an inherently valuable relationship to another, such as the parental nurturance of one's child, is expressed in special concern for the other, even when this reduces one's contribution to total value. I would not properly value my relationship to my daughter if I were willing to abandon her if this were a necessary part of a strategy for introducing nurturant relationships into the lives of two other parents and their children.[6]

Similarly, I do not just mean to insist on the value of a system of social norms that enjoin special beneficence in special relationships such as parenthood. A "rule utilitarian" might acknowledge this, while arguing that facts of global poverty and inequality justify the inculcation of a norm of beneficence that is much more demanding than the Principle of Sympathy. But the rule utilitarian's determination of right and wrong by the most beneficent set of social rules is unsatisfactory. If the efficiency of raising children in group nurseries without the intense particular attachment of parental love were, in fact, a means of increasing total well-being, people could still rightly refuse to swallow a pill that allows them to blithely participate in the project, refusing because of their actual enmeshment in their children's lives or because of goals of parenting with which they actually identify. And similarly for children's loyalty to their parents, friends' mutual loyalties, and other pills. There is also the notorious difficulty of explaining why the overall productiveness of inculcating a social rule is decisive in an atypical case in which more good comes from departing from it. Why should the fact that special concern for family typically makes people more efficient engines of the good make it all right for the physician to desert her atypical opportunity to do great good while neglecting her family? In any case, obsession with the typical and social will not save rule utilitarianism from injustice. A system of slavery that maximizes the sum of well-being because it is needed to sustain a highly productive division of labor is, still, wrong.

Peter Singer and I agree that the mere warm glow of attachment to others—celebrated, for example, in songs of Nazi storm troopers—has no serious moral standing. Special attachments generating special duties must be valuable. To be valuable, they must be well enough integrated with other moral duties and obligatory goals. Our disagreement concerns whether a single impartialist test, such as the production of maximum overall well-being, is what we must impose and the only test we ultimately need.

RESCUE AND CLOSENESS

Like a sneaky lawyer, I have, so far, made my case for a moderate duty of general beneficence while pretending that a certain powerful contrary argument did not exist, namely, Singer's famous argument from a duty to rescue a drowning toddler that nearly all of us would strongly affirm to his Principle of Sacrifice. It is time to confront it. (In the course of my struggle, I will also confront Peter Unger's similar reasoning from another story of impending catastrophe, which Singer now uses to strengthen his own, pioneering argument.)

If I were rushing to a lecture and encountered a toddler drowning in a pond, it would be wrong of me not to stop and rescue him, even if I had to ruin a three-hundred-dollar suit. The lives of children in distant villages who are currently imperilled by lack of access to safe water and basic medical facilities are no less valuable because they are not near. So mustn't I be willing, now and so long as I live in such a grim world, continually to make sacrifices to rescue such people from peril, whenever the sacrifices are on the same scale as nearby rescue can require?

The description of moral duty that appeals to moral codes that no one could reasonably reject is a helpful framework for responding to this challenge. (Thomas Scanlon's writings have revealed the fundamental role in moral reasoning of this aspiration to reconciliation by shared principles.)[7] A choice is wrong if and only if it would be prohibited, under the circumstances, by any moral code that no one could reasonably reject as providing shared terms of self-governance for each to impose on herself. Any such code would include both the Principle of Sympathy, as its description of the duty of general beneficence, and a principle asserting a special connection between nearby peril and a definite, potentially demanding duty of rescue:

> (The Principle of Nearby Rescue). Rescue someone encountered close by who is in imminent peril of severe harm and whom one can rescue with means at hand, if the sacrifice of rescue does not itself involve a risk of harm of similar seriousness or of serious physical harm and does not involve wrongdoing.

The case against rejecting either principle in our moral code provides grounds for insisting on the duty to save the nearby toddler (which Nearby Rescue demands) without requiring saving all equally imperilled people near or far whenever the sacrifice of rescue is no greater (which exceeds the demands of Sympathy).

One alternative to such a moral code, the alternative most directly evoked by Singer's argument, would delete the restriction to those nearby in the Principle of Nearby Rescue, requiring rescue of those in peril near or far. Because of the facilities of aid agencies, this distance-deleted requirement would impose beneficent sacrifices on the scale of the Principle of Sacrifice. For reasons that I brought forward in my critique of the latter imperative, relatively well-off people could reasonably reject the distance-deleted alternative as too demanding. In contrast, in the normal circumstances of human life (which are presupposed in the Principle of Nearby Rescue), the net expected costs of sharing in a general commitment to the Principle of Nearby Rescue are trivial, at most. The small likelihood of costly rescue dictated by the principle is virtually balanced by a prospect of need for rescue that we all face because of human vulnerability.

This is not to deny that the Principle of Nearby Rescue could come due in burdensome ways in particular, exceptional circumstances. This is Bob's fate in Peter Unger's story of the man who must sacrifice a Bugatti in which he has invested his savings in order to save a child from being crushed by a train. However, when we identify demands of equal respect by asking what principles would be part of a moral code that no one could reasonably reject, the acceptances and rejections that concern us are not judgments of what to do in response to particular circumstances. The moral code that someone accepts is in the background of her responses to particular current circumstances, defining an enduring commitment that a person of moral integrity brings into interactions with others as they arise. Correspondingly, the rejection of a moral code as too demanding should be tied to the assessment of likely costs and benefits in light of the background of resources and underlying goals with which the agent approaches particular circumstances and the likelihood, before the fact, that circumstances of various kinds will arise. From this perspective, Bob, like the rest of us, could not reasonably reject the Principle of Nearby Rescue, since the relevant expected cost of shared compliance is trivial, at most.

The Principle of Nearby Rescue, then, is not to be rejected as excessively demanding, while some could reasonably reject, as too demanding, its replacement by an otherwise similar distance-neutral requirement. Still, the principle's special emphasis on nearby perils and nearby means of rescue might be objectionable as elevating one personal policy for rationing the demands of Sympathy into a policy that all must follow. Why can't anyone reasonably reject a specific commitment to help those encountered in peril, on the occasion of encounter, so long as he commits himself to the Principle of Sympathy, which requires a general level of concern without demanding aid on any specific occasion? If there is no good answer, then the Principle of Sympathy itself is threatened. For the duties to save the imperilled children remain to be explained, and rival, demanding principles of general beneficence are waiting in the wings to explain them, such as the Principle of Sacrifice or the even more demanding principle that would dictate Bob's sacrifice of his Bugatti.

If someone were to reject the Principle of Nearby Rescue because he does not want to make a specific commitment to help those encountered in nearby peril, he fails to adequately appreciate certain values that are tied to closeness in the normal human background circumstances that are presupposed. For one thing, such a person would not properly value the relationship of encounter, the minimal relationship among humans that is our pervasive basis for mutual recognition. Quite apart from any actual need for aid, any self-respecting person cherishes participation in a milieu in which people who encounter one another can expect the goodwill that *would* be expressed by aid like that dictated by the Principle of Nearby Rescue should the need arise. Even if a cerebral hemorrhage instantly kills me in ripe old age, ending a life in which I never needed help from a stranger, I would be profoundly deprived by a milieu in which passersby would simply have stepped over me if I had collapsed on a sidewalk. Someone who adheres to the Principle of Sympathy but is not especially attentive to the needs of those close by fails to do his part in sustaining a milieu that all should cherish.

In the second place, the failure to adopt the special policy of aiding those in peril close by that the Principle of Nearby Rescue prescribes would be a failure to participate in a current, widely shared disposition that is part of the best feasible basis for effectively coordinating individual aid initiatives. A joint project of alleviating neediness is considerably advanced by a prevalent means of allocating responsibilities that tends to assign responsibilities to those who are in a position to help. Without such coordination, people are apt falsely to assume that someone else will come to the aid of a victim and people who do help are apt to find that the difficulties of aid are more severe because those who could have helped earlier and more easily did not. A strong inclination to help those in imminent physical peril who are close at hand is, in fact, widely shared, and serves as a fairly effective coordinative mechanism, playing an important role in the joint project of relieving neediness that the Principle of Sympathy describes. So it would be unreasonable, in a parasite's way, for a person of moral integrity, who must be committed to this project, to refuse to share this relevantly undemanding coordinative disposition.[8]

Finally, special attentiveness to needs in one's immediate environment is acceptance of a responsibility corresponding to a self-respectful person's insistence that others be especially willing to respect her space. We expect others to be strongly (though, of course, not absolutely) disinclined to stop us in our tracks or to impose immediate barriers to our physical activities. It would be unreasonable to insist on this special solicitude for control over one's immediate environment without accepting a corresponding spatial trusteeship, a special responsibility to attend to events within one's immediate environment that are cause for concern.

Granted, human fellowship would be even greater and neediness would be relieved even more effectively if all of us had a demanding inclination to relieve dire burdens whenever there is an opportunity to do so. But these are not prevalent inclinations, and a proposal that we should all be so responsive could reasonably be rejected by some, as imposing a significant risk of worsening their lives.

Singer and I do not entirely disagree about the moral status of mere closeness. In imaginable circumstances, very different from the normal circumstances of human life, nearness (I accept) would not characterize a special duty of aid. For example, imagine a future form of life in which people grow up with monitors and keyboards grafted onto their bodies, communicating via the Internet, with only the most awkward and obscure awareness of their immediate environments. In this world, a special duty of nearby rescue would be out of place, even though the Principle of Sympathy would still bind these cybernauts. The Principle of Nearby Rescue presupposes the background circumstances of people who are embodied, aware, and capable in the actual human way. In these circumstances, there is a special connection between closeness and the morally important values of personal encounter, coordinative efficiency, and spatial trusteeship, a connection that would have lapsed among the cybernauts.

LIMITS TO GLOBAL BENEFICENCE

Now that the differences in general approach are clearer, it is time to reexamine the gnawing question of duties of relatively affluent people in per-capita rich countries to give up advantages in the interest of needy people in poor countries, approaching the issue from the standpoint that I have begun to defend. This approach certainly does not lead to demands for aid to needy foreigners that are as extensive as Singer's. I will begin by examining the reasons in more detail, describing ways in which limits to responsiveness to foreign needs are justified by personal prerogatives and by special responsibilities to others. Yet, ironically (as I will try to show, in conclusion), a deeper understanding of these prerogatives and responsibilities, which Singer's argument underrates, also establishes a demanding duty to help needy people in poor countries, a duty that is especially demanding now because of the relationships that bind relatively affluent people in rich countries with needy people in poor ones.

Since people in the per-capita richest countries are typically attached to personal goals that are both relatively expensive and worthwhile, the restriction of obligatory concern for neediness to what does not pose a significant risk of worsening the benefactor's life is an important limitation on the duty to respond to global poverty regardless of special relationships toward the needy. Other features of the Principle of Sympathy lead to two other important limitations.

Many different needs provide worthy objects of giving. Once one considers their diversity, a corresponding freedom in allocating what Sympathy requires further limits the duty to help needy people in poor countries. For the duty to respond to neediness does not entail an exclusive concern with those who are neediest or whose urgent needs are most readily relieved— people who live, quite disproportionately, in developing countries with meager local resources. Those who have serious needs of other kinds could reasonably complain of a moral code requiring such an exclusive focus. So could benefactors who seek to honor other worthy causes, close to their hearts. When benefactors express their love of opera by giving that avoids cultural deprivations or express their attachment to their town by contributing to the local United Way, they do not place a lesser value on the lives of the world's neediest, even if Oxfam would use that money to relieve more urgent needs more efficiently. Of course, they would also do no wrong by embracing the cause of the world's poorest more wholeheartedly, and giving to Oxfam. But in practice, the exercise of the prerogative to favor worthwhile causes closest to one's heart strongly favors giving within the borders, even in the per-capita richest countries. In the United States, only about 4 percent of donations to tax-exempt nonprofit organizations go to those whose primary interest is international, including those concerned with international security, foreign affairs, and cultural exchange rather than development and humanitarian assistance.[9]

Finally, the concern for neediness that Sympathy requires is limited by one's other responsibilities, including responsibilities to be especially concerned for those to whom one stands in special relationships. In arguing for the Principle of Sympathy itself, I emphasized intimate relationships, such as parenting and friendship, which are the clearest sources of special responsibilities. However, the assessment of political duties toward those with whom one shares the cooler relationship that binds compatriots is exceptionally important in assessing duties of foreign aid. In the first place, aid financed by taxes in developed countries is, potentially, the most powerful device for helping needy people in developing countries. It overcomes individuals' reluctance to give voluntarily to needy foreigners. It can sustain the large-scale, coordinated projects improving infrastructure on which development depends. And by imposing burdens of giving uniformly and fairly among compatriots, it can limit the force of complaints that one's giving to the foreign poor will worsen one's life by reducing resources to compete with compatriots who are not so ready to give. In addition, duties toward compatriots are the prime example, in ordinary moral thinking, of duties of aid that can properly override the familiar partialities of private life, even those binding parents and children. The thought that effective educational help to disadvantaged children in my school district will make it harder for my child to get into a good college should not lead me to vote against a candidate for the school board who is committed to improving educational opportunities for the disadvantaged. Unless a special political obligation to relieve disadvantages of compatriots can be shown to reflect the special relationship that binds compatriots, an extrapolation of this duty to the world at large might generate an extremely demanding duty of foreign aid.[10]

Unlike Peter Singer, I share the common view that people have a special responsibility to help needy compatriots through tax-financed aid, even if they live in one of the per-capita richest countries and others, in poor foreign countries, could more effectively be helped to cope with even more serious needs (such as the health needs of children in low-income countries, where 12 percent die before the age of five).[11] This duty of special concern for compatriots is political, a matter of choices concerning what laws to support. Only a patriotic nut would object to an American's checking the "Where the need is greatest" box, not the "United States only" box, when sending a private donation to the Save the Children Foundation. The duty has its sources, correspondingly, in political relationships of mutual coercion and mutual expectations of political loyalty.

If I am politically active, as I ought to be, then, if my political projects succeed, I will have helped to create laws that people living in the territory of my government are forced to obey, on pain of dangerous encounters with cops, courts, and jails. These laws describe permissible ways of getting ahead economically. In order to show respect for those whom I help to coerce, I must be responsive, in my political choices, to complaints of disadvantage due to the laws that I help to impose. Suppose compatriots are burdened by inferior life-prospects due to the current system of laws; their life-prospects are significantly less because their parents did not do well under the imposed terms of self-advancement and because those terms tie life-prospects to family resources. If these burdens could be relieved by changes that do not impose losses on the same scale on those who are socially advantaged, then I would be wrong to support the current system. As a politically active person, I must support the change in the benefits and burdens of the system, on pain of taking part in unjust coercion. After all, if someone significantly disadvantaged by laws imposed on her finds that her compatriots do not take her disadvantage to be a serious reason for change, she cannot reasonably be expected to loyally, actively, willingly support her country's political arrangements, and a political system that does not merit such support is unjust.

Institutional loyalty also gives rise more directly to special duties to compatriots. Within any reasonably just political community, stability is based on loyalty. People expect their compatriots loyally to support their shared institutions, engaging in principled compromise on the basis of shared political values, making sacrifices when the shared arrangements are under special stress, even, in some circumstances, risking their lives for their country. In general, the proper valuing of others' expected loyal participation in a shared institution on whose thriving one's own well-being depends is expressed in loyalty to co-participants, a special concern to use the shared arrangement to help them when they are in need. This connection between loyalty to a shared arrangement and loyalty to fellow members is quite general. It generates duties of special concern among department colleagues and fellow members of a team, as well as compatriots. However, the strength of one's duty of special concern depends on the importance of the shared arrangement to one's well-being and on the potential demands of loyalty to it. On both dimensions, loyalty to shared political arrangements is especially important, creating especially demanding duties of special concern.

If, in my political choices, I do not choose to relieve significant burdens of social disadvantage due to norms that are imposed on my compatriots or do not display special loyal concern for needy compatriots, and my only reason is that resources could be used more effectively to relieve more serious needs among the foreign poor, then I am like a feudal overlord who exploits his serfs to extract revenues that he uses to help the much more miserable serfs in the neighboring valley. In all or virtually all developed countries, certainly including the United States, there are people whose life prospects are threatened by serious social disadvantages and by misfortunes with which they cannot adequately cope without tax-financed aid. So patriotic responsibilities properly restrict aid to the world's neediest, who tend to live in developing countries.

GLOBAL SOCIAL JUSTICE

These are, I think, the main limits of the duty of relatively affluent people in the per-capita richest countries to do what they can to relieve the burdens of desperate neediness worldwide, regardless of specific transnational relationships. It might be feared that this approach justifies Scrooge-like neglect of the foreign poor. But in fact, an accurate understanding of the prerogatives and responsibilities generating those limits establishes a demanding duty to help needy people in poor countries—not as demanding as Singer's requirement but far more demanding than what most people in developed countries now impose on themselves, either in personal giving or political choices.

For one thing, giving to causes other than the effective relief of the most urgent needs is often more extensive than it has to be to express the strength of the benefactor's intelligent attachment to a worthy cause. If so, then too much flows into these other channels. For giving to help the neediest or those whose urgent needs are most readily relieved—the cause that strongly favors the needy in developing countries—is not just one worthy practice of giving among others. This concern is, as it were, the default stance of those who are adequately responsive to neediness. My giving to the opera, the United Way, or my alma mater can be justified in light of the legitimate strength of attachments of mine. But my giving where the need is greatest does not require any special justification in light of my personal history and values. If we were to ask whether the departure of our giving from the default stance is due to the legitimate strength of our attachments to other worthy causes, most of us, on reflection, would have to concede that it partly responds to irrelevant enticements and pressures (such as the regular calls from the class agent that lead to my disproportionate donation to Amherst College). If we could keep a clear head about what actually poses a significant risk of worsening our lives and what actually draws us to local causes, the commitment to Sympathy would lead us to do more for the world's neediest.

Still, personal causes, goals, and relationships can impose large and legitimate demands. The question of the extent to which a relatively affluent person overestimates the legitimate force of these personal concerns is both hard to answer and dependent on features of his outlook into which a government should not inquire in pursuing political projects such as

tax-financed foreign aid. Because of limits to the appeal to general beneficence, the moral obligations of relatively affluent people in the richest
countries to give up advantages in the interest of needy foreigners in poor
countries largely reflect specific interactions with them. This major part of
the case for transnational aid takes the argument from compatriots' relationships to duties of patriotic concern as its model; it treats measures helping people in poor countries as means of preventing or repairing defects in
relationships to them. Here are some aspects of the current vast failure to
fulfill responsibilities based on transnational relationships.[12]

Transnational coercion. The bearing on foreign needs of the rationale
for patriotic concern is most direct when a government coercively imposes
its rules on foreigners. This is a routine practice at borders, where many
who want to enter in order to take up opportunities to make an honest
living would be stopped by officials with guns. Such uses of political coercion by developed countries mainly burden poor people in developing
countries. They exclude them from important opportunities for legitimate
self-advancement. (In one study of legal immigration from Mexico to the
United States, Mexicans left jobs paying on average $31 a week and on
arrival immediately earned $278.)[13] And they worsen wages, working con-
ditions, and unemployment in developing countries, by increasing the competition among those desperately seeking to sell their labor. So the same
argument from coercively imposed disadvantage that generates a political
duty of concern for compatriots generates a political duty among citizens of
developed countries to relieve the burden that these countries jointly impose
on needy foreigners through immigration restrictions, either by reducing
the restrictions or by reducing the poverty that makes them burdensome.
In part because of the special dictates of civic loyalty, this duty should be
discharged in ways that are sensitive to the special vulnerabilities of needy
compatriots to competition from immigrants. But the force of patriotic concerns in apportioning the costs of a task of transnational justice does not
negate the task itself. No one, rich or poor, has a right to benefit from others' unjust coercion.

Exploitation. The difficulty of reconciling physical coercion with respect is especially clear and especially well established as a topic of political
philosophy. But exploitation of advantages other than superiority in physical coercive power can also express disrespect. If I am dying of thirst in a
desert, someone might be able to use his special knowledge of where the

water is to get me to accept an arrangement in which I wait on his caprices for the rest of my life. Even if he does not use or threaten physical coercion, he wrongs me by taking advantage of me. He wrongs me even if I am better off as a result of the bargain than I would be if I never met him. Similarly, unless they support special measures giving up advantages in the interests of people in developing countries, relatively affluent people in developed countries, who benefit from globalization, will unjustly take advantage of needy people in developing countries. The price of goods imported from developing countries is less and the return on investments there is greater because desperately poor people are driven by the urgency of their needs to accept low wages and miserable working conditions to avoid even worse fates. Relatively affluent people in developed countries are no better than the exploitive desert dweller if we are not willing to use benefits from others' bargaining weakness to alleviate the dire need that generates the weakness.

Threats vs. reasonableness. The process molding the institutional framework of international economic life also generates special duties to improve current life-prospects in developing countries, to avoid undue influence of threat-advantages of developed countries, especially the United States. For example, the trade, investment, and patent and copyright agreements that are now administered by the World Trade Organization were instituted in negotiations in which the United States exploited to the hilt threats addressed to needs and weaknesses in other countries, both threats of retaliatory tariffs (such as the warning that the United States would play a leading role in "trade wars over all sorts of silly things" if it did not get its way[14]) and threats to exclude the recalcitrant from new, narrow circles of favored partners ("'a market liberalization club' approach, through minilateral arrangements"[15]). In international political relationships, as in domestic ones, someone who adequately respects others' capacity for choice will not be satisfied by joint arrangements whose acceptance depends on fear of threat-advantages she enjoys. She will seek outcomes that could be justified through reasonable deliberations over the best interpretation of relevant shared moral values. Such an outcome of reasonable deliberations over rules for trade, investment, and property rights would substantially differ from current arrangements, in ways that would greatly help needy people in developing countries. For example, current outcomes combine prohibitions of government subsidies to strengthen exports in developing countries with farm subsidies in rich countries that equal a third of the value of their total farm product and substantially exceed the GDP of the fifty poorest countries, devastating farms in developing countries by undercutting farm prices.[16] Principled deliberation based on appeals to relevant shared moral values could not have this outcome. Nor could the reasonable outcome of trade deliberations resemble the current one in which developing countries' exports face higher trade barriers in high-income countries than those faced by other high-income countries, three times higher, on average, on a value-weighted basis in 2000.[17]

Subordination and inequality. In seeking processes and outcomes that respect other peoples' capacity for choice, rather than taking advantage of their weaknesses, a morally responsible citizen of one of the per-capita richest countries will also seek to reduce vast inequalities of income and wealth, which promote subordination in international politics as surely as they do domestically. Thus, her interest in political justice, not just her compassion for the world's needy, will lead to concern with the scale of such inequalities. (For example, in 2007, the ratio of the Gross National Income in the highest-per-capita-GDP countries, where 16 percent of the world's people lived, to GNI in the bottom 20 percent was 53 to 1, converting to dollars at foreign exchange rates, 20 to 1 at purchasing power parity.)[18]

In these and other ways, whatever worthy causes are close to her heart, a morally responsible person in a developed country must be willing to improve the situations of people in developing countries to avoid taking advantage of them. Unlike the plea "Take pity on us," the protest "Don't take advantage of us," is not met by noting, "I'm sorry, but I have other, legitimate goals."

CONCLUSION

Of course, a concern to repair relationships in which one would otherwise take advantage of others is quite compatible with a concern to relieve suffering as such. It is hard to imagine an effective movement to help people in poor countries that is not inspired by both motivations, and appalling to contemplate someone who cares about injustices done to people in poor countries but not about their suffering as such. Still, given the limitations of the duty of general beneficence, arguments from transnational relationships are an especially fruitful source of transnational duties to do more to help needy people in poor countries.

Some may think that the complex reasoning that I have sketched is messy. Maybe so, but it involves the interpretation of vague general principles in light of more specific findings that is the hallmark of sound legal reasoning, and the tolerance for the theoretical complexity that specific observations require that is the hallmark of good science. Perhaps this reasoning has practical benefits as well, in the project of persuading people to do much more to relieve global poverty. The less radical, though demanding, view of our duties to the foreign poor may be less apt to produce a cynical backlash based on the sentiment, "If this is what morality requires, morality isn't for me." The arguments for vast unmet transnational responsibilities honor and appeal to the valuing of special relationships that is central to people's lives, including the valuing of ties to compatriots that is at the center of most conscientious people's political choices. Given the moral force they already ascribe to relationships within borders, it would be arbitrary not to attribute similar force to other relationships across borders.

I have called for many departures from Peter Singer's classic discussions of sacrifice and beneficence. But my effort, like his, is an attempt to derive from ordinary strong moral convictions duties of aid that most of us are reluctant to acknowledge. In this way, my rival to his account of aid and obligation pays homage to his groundbreaking work.

Part II

HOW MUCH INEQUALITY DO WE NEED?

(Some) Inequality Is Good for You

Richard B. Freeman

Economists have a more favorable view of inequality than moral philoso-phers, theologians, other social scientists, and human beings in general. They do not have a more favorable view of inequality because economists are hard-hearted and care less about the poor than other people, though some economists fit that description. Nor do economists have a more favor-able view on inequality because they—or more properly, we—are highly paid beneficiaries of inequality or consultants to corporate America, though again some of us fit those descriptions.

Economists look favorably on inequality because economic analysis stresses that inequality creates incentives that induce people to work hard, invest in skills, and choose work activities where the economy most needs

Richard B. Freeman holds the Ascherman Chair in Economics at Harvard University and is currently serving as faculty codirector of the Labor and Worklife Program at the Harvard Law School. He directs the Science and Engineering Workforce Project at the National Bureau of Economic Research. He is a senior research fellow in labor markets at the London School of Economics' Centre for Economic Performance and a fellow of the American Academy of Arts and Science. He received the Mincer Lifetime Achievement Prize from the Society of Labor Economics in 2006, and in 2007 he was awarded the IZA Prize in Labor Economics. In 2011 he was appointed Frances Perkins Fellow of the American Academy of Political and Social Science. His recent publications include *International Differences in the Business Practices and Productivity of Firms* (with Kathryn Shaw), *Science and Engineering Careers in the United States* (with Daniel Goroff), *Reforming the Welfare State: Recovery and Beyond in Sweden* (with Birgitta Swedenborg and Robert Topel), and *Shared Capitalism at Work: Employee Ownership, Profit and Gain Sharing, and Broad-Based Stock Options* (with Douglas Kruse and Joseph Blasi).

labor. Unlike theologians, economists know why archeologists have found no relics from the Garden of Eden. It is because Adam and Eve had no incentive to produce anything in the Garden. They had no incentive since all consumption was freely available.

Most other members of our species see inequality differently. Many recognize that economic incentives motivate people, but associate inequality more with morally offensive differences in living standards than with incentives. Many regard inequality as arising largely from random luck—who happens to own the land where oil is located or where an earthquake strikes, who happens to have been born into a wealthy or poor family or to have received a particular genetic endowment—rather than as incentives to perform. Some psychologists worry that economic incentives weaken the intrinsic motivation to work and thus do less than economists believe they do to induce people to work. Some argue that monetary incentives have perverse effects on work by undermining intrinsic motivation.

Exhibit 1 documents these differences with a set of quotations from economists and non-economists. Economists defend inequality/incentives as virtuous because it motivates people to undertake the activities that society wants. Moreover, to the extent that it does that, inequality is in part self-correcting. If the pay for star professional wrestlers rises above that for sociologists, which leads to greater inequality, more young persons will train in the squared circle. This will increase the supply of wrestlers, lowering their pay and dampening the wage gap between wrestlers and sociologists. Non-economists object to inequality because they see that inequality is associated with some people living as paupers while others live as princes or princesses. When individuals are poor through no fault of their own, the resultant inequality has nothing to do with incentives and everything to do with morality.

How strong is the evidence regarding the incentive effects of inequality? Does an analysis that treats inequality solely as incentives imply that more inequality is invariably better for production than less inequality? Per the title of this essay, how much inequality is good for a society? And where does the United States fit on the inequality spectrum—too much inequality, too little inequality, or just the right amount?

THE VIRTUES AND SINS OF INEQUALITY

Consider first the virtuous side of inequality as seen through the eyes of an economist. Imagine a world with no inequality of pay. Regardless of

A. Economists

Inequality of wealth and incomes . . . forces all those engaged in production to the utmost exertion in the service of the consumers. It makes competition work . . . [Countries like the United States] enjoy the highest standard of living ever known in history because for several generations no attempts were made toward "equalization" and "redistribution." Inequality of wealth and incomes is the cause of the masses' well-being, not the cause of anybody's distress. —Ludwig von Mises

The inequality of reward which the market system engenders does not seem to me something which persons of good sense should worry about over-much . . . Let us . . . suppose that equality of reward all round is *decreed* to be the order of the day . . . We should expect a tendency to a decline in output per head. If the reward remains the same *whatever the degree of productivity*, we are surely warranted in supposing that there will be at least some diminution of production. —Lionel Robbins

Inequality is necessary for motivation and reward, which contribute to the organization of society for survival and progress . . . —Harry G. Johnson

It is not too much of an exaggeration to say that all of economics results from inequality . . . Increasing dispersion can offer increased opportunities for specialization and increased opportunities to mesh skills and activities. —Finis Welch

B. Non-economists

It is the belief that extremes and excesses of inequality must be reduced so that each person is free to fully develop his or her full potential. This is why we take precious time out of our lives and give it to politics. —Paul Wellstone, U.S. political leader

We can either have democracy in this country or we can have great wealth concentrated in the hands of a few, but we can't have both. —Louis Brandeis, U.S. Supreme Court justice

I strongly believe in fighting inequality. —William J. Wilson, sociologist

(continued)

EXHIBIT I (*continued*)

Inequality makes everyone unhappy, the poor most of all, and that is well within the remit of the state. More money gives less extra happiness the richer we get, yet we are addicted to earning and spending more every year. —Polly Toynbee, journalist

However, as long as poverty, injustice and gross inequality persist in our world, none of us can truly rest . . . Massive poverty and obscene inequality are such terrible scourges of our times—times in which the world boasts breathtaking advances in science, technology, industry and wealth accumulation—that they have to rank alongside slavery and apartheid as social evils. —Nelson Mandela, speech to Trafalgar Square Crowd, February 3, 2005

(I)ncreasing income inequality is bad for the economy, bad for crime rates, bad for people's working lives, bad for infrastructural development, and bad for health—in both the short and long term. —*British Medical Journal*

SOURCES

Brandeis, Louis. http://www.demos.org/inequality/quotes.cfm.
British Medical Journal (1996 editorial): http://www.demos.org/in equality/quotes.cfm.
Mandela, Nelson. http://www.makepovertyhistory.org/docs/mandelaspeech.doc.
Von Mises, Ludwig. *Essays on Liberty*, vol. 3. Irvington-on-Hudson, NY: The Foundation for Economic Education, 1958. Available at http://www.fff.org/freedom/1098f.asp.
Welch, Finis. "In Defense of Inequality." *The American Economic Review* 89, no. 2, Papers and Proceedings of the One Hundred Eleventh Annual Meeting of the American Economic Association: 1–17.
Wellstone, Paul. http://www.brainyquote.com/quotes/quotes/p/paulwellst361467.html.

whether people work hard or take it easy, whether they work in sewers or palaces, do brain surgery or flip burgers, they are paid the same. Would many people work hard or choose the more onerous job and produce much in such a world? Economic analysis suggests that most people would not work hard. They would avoid unpleasant or demanding tasks and shun training for careers that require great knowledge or skill. The result would not be socialism at its idealistic best—from each according to their ability and to each according to their need—but a nonproductive economic mess, in which people would not give their full effort to work, and where the Soviet-era workers' apothegm about pay and effort would hold: "They pretend to pay us, and we pretend to work." Output would increase if the society paid more to those who would work harder or who would gain more skills or who would accept more onerous tasks—i.e., if the society accepted greater inequality. In fact, economies that operate by the market rule "to each according to their ability and effort" outperform those that have relied on moral suasion or altruism to motivate productive effort, at least insofar as the performance of "existing socialism" speaks to the question.

Generalizing from this, economists see efforts to reduce inequality below what the market produces as costing society in terms of output. The efficiency-equity trade-off creates a choice between lower output and a more desirable distribution of income and higher output and a less desirable distribution.[1] If the gain in output from higher inequality is sizeable, the rate of poverty could be lower in a high-inequality society than in a low-inequality society. In fact, when China chose a more market-oriented economy over Communist central planning after the death of Mao Tse-tung, the rate of poverty fell sharply even though inequality rose at one of the fastest rates in recorded history. What matters is the steepness of the efficiency-equity trade-off and the link between poverty and inequality to economic growth. If inequality incentives induce great growth compared to the rise of inequality, poverty will fall as inequality rises. If inequality incentives induce modest growth compared to the rise of inequality, poverty will rise as inequality rises.

Turning to the vice of inequality as seen through the eyes of the non-economist or of economists with an egalitarian bent, consider a world in which most inequality results from random chance. Society hands large sums of money to some people and little to others for no particular reason. You were born a Rockefeller or not, a superstar entertainer or not. You bought the winning lottery ticket or you got the ticket worth nada. To the extent that inequality is due to luck unrelated to incentives, it is hard to justify and costs society little to reduce. Indeed, one of the main precepts of public finance is that it is better to tax factors that are in inelastic supply than factors in elastic supply because taxing the former does not affect their supply of services. Henry George advocated the abolition of all taxes save those on land value because he believed that land was completely inelastic.[2] Some economists favor a head tax on similar grounds. This perspective makes the elasticity of supply responses to marginal incentives a critical factor in assessing government efforts to tax and redistribute income.

Psychologists who study motivation have a different objection to the economic case for inequality in economic rewards. Differentiating between the extrinsic and intrinsic incentives for undertaking actions, they argue that increases in extrinsic economic incentives adversely affect intrinsic motivation and thus are to some extent self-defeating.[3] Reward children for learning math and the children end up disliking math and shunning the subject later. Pay athletes huge sums for performing in the clutch and the pressure leads them to choke. Posing the issue in this way directs attention at the impact of extrinsic incentives on intrinsic incentives and on their net effect on economic behavior.

In sum, the critical issue in the debate over inequality is the extent to which it acts as an incentive and affects total production as opposed to the extent to which it reflects an uneven distribution of resources and consumption. Economists see incentives as being more important in behavior than do most other people and thus generally favor higher levels of inequality than most others. But economic analysis does not predict that increasing equality inevitably increases output or that a society should only choose more unequal outcomes along the equity-efficiency frontier. Economics is more subtle in its predictions about the relation between inequality and output and more catholic in its assessment of social choice and preferences than is indicated by some of the statements of blanket support for inequality in Exhibit 1.

The Relation Between Inequality and Output

Economic analysis suggests that the relation between output and inequality follows an inverse-U-shaped curve. At very low levels of inequality, increases in inequality generate greater social output. The equity-efficiency trade-off operates in that area: society gets more output with more inequality. It chooses the most desirable point. But the gains in output from inequality decline and then drop. Beyond the level of inequality that maximizes output, increases in inequality reduce output. Exhibit 2 illustrates this relation. The horizontal axis displays the level of inequality in an economy. The vertical axis shows output, defined as the sum of the production of each person in the economy based on the incentive determined by the level of inequality.[4] When inequality is zero, output is zero: no incentive → no production. At the maximal level of inequality, where all of the output goes to a single person, output is higher than zero but low. As inequality increases from zero incentives, output increases. People have an incentive to work harder or take on more onerous and productive tasks. As rewards go increasingly to the more productive, some less able workers might reduce their effort but total output would rise as those with greater chances of gaining the larger

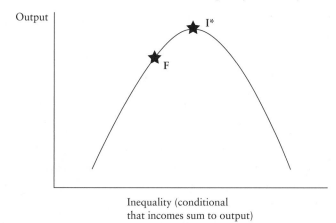

EXHIBIT 2   The inequality-output inverse-U curve

rewards produce more. Then the gains from inequality end and society reaches the output of I*, which is the output-maximizing level of inequality.

To the right of I*, output falls as inequality increases toward the maximum level. The higher inequality will induce a few "superstars" with a chance to reach the top of the income hierarchy to work harder and produce more, but it will demotivate everyone else. Since there are more normal workers than superstars, total output falls. At the extreme, where one person or entity earns nearly everything—the feudal lord, the slave owner, a small group of billionaires—and where most people earn subsistence wages, there is an incentive to become the dominant person or group but not to do much of anything. Run a golf tournament where there is a single prize, and Tiger Woods and a few other players will enter and try hard. But most players, with little or no chance of gaining the prize, will drop out of the tour. In fact, of course, golf and other tournaments give prize moneys to people who rank tenth, twentieth, fiftieth, and so forth (in declining amounts) so that all players have an incentive to enter the tournament and do their best.

A numerical example clarifies the economics. Say a firm has five workers, two of whom are very able and three of whom are less able. The firm has $30 to motivate them to try hard. Under maximal inequality, it offers $30 to the worker who produces the most and none to anyone else. The two workers with a chance of winning try hard. One produces say, 10 units of output beyond what they otherwise would do, and the other produces 9 units of output beyond what they otherwise would do. The three other workers give up and produce the bare minimum. Total output is 19 units higher than it would have been if the firm had not spent $30 on prizes for performance. Now change the prize structure so that there are four prizes: $15 to the top person, $8 to the second, $4 to the third, and $3 to the fourth person. Everyone has an incentive to try to do better. The top two people have less incentive than when there was a single large prize that they might win. Accordingly, they would give less effort and produce less, say 8 and 7 units above what they would have done without any prize. But all of the other workers have an incentive to try harder. Say they produce 5, 4, and 3 units more. Total output is 27 units higher with the new prize structure. The more egalitarian reward system led to 8 units greater output than the winner-take-all reward system.

To be sure, a numerical example can demonstrate only that something is possible. Assume more superstars capable of winning the tournament or a greater gap between the output of the more able and less able, and you can generate the result that rewarding those at the top of the distribution all of the prizes produces greater output than giving incentives for persons throughout the distribution. Contrarily, assume more regular workers, and the less unequal reward system would have looked better than it did in my example. Both economic theory and evidence suggest that the inverse-U-shaped inequality-output curve is a realistic representation of economic reality.

What Economic Theory Says

The relevant theory is the theory of prizes in tournaments when competitors vary in their abilities.[5] Like much economic theory, the analysis is fairly mathematical but structured around a comprehensible idea that can be explained without any math. The analysis specifies the conditions under which it is better to give incentives to many people (multiple prizes in a tournament)—lower inequality—than to concentrate incentives for the top person in the income distribution (single prize in a tournament)—high inequality. The technical condition for multiple prizes to induce greater output than single prizes is that each worker's marginal productivity declines with effort or, equivalently, that their cost of effort rises with the level of effort so that the highly productive squeeze out less additional output when they are given increasingly large incentives compared to the more numerous less productive.

The analysis depends greatly on the uncertainty of gaining greater rewards from increased effort. If there was no uncertainty, the top person would always win, and once everyone knew who the top person was, the other highly productive persons would give up; and similarly for persons lower in the distribution. That uncertainty or luck is a positive contributor to production in a tournament model shows that, contrary to the general view that luck is a nonproductive factor in the distribution of income, some uncertainty/luck is in fact productivity-motivating ex ante. Tournaments are often structured to make sure that uncertainty or luck plays a role in who wins. Tournaments seek to enlist persons of roughly similar abilities so that everyone has some plausible chance of winning (Lazear and Rosen).[6] In some cases, tournaments handicap competitions by giving the less able a leg up in the race, as is common in horse racing.

Finally, while analysis of behavior in tournament settings focuses on individual efforts, much production in the world occurs through the joint activity of persons cooperating together in some form of team production. Assembly line output depends on the inputs of all workers, but even in more individualistic activities, such as research and development, what one person does affects another person's productivity. And while golfers compete as individuals in tournaments, the entire product relies on the activity of many persons beyond the players: caddies, grounds personnel, the transportation sector that enables people to travel to watch the tournament, the producers of clubs and balls, and so forth. The fact that people cooperate in most real production activities suggests that the outcome-maximizing level of inequality is lower than the outcome-maximizing level of inequality in a tournament, where individuals engage solely in competitive activities and which generates no productivity spillovers or interactions.

In short, economic analysis predicts that under reasonably general conditions, there is a level of inequality that is output maximizing. This level depends on the distribution of abilities, uncertainty or luck, and team production, among other factors. The general proposition is more far-reaching than a numerical example, but it still is argumentation, not evidence. To demonstrate that the output is related to inequality in a U-shaped relation in the real world, we must examine the link between inequality and actual economic outcomes and behavior.

EVIDENCE

Analysts have investigated the relation between inequality and economic outcomes in two ways: through studies of aggregate data linking measures of inequality and output generated across countries or states; and through experiments that manipulate incentives in laboratory or field conditions. Each has advantages and disadvantages. Studies that analyze the relation between inequality and productivity at the national or regional level cannot readily pin down the link because so many things differ among countries or regions. Experimental studies can pin down the inequality-behavior link but in potentially artificial settings or in situations that may not generalize beyond the specific experiment.

Aggregate Economic Relations

The aggregate studies yield one consistent empirical finding. In cross-section comparisons of countries, inequality is invariably lower among countries with higher levels of per capita GDP. The particular shape of this relation is less clear. There is a mixed bag of evidence on the famous Kuznets curve,[7] which posits that inequality rises with GDP per capita from very low levels and then falls at higher levels of GDP per capita, which produces the inverse relation of GDP per capita with inequality that dominates most data sets. While it is always valuable to have established an empirical regularity in data, the fact that inequality is lower in countries with higher GDP per capita does not provide much insight into the incentive effect of inequality of interest to us. Analysts interpret the falling inequality with per capita income as largely reflecting the impact of the level of economic development on inequality rather than the impact of incentive inequality on output; and they are undoubtedly correct.

Aggregate studies with a better chance of identifying any causal relation from inequality to growth look at the relation between inequality in a given year and ensuing growth of GDP per capita. By measuring inequality before the period of growth, and focusing on changes in GDP, these analyses eliminate the base-level link from GDP per capita to inequality and any potential impact of fixed country/state factors on inequality and GDP per capita. As Exhibit 3 shows, studies that relate inequality to ensuing economic growth across countries and states generally find a negative relation. This suggests that the average economy is on the right side of the optimal inequality point so that lowering inequality increases output. But the pattern is complicated, and dependent on the data set. The most extensive data on inequality across countries is from Deininger and Squire. Taking all of their data, analysts obtain negative relations between inequality and growth. But analyses limited

EXHIBIT 3

Cross-country studies of the effect of inequality on growth

Reference	Effect of inequality on growth	Source of inequality data
REGRESSIONS WITH LEVEL OF INEQUALITY		
Venieris and Gupta (1986)	--	Fifty observations on fifty countries (one observation per country), between 1958 and 1971 (inclusive); equally balanced between developing and developed countries
Clarke (1992)	--	SOCIND, Jain (1975), U.N. (1981), U.N. (1985), Lecallion et al. (1984); data lie between 1958 and 1976 (inclusive)
Persson and Tabellini (1992)	--	Paukert (1973), Taylor and Hudson (1972), Taylor and Jodice (1983)
Perotti (1994)	--	Flora, Kraus, and Pfenning (1987), Jain (1975), Kuznets (1963), LeCaillon et al. (1984), Paukert (1973), Pryor (1989), U.N. (1981), van Ginneken and Bak (1984), World Development Report (1979), World Development Report (1986)
Alesina and Rodrik (1994)	--	Fields (1973), Jain (1975)
Persson and Tabellini (1994)	--	Paukert (1973), Lindert and Williamson (1985), Hartog and Veenbergen (1978), U.S. Dept. of Commerce (1975), Jain (1975), Flora et al. (1987)
Benhabib and Spiegel (1994)	-	Paukert (1973), Lindert and Williamson (1985), Hartog and Veenbergen (1978), U.S. Dept. of Commerce (1975), Jain (1975), Flora et al. (1987)
Perotti (1996)	--	Data of Persson and Tabellini (1994)
Li and Zou (1998)	+++	The portion of Deininger and Squire high-quality data that contains inequality observations on two consecutive five-year periods
Deininger and Squire (1998)	--	Deininger and Squire high-quality
Sylwester (2000)	--	Deininger and Squire high-quality, Deininger and Squire low-quality
Easterly (2000)	--	Deininger and Squire high-quality, Deininger and Squire low-quality
Keefer and Knack (2000)	--	Deininger and Squire high-quality

(continued)

EXHIBIT 3 (continued)

Reference	Effect of inequality on growth	Source of inequality data
Barro (2000)	+++ in countries with per capita GDP > US $2,000 --- in countries with per capita GDP < US $2,000	Deininger and Squire high-quality, plus extra observations mainly drawn from developing countries
Banerjee and Duflo (2000)	Growth inversely correlated with changes in inequality level	Data used by Forbes (2000)
Deininger and Olinto (2000)	+++	Deininger and Squire high-quality
Castello and Domenech (2001)	++	Deininger and Squire high-quality
REGRESSIONS WITH CHANGES IN INEQUALITY		
Forbes (2000)	+++	The portion of Deininger and Squire high-quality data that contains inequality observations on two consecutive five-year periods
Panizza (2002)	---	U.S. state data from IRS Statistics of Income

NOTE: +++, ---: significant sign; ++, --: sometimes significant; +, -: generally not significant to their "high quality" data (which eliminates many developing countries) often yield a positive relation between inequality and growth. Dividing the countries by GDP per capita, Deininger and Squire, and Barro also, find that advanced countries have growth either unrelated or positively related to inequality, while developing countries have growth negatively related to inequality.[8] There is also evidence from Sweden that in a country with very low inequality higher levels can add to growth: in the 1980s and 1990s, growth was higher in Swedish counties with higher inequality.[9]

An alternative and arguably better way to identify the effect of inequality on growth rates is to compare changes in growth rates with changes in inequality. This design has the virtue of examining how changes in inequality affect growth rates in the same country or geographic unit rather than contrasting growth rates across areas with differing levels of inequality and possibly other unmeasured factors. Analyses using this difference in design yield contradictory results. Using the Deininger-Squire "high quality" data, Forbes found that increases in inequality raise growth rates, while Banerjee and Duflo found that changes in inequality around an initial level reduce growth.[10] But using state data from the United States (which is invariably of high quality on an international scale), Panizza found that increases in inequality reduced growth rates.[11]

In short, the results from analyses of aggregate data are largely inconclusive. One reason is that there is significant measurement error in both the inequality data and growth data in aggregate cross-country analyses. Another reason is that, even when well measured, the Gini coefficient of inequality for any country reflects much more than the incentive inequality of concern to us. Measured inequality (and changes in inequality) consists of incentive inequality and other factors—luck, random or unexpected shocks, and shifts in industry or occupational composition, as well as measurement error—that are unrelated to incentives. Even if these problems could be resolved, there is no single growth equation to which an inequality measure can be simply added as another explanatory factor. Some growth equations focus on investment in human capital, others on research and development, still others on institutional factors, any of which could interact with inequality in substantive ways. Given these problems and the inconclusive empirical results, I put little weight on this evidence and find more compelling evidence from experimental studies that vary incentives in controlled settings to see how high and low levels of inequality affect economic performance.

The Maze Tournament

To illuminate the incentive-output relation, Alex Gelber and I undertook a set of maze experiments at the Harvard Business School Computer Lab for Experimental Research in 2004–2005.[12] In each experiment, we gave six participants the task of solving packets of paper mazes in two rounds: a first round that would identify the participants' maze-solving ability and a second round in which we had subjects compete in a tournament with three incentive treatments, each of which distributed $30 in total prizes.[13] Our *no-inequality* treatment gave each participant $5 regardless of their performance. The only incentive was the intrinsic desire to do well, either absolutely or relative to others. Our *high-inequality* treatment gave $30 to the top scorer and nothing to anyone else. This is the most unequal possible distribution of $30. The no-inequality and high-inequality treatments pin down the end points for the hypothesized curve relating output to inequality. In the *medium-inequality* condition, we gave out multiple prizes. There are many ways to do this. We chose a reward structure in which the winner received $15, the second-prize winner received $7, the third-prize winner received $5, the fourth-prize winner received $2, the fifth-prize winner received $1, and the sixth-prize winner received nothing. This gave incentives to persons in all parts of the distribution of first-round maze performances.

Thus, we presented people with one of the following three incentive/inequality schemes (see Exhibit 4) in the tournament round of our experiment:

In the high-inequality treatment, the incentive is $30 to finish first but there is no incentive to get the second, third, or worse score. In the medium-inequality treatment, there is an incentive to do better throughout the distribution, with the highest marginal incentive at the top of the tournament. In the no-incentive treatment, there is no incentive to do well, beyond intrinsic motivation.

We also varied the amount of information the subjects had about their relative standing in the distribution of maze-solving skills. At the end of

EXHIBIT 4
Position in tournament

Incentive/inequality	1 ($)	2 ($)	3 ($)	4 ($)	5 ($)	6 ($)
High	30	0	0	0	0	0
Medium	15	7	5	2	1	0
None	6	6	6	6	6	6

Round 1, in half of the groups we informed subjects of the scores of all group members in the first round. Since individuals knew their own score, this enabled them to place themselves in the distribution and assess their chances of ranking high or low in the second round. We refer to this treatment as "full information." In the other half of the experiments, we said nothing about how others performed.

We presented the exercise to the subjects in paper-and-pencil form. We asked subjects to report the number of mazes they solved and told them that they had to solve them in the order they were presented in the packet. Serendipitously, this provided an independent test of the effect of incentives on behavior, since it gave subjects the potential to fudge or cheat in the experiment, consciously or unconsciously.

The upper part of Exhibit 5 gives the main results from our experiment in terms of the change in the number of mazes solved per person from the first round to the second round in the three inequality incentives in the full information and no information conditions. The changes per person use the first-round numbers of mazes solved as a control for the individual's maze-solving ability. The results under full information show the inverted U relation. There is a modest increase in the number of mazes solved for the no-inequality group (due presumably to learning); a large increase in the number of mazes solved for the middle-inequality group; and a moderate increase in the number of mazes solved for the high-inequality group. The results under no information show only modestly different responses among the treatments: when subjects have no information about their relative position in the distribution of maze-solving, they have no clear incentive to try harder under the different inequality treatments.

As noted, because the experiment was conducted with paper and pencil mazes rather than with computer mazes, subjects had an opportunity to cheat or fudge on their answers. One way they could do so was to jump their pencil over a line and complete a maze incorrectly. Another way was to skip a maze and do additional mazes and count them in their total, even though the instructions said they could not count any mazes after an incomplete one. In the first round, twenty-six subjects fudged in maze-solving and counted forty-eight mazes as solved that they had not solved properly. There was no statistical difference in the number of people or mazes in which respondents fudged or cheated across the groups by their classification in the second round. By contrast, in the second round, nearly three

Changes in numbers of mazes

A: Mean score increase from Round 1 to
Round 2 for full information treatments

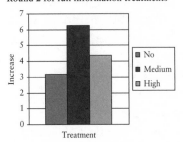

B: Mean score increase from Round 1 to
Round 2 for no information treatments

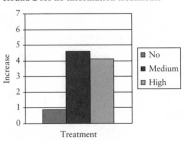

Changes in number of mazes, where person cheated

A: Increase in cheating per person from Round 1
to Round 2 for full information treatments

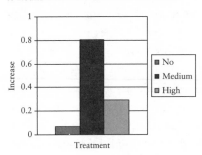

B: Increase in cheating per person from Round 1
to Round 2 for no information treatments

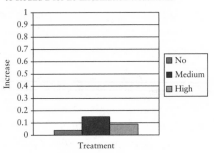

EXHIBIT 5   Changes in numbers of mazes solved and in numbers where person cheated, by incentive treatment and information (per person)

times as many people (76) fudged/cheated on 151 mazes, with a distinct pattern across the treatments. The bottom panel of Exhibit 5 shows that in the full-information case, the largest increase in fudging/cheating occurred for the middle-inequality incentive group, in which all subjects can gain by doing better. Moreover, there is much less cheating and little difference among the groups in the no-information case.

In sum, in the maze tournament, when people know where they stand relative to others and can thus roughly estimate how much they might gain from doing better, inequality/incentives operate to produce the inverted-U pattern shown in Exhibit 2. We decomposed the gains by the position of persons in the distribution of maze-solving and showed further that the difference in the increased number of mazes solved and fudged is driven by persons in the distribution of maze-solving most likely to be affected by the different incentives given by the treatments. For instance, the increased maze-solving in the medium-inequality treatment occurs largely among persons in the bottom of the distribution of mazes solved in the first round. Those are the subjects who can gain from doing better in this treatment. In the high-inequality or no-inequality treatments, where subjects are unlikely to gain from moderately better performances, there is no comparable change in mazes solved among persons in the bottom.

While this is the only experiment with which I am familiar to focus on the predicted inverse-U inequality/output relation, previous experimental investigations of tournament incentive schemes, in which subjects are given "cost-of-effort" functions instead of performing real tasks such as maze-solving, show considerable responsiveness to incentives in ways that would produce inverse-U relations. Harbring and Irlenbusch compare a tournament in which one prize is given to the winner and the sum of the prizes is smaller, with a tournament in which two prizes are given and the sum of the prizes is larger. Subjects put forth more effort in the setting with higher total prize money and multiple prizes.[14] Nalbantian and Schotter find that relative performance schemes outperform target-based schemes.[15] Müller and Schotter find that some participants work hard in tournaments while others effectively drop out.[16] Analogous results to ours are also found in the context of all-pay auctions, which have the same incentive structure as tournaments.[17] The Niederle and Vesterlund experiment, which also has subjects perform a real-effort task (addition problems), focused on the supply decision of men and women to enter a tournament rather than on the response of subjects to variations in tournament incentives. This experiment found different responses of the genders to incentives.[18]

In contrast to these results, there are some psychology experiments that point out the limitations that extrinsic incentives, such as economic rewards, have in motivating behavior. In *Punished by Rewards*, Alfie Kohn uses these studies to argue against employee incentive plans and thus against inequality as incentives.[19] My reading of the experiments in this area is different than his. Some of the studies that convince him that extrinsic rewards such as money do not work show that people behave in a specified way when they are rewarded but desist from that behavior once the rewards are removed. This may be disturbing to someone who wants to alter people's long-term attitudes, but not to an economist. For better or worse, most economic analysis is based on people with fixed preferences responding to rewards, not on changes in preferences and long-term behavior irrespective of ensuing rewards. The prediction of economics is that workers will do more of X when X is rewarded and more of Y of when Y is rewarded. Another set of studies argues that extrinsic rewards undermine intrinsic motivation, so that in the long run economic incentives are bad. Some experiments reward/pay children to play with toys and then examine whether they choose those toys later. Without gainsaying the specific experimental results (which may be confusing declining marginal utility from playing with toys with the hypothesized negative effect of rewards on intrinsic desire), such experiments do not tell much about economic incentives to work, which are designed to induce people to choose onerous and less desirable tasks. And the opposite pattern is also found in some learning experiences: we reward someone to go through the difficult task of learning a language—with good grades, gold stars, whatever—and then they go on to enjoy the period of speaking, reading, and using it later.

Ariely et al. show that, under some conditions, extremely high reward levels can reduce performance.[20] This is presumably because overarousal, nervousness, or "choking" undermine the relationship between effort and performance. If extremely high rewards lead to such overarousal, then the incentive-output relationship will again assume a curvilinear form.

Finally, consider what would happen in an educational setting if some faculty conducted the following experiment in grading classes. In one class, the professor announces that everyone would get a B grade regardless of performance. In another class, the professor announces that the best student would get an A and everyone else would fail. In a third class, the professor announces that grades would follow a grade curve, with the top 20 percent getting As, the next 40 percent getting Bs, the next 30 percent Cs, and 10 percent would fail. Measuring class output by the total number of correct answers on a final exam, in which case do you imagine output would be highest? Every time I have asked colleagues and friends in academe what they would expect, I get the same answer: virtually no output in the first case, with many students skipping the irrelevant exam; large dropout from the second class and mass student protest by those who could not switch to some other class; and the largest number of correct answers in the third case. This is the inequality/incentive inverse-U relation.

OPTIMAL INEQUALITY

Economics does not privilege the output-maximizing level of inequality as the level of inequality that society should seek. The level of inequality is a social good about which individuals can have legitimate varying preferences. A Rawlsian would favor an income distribution that improved the well-being of the very poor even if it lowered the income of most citizens; the average citizen would presumably favor an income distribution that gave more to the middle of the distribution, while the self-made entrepreneur would presumably favor a more unequal distribution to ones that privileged the very poor or the average citizen. The contribution of economists to discussion of inequality in society is to point out the cost of attaining different levels of inequality in terms of reduced incentives and lower social output. If the cost of lowering inequality is modest, even many economists enamored of incentives would, I believe, favor policies that benefit the poor at the expense of the rich. The debate among economists over the minimum wage is not over the goal of raising the incomes of low-income workers but of the possible loss of jobs from the minimum, which harms some low-income workers, and of the potential greater efficacy of other modes of intervening on their behalf—for instance, through an Earned Income Tax Credit.

To be sure, economists are leery about interpersonal comparisons of utility, but the declining marginal utility of income that helps explain individual behavior fits naturally with the commonsensical view that poor persons value additional money more than the Rockefellers and thus getting more resources to the poor should weigh more heavily in the social maximand. Analyzing risk behavior, financial economists assume that people have utility functions in which the marginal utility of income falls fairly sharply and often recognize that people "require" a base level of income for an acceptable standard of living, so that there is high marginal utility at low levels of income.[21] Economists aside, the inequality in the income distributions suggests that the median voter is likely to prefer less inequality than the market generates and thus that in a democracy the socially desired level of inequality will be less than the output-maximizing level. Exhibit 2 displays this relation by locating the desired (fair) level of inequality, F, to the left of I*. With this specification, society pays a price in efficiency for a "fairer" income distribution, giving the equity-efficiency trade-off.

The trade-off is reflected in the slope of the inequality-output curve, which increases the further one moves from I* to other levels of inequality.

WHERE DOES THE UNITED STATES STAND?

The natural question to ask next is how income inequality in the United States compares to the output-maximizing level and to the socially desirable level. This is difficult to answer. There is no natural way to move from small laboratory experiments, such as that in the maze tournament, to measured levels of inequality in society. What is clear is that the United States has the highest level of inequality among advanced countries. Indeed, the level of inequality in the United States exceeds that in many developing countries, where as noted inequality tends to be higher than in advanced countries. My suspicion is that the level of inequality exceeds the output-maximizing level, and that many of the ways in which top earners make their money in response to incentives are counterproductive—giving them reasons to fudge financial reports, hide bad outcomes through financial chicanery, release good news when they can cash in their options, and otherwise exploit the incentive compensation system rather than to act productively. The recent financial crisis might be partly interpreted in just those terms.

One reason for my suspicion is that so much of recent inequality has taken the form of huge increases in earnings at the top of the income distribution, where incentives are already larger than for any other workers. It is hard to imagine that top CEOs need increasingly more pay to motivate them. Another reason is that some of the rise of inequality occurred through modes of payment that do not work as efficient incentives. Much of the high earnings of executives is in stock options that pay off if the firm's share prices rises. They are designed to align the interests of executives with shareholders. But the options are written in ways that seem to raise executive pay regardless of their actual performance. Options pay off when share prices rise above some specified absolute level, so that if inflation or reductions in interest rate raise the prices of all shares, the options increase in value, and even executives in low-performing firms are richly rewarded. When the stock of a company falls, moreover, stock options are often re-priced, which gives a perverse incentive to add volatility to share prices. In summer 2006 a new scandal regarding options surfaced that shocked even aficionados of executive compensation. This is the backdating of options, by which a firm gives shares to executives when share prices are high, and backdates the option as if it had been granted earlier when share prices were lower.

Economists aside, how do the American people see inequality? Do they appreciate the incentive effects? Are they favorable to efforts to reduce U.S. inequality?

First, the facts: Inequality began rising in the United States in the late 1970s/early 1980s and continued increasing through the early 1990s, stabilized or fell slightly in the 1990s' boom, and then drifted upward in the 2000s, depending on the measure of income and of inequality. In 1979 the top 10 percent of wage and salary workers earned 3.5 times per hour what the bottom 10 percent earned. In 2005 the top 10 percent earned 5.8 times as much as the bottom 10 percent.[22] In 1979 college graduates earned 1.4 times as much as high school graduates. In 2005 college graduates earned 1.74 times as much as high school graduates.[23] In 1980 the pay of CEOs was about 42 times that of average workers. In 2004, CEO pay was 262 to 431 times the pay of an average worker, depending on whose estimates of CEO pay one takes.[24]

In the 1980s, the rise in inequality was roughly equally divided between decreases in the income of the lower paid relative to the median and increases in the income of the higher paid relative to the median. This polarization of the income distribution generated widespread concern about the decline of the middle class. When the top of the earnings distribution and the bottom of the earnings distribution pull away from the middle, almost any measure of the middle class will show a declining proportion of workers in the middle.

In the 1990s, the increase in inequality took a very different form: huge increases in the earnings of persons at the very top of the income distribution compared to everyone else. Between 1987 and 2005, the wages of persons in the upper 5 percent of the wage distribution increased from 2.5 times the median to 2.9 times the median earnings. But the gains of the upper 5 percent were not equally shared. The upper 1 percent gained relative to the rest; and within the upper 1 percent it was the upper one-tenth of 1 percent who did really well. It was a great time to be super-wealthy.

The increase in inequality in the United States was sufficiently large that despite healthy economic growth, the living standards of most workers stagnated or declined, breaking with the historic pattern in which real wage growth tracked productivity growth. The rate of poverty barely changed despite increased GDP per capita. It was not a great time to be a normal worker.

To see how Americans view inequality and its rise, I examined the results of two surveys of attitudes toward inequality (see Exhibit 6). The first survey comes from the Campbell Public Affairs Institute of Syracuse University, which has conducted surveys on American attitudes toward inequality since 2004. The 2006 Campbell survey showed that most Americans recognized that inequality was increasing, and that many were worried about its impact on the society. Seventy-one percent said that the United States was becoming a nation of haves and have-nots. Asked whether inequality was a serious problem, an increasing proportion reported that it was a very serious problem, while, asked about the factors that led to achievement, a decreasing proportion believed that abilities and hard work were the key to achievement. Finally, an increasing proportion of Americans favored more government efforts to reduce inequality. The survey shows striking political

EXHIBIT 6

Percentage of Americans with specified attitudes toward inequality and toward the role of ability and hard work in economic achievement

	2004	2005	2006
INEQUALITY AS A PROBLEM			
Serious problem	38.3	46.8	51.6
Somewhat of a problem	43.1	38.5	30.6
Not much of a problem	17.1	12.6	15.3
No opinion	1.6	2.0	2.6
DETERMINANTS OF ACHIEVEMENT			
Family background	7.5	11.6	13.2
Both	27.3	27.6	39.4
Abilities and hard work	63.2	59.8	45.4
No opinion	2.0	1.1	2.0
DIRECTION OF GOVERNMENT EFFORTS TO REDUCE INEQUALITY			
More	53.8	55.1	61.5
About what is done now	22.4	19.0	18.6
Less	17.5	21.5	14.5
No opinion	6.3	4.4	5.4

SOURCES: Maxwell Polls 2004–2006, Campbell Public Affairs Institute, based on questions: "Do you see the current extent of income inequality in our society as a serious problem, somewhat of a problem, or not much of a problem?"; "Do you think what you achieve in life depends largely on your family background, or on your abilities and hard work?"; "Should government do more to try to reduce inequality, about what it is doing now, or less than is done now?" Jeffrey Stonecash, "Inequality and the American Public: Results of the Third Annual Maxwell School Survey Conducted September–October 2006," Working Paper 2006-01. Revised January 2007.

polarization around these issues, with Republicans seeing inequality as a modest problem about which government should do little, while Democrats and independents view it as a problem about which something should be done.

The second survey comes from the 1999 International Social Science Programme Survey (ISSP). Each year members of the ISSP carry out the same survey around the world focused on a particular issue. In 1999 the issue was social inequality. The ISSP surveyed respondents in about twenty-five countries on various aspects of inequality and their views of it. I categorized three statements from the survey as reflecting perceptions of the role of incentives as inequality: people get rewarded for effort; people get rewarded for skill; and people study to earn a lot of money. Many more Americans agree than disagree with these statements, indicating widespread recognition of the incentive role of inequality. On the first two statements, moreover, Americans are far more likely to agree than the citizens in the other countries in the survey. I categorized two statements as reflecting perceptions of inequality as inequity: inequality continues to exist to benefit the rich and powerful; and to get to the top, you have to be corrupt. Americans are much less likely to agree with these statements than persons in other countries. Overall, Exhibit 7 shows that Americans may be closer to economists than to persons in other countries in their views of the relative importance of incentives and inequity in inequality. This would be consistent with the United States accepting greater inequality than other countries, though with levels of inequality coming to exceed those in many developing countries, this tolerance may be changing.

CONCLUSION

Inequality is Janus-faced. On the one side, it is an incentive that motivates people to produce more and to undertake productive tasks that they might otherwise have rejected. Economists stress the role of inequality as incentive. On the other side, inequality creates differences in living standards that many view as inequitable. Non-economists stress the role of inequality as inequity. The analysis in this essay has brought these two visions of inequality together. It has shown that inequality is an incentive for greater production up to a point—the output-maximizing level of inequality, beyond which additional inequality reduces total output. It has further argued

EXHIBIT 7
Americans see inequality more as incentives than as inequity

	U.S. (n = 1,272)		ALL COUNTRIES (n = 34,178)	
	Agree (%)	Disagree (%)	Agree (%)	Disagree (%)
INCENTIVE INEQUALITY				
People get rewarded for effort	61	11	33	45
People get rewarded for skill	69	8	40	35
People study to become lawyers or doctors to earn a lot more than ordinary workers[a]	58	22	68	16
INEQUITY INEQUALITY				
Inequality continues to exist because it benefits the rich and powerful	45	20	66	14
To get to the top, you have to be corrupt	16	56	34	41

SOURCE: Tabulated from International Social Science Programme Survey ISSP 1999, "Social Inequality III," ZA No. 3430, http://www.gesis.org/en/data_service/issp/data/1999_Social_Inequality_III.htm.

[a] I reverse-coded this for ease of interpretation. The actual question was, "No one would study for years to become a lawyer or doctor unless they expected to earn a lot more than ordinary workers."

that the socially ideal level of inequality will tend to be lower than the output-maximizing level, generating an equity-efficiency trade-off.

The difficult problem is in moving from the theory and experimental evidence to the actual status of inequality in the United States or in other countries. From the 1970s through the 2000s, inequality rose greatly in the United States, placing the country at the top of the league tables in inequality. While Americans are more attuned to inequality as incentive than persons in most other countries, survey evidence shows rising concerns over the level of inequality. As noted, I suspect but cannot prove that inequality has gone past the output-maximizing level. For the typical American, who has obtained just a small share of the gains of economic growth, inequality has almost certainly gone past the level that maximizes his or her income. The country has experimented with tax cuts and spending decisions favoring high-income citizens with the result that they have benefitted handsomely, while earnings growth has been relatively stagnant for most of the rest of the population. If future U.S. governments experiment with tax and fiscal policies favorable to the average citizen, shifting incentives down the income distribution as in the middle-inequality maze experiment, my guess is that the economy will grow as or more rapidly than it would with continued policies that privilege the wealthy few. If I am wrong and policies that gave more income to the average citizen reduced aggregate growth, I expect that the average citizen would still benefit. A policy that reduces the billionaire's income by, say $100 million, but increases the income of regular workers by $90 million and thus lowers GDP by $10 million would seem to be socially more desirable than policies that increase the billionaire's income by $100 million at the expense of $90 million of lost income for others, even though the result is a $10 million increase in GDP. Of course, some billionaires might disagree with this statement about the location of the "fair" income distribution shown in Exhibit 2.

Inequality and Economic Growth in Comparative Perspective

Jonas Pontusson

One of the big controversies about inequality concerns its implications for economic efficiency and growth and, by extension, its implications for average living standards. Most of us would agree that a more egalitarian society is preferable to a less egalitarian society, everything being equal. But if we care about the welfare of people at the bottom of the socio-economic hierarchy, we must care about average living standards as well as the distribution of living standards across the socio-economic hierarchy. Put differently, we must care about the median income as well as the distance between the median and the bottom.

Consider two hypothetical countries with a median household income of \$20,000 and identical distributions of market income.[1] With poverty defined as a household income of less than 40 percent of the median household income, 20 percent of the population lives in "poor" households before taxes and transfers. While country A engages in redistributive tax and spending policies that bring the poverty rate down to 10 percent, country B does not engage in any redistribution and so the poverty rate remains 20 percent. In an immediate sense, the poor are better off in country A than in country B. But suppose that redistribution by the government has

Jonas Pontusson is a professor of comparative politics at the University of Geneva. He received the American Political Science Association's Gladys M. Kemmerer Award for *Inequality and Prosperity: Social Europe Versus Liberal America* (2005) and the Heinz Eulau Award for "The American Welfare State in Comparative Perspective" (*Perspectives on Politics*, 2006). Coauthored with Noam Lupu, his most recent article, "The Structure of Inequality and the Politics of Redistribution," appeared in *American Political Science Review*.

the additional effect of reducing the rate of economic growth so that, ten or fifteen years later, the median household income of country A is $25,000 as compared to a median income of $30,000 in country B. It is no longer clear that the poor in country A are better off than the poor in country B.

Conventional wisdom teaches us that egalitarianism will, at least if taken to extremes, interfere with the dynamics of (capitalist) economic growth. Our intuitive notion that there is some kind of trade-off between equality and growth resonates with many of the premises of mainstream economics. The basic argument is familiar, indeed so much taken for granted that it is seldom explicitly articulated: inequality creates incentives for individuals to work hard, to innovate, and to invest (in human capital as well as other forms of capital). Although I will take issue with some of Richard Freeman's contribution to this volume, I appreciate the lucidity with which he articulates an argument that is too often left unstated.

It is hard to argue with Richard Freeman's proposition that if an instructor announces in advance that everyone will get a B for the course regardless of their performance on the final exam, no one will study for the final exam. This proposition seems almost certain to be true, but it also seems rather trite. The important questions are, first, whether the trade-off between equality and effort observed in such an experiment translates into a trade-off between equality and growth at the level of national economies and, second, whether this trade-off is continuous in the sense that less equality always translates into more growth.

The simple version of the trade-off thesis would lead us to expect that more egalitarian countries tend, on average, to grow less rapidly than less egalitarian countries. As I demonstrate ahead, cross-national comparison of OECD countries does not at all bear out this expectation. A second, more subtle version of the trade-off thesis focuses on the disincentive effects of political efforts to create a more equal distribution of economic rewards, through either progressive taxation or income transfers to poorer individuals or households. In this version of the trade-off thesis, equality does not necessarily preclude economic dynamism; equality of rewards is fine so long as it reflects the distribution of wealth and educational endowments. The problem arises when governments intervene to offset or alter the distributive effects of market dynamics. If this argument is correct, more redistribution should be associated with less growth on a cross-national basis. Again, this prediction is not borne out by data for the OECD countries.

In his contribution to this volume, Richard Freeman advances yet a third version of the trade-off thesis, positing a hump-shaped relationship between inequality and growth. In Freeman's account, inequality promotes economic growth, but only up to a certain point. Beyond that point, increasing inequality becomes counterproductive from the point of view of economic performance. This argument strikes me as a reasonable and attractive compromise, but I do not find any support for it in my cross-national data.

The question becomes, why is it that aggregate data on inequality and growth do not yield patterns of association predicted by any of the variants of the trade-off thesis? In what follows, I will present several arguments to the effect that egalitarianism may have positive as well as negative consequences for economic growth. Also, I will consider the proposition that countries with more egalitarian income distributions have developed policies that offset or compensate for the disincentive effects that egalitarianism entails.

My discussion ends up emphasizing two points. First, in thinking comparatively about the relationship between inequality and growth, it is essential to distinguish between different forms of inequality. Some income differentials are more "productive" than others, and the relative importance of productive income differentials is likely to vary across countries. Secondly, the size of the material rewards necessary to elicit a certain amount of effort (or some other behavioral response) is also likely to vary across countries. The cross-national evidence presented ahead suggests that responsiveness to material rewards increases as inequality declines.

OKUN'S BIG TRADE-OFF

Arthur Okun's book of 1975, entitled *Equality and Efficiency: The Big Trade-Off*,[2] is commonly cited as the classic statement of the trade-off thesis. Observing that "the market creates inequality and efficiency jointly,"[3] Okun flatly asserts that "we can't have our cake of market efficiency and share it equally."[4] It deserves to be noted, however, that Okun quickly qualifies the trade-off thesis. In his words,

> the presence of a tradeoff between efficiency and equality does not mean that everything that is good for one is necessarily bad for the other. Measures that might soak the rich so much as to destroy investment and hence impair the quality and quantity of jobs for the poor could worsen both efficiency and equality. On the other hand, techniques that improve the productivity and

earnings potential of unskilled workers might benefit society with greater efficiency *and* greater equality. Nonetheless, there are places where the two goals conflict, and those pose the problems.[5]

Curiously, the chapter in which Okun promises to lay bare the conflict between equality and efficiency focuses on the virtues of market allocation of economic resources and the inefficiencies of economic planning, i.e., the superiority of capitalist market economies over socialist planned economies. From the perspective of this capitalism-socialism comparison, the proposition that markets are a source of both efficiency and inequality seems undisputable. However, the trade-off thesis implies something else: namely, that efficiency and inequality are associated with each other *in the context of capitalist market economies*. Do more efficient markets generate more inequality than less efficient markets? Or, alternatively, does inequality render markets more efficient? Like many mainstream economists, Okun does not seem to perceive any pressing need to justify the assumption that inequality is either a source of efficiency-enhancing incentives or a "proxy" for such incentives.

Okun is a liberal, in the American sense of the word. His liberalism manifests itself first and foremost in the emphasis that he places on the distinction between "equality of opportunity" and "equality of rewards." Okun argues persuasively that inequality of opportunity (for example, in college admissions) is an important source of economic inefficiency in contemporary American society, since it implies a misallocation of "natural talent." In other words, inequality of opportunity prevents talented people from rising to positions in which their talents would contribute most fully to efficiency. As conceived by Okun, the trade-off between equality and efficiency pertains specifically to equality of rewards, i.e., monetary returns to investment, innovation, and hard work. In essence, Okun's political project is to eliminate inequality of opportunity while preserving inequality of rewards.

The obvious question that arises is whether the two forms of inequality identified by Okun can in fact be so neatly separated. After all, the ability to do things for one's children, to help them get a "head start" in any number of different ways—and, ultimately, to pass on one's accumulated wealth—is itself a major incentive motivating individuals in our society. Moreover, inequality of opportunity involves more than simply discriminatory college admissions practices such as "affirmative action" in favor of children of alumni. It is difficult to see how inequality of opportunity could truly be eliminated in a society characterized by large income differentials.

This introduces the possibility that redistributive policies may have positive effects on efficiency by reducing inequality of opportunity even if they also have negative effects by reducing inequality of rewards.

CROSS-NATIONAL EVIDENCE: A FIRST CUT

As formulated by Okun, the trade-off is between equality and efficiency. To the extent that economists have explored this problem empirically, however, their investigations have dealt with the relationship between income distribution and economic growth. As every economics textbook tells us, growth is a function of the amount of capital and labor that is put into productive activities as well as the efficient utilization of these factors of production. The shift in focus from efficiency to growth reflects the fact that efficiency is notoriously difficult to measure. Moreover, it is a matter of definition that, everything else being equal, more efficient economies will grow more rapidly than less efficient economies.

At least as a first cut, then, the trade-off thesis might be empirically evaluated by asking whether inequality is positively associated with higher rates of economic growth on a cross-national basis. If we were to find that such an association exists, we would want to ask whether efficiency is really the causal mechanism involved, but this line of inquiry becomes moot if there is no positive association between inequality and growth. (An alternative mechanism linking inequality and growth would be that inequality is associated with lower absolute incomes at the bottom of the income distribution, inducing low-income households to work more.)

The preliminary analysis presented in Exhibits 1–3 is restricted to industrialized countries or, in other words, long-time members of the Organization for Economic Cooperation and Development (OECD). There are two reasons why I restrict my analysis in this manner. First, the data on income distribution in the OECD countries are more reliable (and more directly comparable) than the data on income distribution in developing countries. Second, the OECD countries share a number of conditions that can be expected to affect the dynamics of economic growth. Most obviously, these countries are all well-functioning democracies and all have well-developed, compulsory systems of primary and secondary education. Holding these considerations constant allows us, again as a first cut, to look at the bivariate association between income distribution and growth (and to observe how specific countries line up in a two-dimensional space).

We are interested in the effects of inequality on growth, yet there are good reasons to suppose that economic growth also affects the distribution of income. The simplest way to deal with this potential for reverse causality is to plot growth against levels of inequality prior to the period for which growth is observed.[6] In all the graphs presented in this essay, growth is measured as the change in real GDP per capita over the ten-year period from 1994 to 2004. In due course, I will address the question of whether findings based on this particular time period are somehow unique.[7]

To begin with, Exhibit 1 plots real growth of GDP per capita over the period 1994–2004 against 90-10 wage ratios in or around 1994. The "90-10 ratio" is the ratio of earnings of someone in the 90th percentile of the earnings distribution (i.e., someone at the bottom of the top 10 percent) to the earnings of someone in the 10th percentile (i.e., someone at the top of the bottom 10 percent). With one exception, the figures presented here refer to gross (pre-tax) earnings from employment and are restricted to full-time employees.[8]

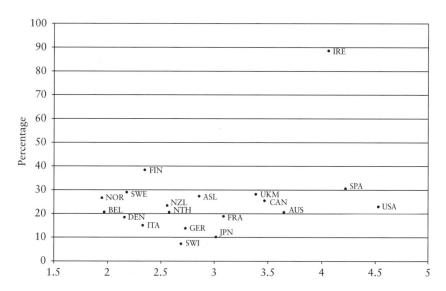

EXHIBIT I   Real growth of GDP per capita 1994–2004 versus 90-10 wage ratios c. 1994

SOURCES: Real growth of GDP per capita (at purchasing power parities) from OECD, National Accounts 2006, v. 1, pp. 332–33; wage ratios from OECD Directorate for Education, Employment, Labour and Social Affairs (electronic database).

NOTE: Wage ratios refer to years other than 1994 for Denmark (1990); Spain (1995); Canada, New Zealand, Norway (1997); and Belgium (1999).

The Irish economic miracle is the most eye-catching feature of Exhibit 1. Over these ten years, Irish GDP per capita nearly doubled, increasing by 89 percent (or, on average, by nearly 6.5 percent per year). The Irish growth rate in this period was more than twice that of Finland, the second-best growth performer among the nineteen countries. At the other end of the spectrum, Switzerland and Japan, both relatively rich countries to begin with, stand out as the two countries with the most sluggish growth of GDP per capita over this period.

Ireland turns out to be not only the best GDP growth performer by a long shot, but also one of the OECD countries with the most unequal distribution of wages. However, the overall picture conveyed by Exhibit 1 clearly suggests that inequality cannot be the main explanation for the Irish miracle. Ignoring the Irish case, there is no indication whatsoever in Exhibit 1 that wage inequality is associated with more rapid economic growth. Belgium, New Zealand, the Netherlands, Austria, and the United States cover the entire range of wage inequality among OECD countries, yet all fall within the range of 20–24 percent growth of GDP per capita. Also, it is noteworthy that three of the five countries with the most compressed wage distributions in the early 1990s—Finland, Sweden, and Norway—have enjoyed above-average growth rates (higher than the U.S. growth rate). If anyone needs any further convincing as regards Ireland, it need only be noted that, during the recent recession, Ireland's high inequality didn't protect against a spectacular decline in GDP (nearly 14 percent) during the Great Recession of 2008–09.[9]

90-10 wage ratios for full-time employees represent a particular, rather narrow, measure of income inequality. For a subset of countries, the Luxembourg Income Study provides the basis for more comprehensive measures of income inequality. In contrast to the OECD data on relative wages, the LIS data pertain to the distribution of income among households. Since the debate about the consequences of inequality for growth concerns its effects on the behavior of individuals who are engaged in productive activities or who anticipate being engaged in productive activities, it makes sense to restrict our analysis to income inequality among working-age households (here operationalized as households headed by someone between the ages of twenty-five and fifty-nine). Also, certain qualities of the LIS data make the Gini coefficient a more appropriate measure of income inequality than decile ratios. Ranging from 0 to 1, the Gini coefficient is a commonly used measure of income distribution. Multiplied by 100, it represents the percentage of total income that would have to be redistributed in order to achieve complete equality.

For eleven countries, the LIS database allows us to calculate Gini coefficients for gross market as well as net market income and disposable income among working-age households. For an additional three countries, it allows us to calculate Gini coefficients for net market income and disposable market income only. "Market income" includes income from financial assets and self-employment as well as income from dependent employment. Needless to say, perhaps, "net market income" refers to market income net of taxes. In addition, "disposable income" includes transfer payments and "near-cash" benefits received from the government, also net of taxes.[10] The results of plotting GDP growth against Gini coefficients for gross and net market income are very similar. With Gini coefficients for net market income on the horizontal axis, to maximize the number of countries included, Exhibit 2 suffices to illustrate that there is no linear association between the

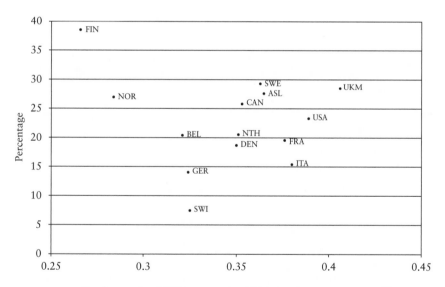

EXHIBIT 2   Real growth of GDP per capita 1994–2004 versus Gini coefficients for net market income, working-age households, in the early 1990s

SOURCES: OECD, National Accounts (see Exhibit 1), and Luxembourg Income Study (own calculations).

NOTE: Years of observations of household income inequality are as follows. 1991: Finland, Norway, United Kingdom; 1992: Belgium, Denmark, Sweden, Switzerland; 1994: Australia, Canada, France, Germany, Netherlands, USA.

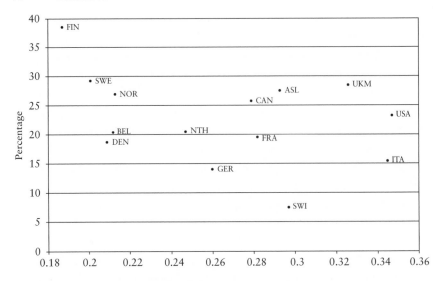

EXHIBIT 3   Real growth of GDP per capita 1994–2004 versus Gini coefficients for disposable income, working-age households, in the early 1990s

SOURCES: See Exhibit 2.
NOTE: See Exhibit 2.

distribution of market income and economic growth over the last decade. With Ireland missing for lack of data on net market income, Finland stands out as the most egalitarian and also the fastest growing of the countries included in Exhibit 2.

Exhibit 3 repeats the exercise with Gini coefficients for disposable income on the horizontal axis. Again, cross-national comparison seems to provide no support whatsoever for the proposition that more inequality spurs efficiency and thereby contributes to faster economic growth.

THE TRADE-OFF THESIS REVISED: REDISTRIBUTION AS THE PROBLEM?

The absence of cross-national support for the simple trade-off hypothesis should not come as news to economists or others familiar with the relevant literature in economics. In fact, several articles by prominent economists have shown, using multiple regression analysis of data for developing as well as developed countries, that more inequality tends to be associated with slower rather than faster economic growth.[11]

Separate contributions by Alesina and Rodrik and by Persson and Tabellini propose a modified version of the trade-off thesis in the face of what would appear to be disconfirming empirical evidence. The specific assumptions of the economic models developed by these authors differ, but the gist of their argumentation is strikingly similar. Crudely put, governments depend on the support (or, in the case of nondemocratic countries, on the acquiescence) of the majority of citizens, and the extent to which governments engage in redistribution of wealth or income is a function of the interests of the median voter. As inequality rises, governments come under increasing pressure to redistribute income. Redistribution in turn reduces the incentives for individuals to work hard and, above all, their incentives to invest in education and other forms of capital accumulation. For Alesina and Rodrik and Persson and Tabellini alike, then, inequality is harmful to economic growth because it generates redistributive policies that have harmful effects on the structure of incentives.

The modified trade-off thesis proposed by these authors seems to hinge on the proposition that it matters crucially whether a given incentive structure is the product of government intervention. This proposition deserves critical scrutiny. In calculating whether to undertake a certain investment—say, a college education—individuals presumably care about the returns to this investment in terms of disposable (post-tax) income. Consider two hypothetical countries. In country A, the gross earnings of those who have graduated from college are, on average, three times as high as the gross earnings of those who have not graduated from college, but progressive income taxation reduces this differential to a factor of two. In country B, the gross earnings of college graduates are twice as high and income taxation is strictly proportional, so that the post-tax college premium remains the same. The modified trade-off thesis appears to stipulate that individuals in country B will be more prone to invest in a college education, but it is far from clear why this should be so. More plausibly, proponents of the modified trade-off thesis might argue that pre-tax earnings differentials indicate that country B is less in need of college graduates than country A.

The latter argument brings out another problem with the modified trade-off thesis: the premise that in the absence of government intervention earnings differentials are determined simply and harmoniously by the interplay of supply and demand. As many scholars have shown, labor-market institutions matter greatly to the structure of relative wages. A great deal of empirical evidence suggests not only that unionization is associated with more compressed wage differentials, within and between firms, but also that the degree of bargaining centralization and the collective behavior of employers matter to the structure of relative wages.[12] Clearly, wage setting within firms is also a deeply politicized process or, in other words, a process in which the exercise of power comes into play, altering the effects of market forces. In "real-existing capitalist economies," the forces of supply and demand are distorted by many factors, at different stages in the process whereby individual earnings and household incomes are determined. Thus it seems rather problematic to imagine that we could identify a pure market allocation of income that would define the appropriate structure of incentives for any particular economy.

Leaving the underlying premises of the modified trade-off thesis aside, how does it hold up against cross-national empirical evidence? The fact that we do not observe any negative association between inequality and growth across OECD countries over the period 1994–2004 raises some questions about the empirical findings presented by Alesina and Rodrik and Persson and Tabellini, but the evidence presented earlier is by no means definitive on this score. In any case, the real question here is whether comparative analysis supports the contention that redistributive government policies are harmful to economic growth. This is clearly the critical step in the arguments developed by these authors. While Alesina and Rodrik's empirical analysis completely ignores this question, the negative coefficients for government spending on income transfers reported by Persson and Tabellini fall far short of any conventional criteria for statistical significance.[13]

Still restricting our analysis to working-age households, the LIS database allows us to calculate the combined impact of taxes and transfer payments on the distribution of household income for eleven countries. Again, it is possible to calculate the redistributive impact of transfer payments only for an additional three countries. These alternative measures of redistribution—total redistribution and redistribution via transfers—appear on the horizontal axes of Exhibits 4 and 5, respectively.[14] Contrary to the modified trade-off thesis, both exhibits suggest that redistribution may have contributed positively to economic growth in the 1994–2004 period. I hasten to point out that Switzerland is clearly an influential case in these exhibits, being characterized by exceptionally little redistribution

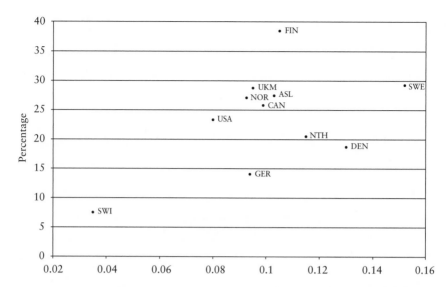

EXHIBIT 4   Real growth of GDP per capita 1994–2004 versus total government redistribution (Gini coefficients for gross market income minus Gini coefficients for disposable income) in the early 1990s

SOURCES: See Exhibit 2.
NOTE: See Exhibit 2.

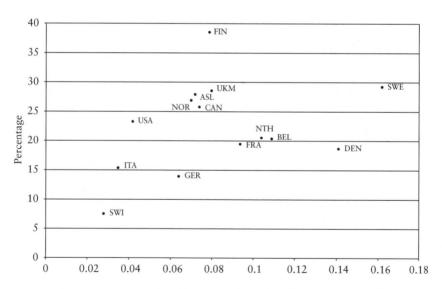

EXHIBIT 5   Real growth of GDP per capita 1994–2004 versus government redistribution via transfers (Gini coefficients for net market income minus Gini coefficients for disposable income) in the early 1990s

SOURCES: See Exhibit 2.
NOTE: See Exhibit 2.

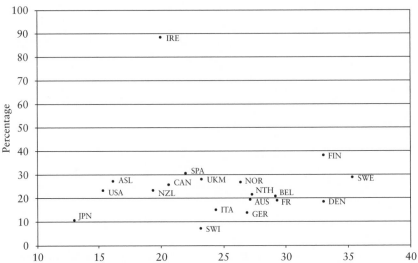

EXHIBIT 6   Real growth of GDP per capita 1994–2004 versus public social spending in percentage of GDP in 1994

SOURCES: Exhibit 1 and OECD, Social Expenditure Database (http://www.oecd.org/els/social /expenditure).

and also exceptionally slow growth. Recognizing Swiss exceptionalism, one should not make too much of the positive association between redistribution and growth. Yet it is surely fair to say that this evidence contradicts the modified trade-off thesis.

Exhibit 6 plots growth of GDP per capita over 1994–2004 against government spending on social programs as a percentage of GDP in 1994. Public social spending in percent of GDP is commonly treated as a proxy for redistribution and allows us to include the full set of OECD countries.[15] With Ireland back in the picture, the positive association between redistribution and growth disappears, but the argument that redistribution is harmful to growth does not seem to fare any better than it did with direct measures of redistribution.

THE TRADE-OFF HYPOTHESIS REVISED (AGAIN): OPTIMAL INEQUALITY?

Whereas the simple version of the trade-off thesis expects growth (or efficiency) to rise as inequality increases, the modified versions proposed

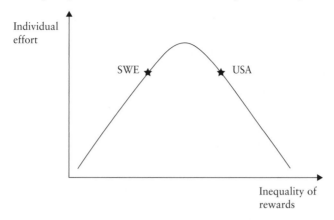

EXHIBIT 7   Illustration of the optimal-inequality thesis

by Alesina and Rodrik and by Persson and Tabellini expect growth (or efficiency) to decline as redistribution increases. In either case, the relationship between inequality or redistribution, on the one hand, and efficiency or growth, on the other, is assumed to take a linear form. By contrast, Richard Freeman's contribution to this volume suggests that the relationship between inequality and efficiency takes the form of a hump-shaped curve or, in other words, a curve shaped like an inverted U. In an article co-authored by Anders Björklund, Freeman puts the argument as follows: "Too little inequality reduces work incentives so much that no one bothers to work; too much inequality means that people work too little because most people are not adequately rewarded for their work."[16] As illustrated by Exhibit 7, this argument implies there is an optimal level of inequality and that inequality falls short of the optimal level in some countries while it exceeds the optimal level in other countries. While more inequality would spur economic growth in more egalitarian countries, like Sweden, it would actually dampen growth in less egalitarian countries, like the United States.

The basic idea behind Freeman's argument might be illustrated by the following examples. Suppose that the instructor in a course announces in advance of the exam that all students will get a B in the course regardless of how they perform. Surely, we would not expect any of the students to study very hard, if at all, for the exam. On the other hand, suppose that the instructor announced that the student with the best performance on the exam will get an A and that everyone else will get a C. Some students would probably study very hard for the exam, but many would decide that their prospects of turning in the best exam performance were hopeless, and therefore they would behave just as they would under the first scenario. This example illustrates the potentially negative effects of competitions based on the "winner-take-all" principle.[17] From the point of view of maximizing effort across the entire collectivity, it is surely desirable to have an incentive structure that provides for a significant number of intermediary rewards. But does the winner-take-all example really speak to the question of the size of differential rewards? Freeman wants to argue that the distance between the rewards of the top performer and worst performer matters even if there is a graduated reward structure between the two, but his argument on this score is not fully developed.

The idea of a curvilinear, hump-shaped relationship between inequality and efficiency or growth is appealing, but why should we assume that that there is a single curve that defines this relationship across all countries? I shall return to this question shortly. For now, let me simply observe that the cross-national evidence presented in Exhibits 1–3 does not conform to the optimal inequality thesis. Based on Freeman's argumentation, one would expect to observe above-average rates of growth among countries in the middle range of the distribution on measures of income inequality. This is clearly not what we observe. Quite the contrary, there is some indication of a U-shaped relationship between inequality and growth in these scatterplots. In Exhibit 1, Switzerland, Germany, and Japan are distinguished by medium levels of wage inequality and particularly slow economic growth. In Exhibit 3, with growth being plotted against Gini coefficients for disposable household inequality, Switzerland and Germany again appear as cases that challenge the optimal inequality thesis.

PREEMPTING SOME OBJECTIONS

To summarize, none of the three versions of the trade-off thesis identified earlier seem to be supported by cross-national comparison based on data from the OECD countries. Among these countries, we do not observe the positive linear association between inequality and growth posited by the simple trade-off argument. Nor do we observe the negative linear association between redistribution and growth predicted by Alesina and Rodrik and by Persson and Tabellini. Finally, we do not observe any trade-off between equality and growth among the subset of countries that fall within the range of low-to-medium levels of inequality, as the idea of optimal inequality would lead us to expect.

The assumptions about material rewards as growth-enhancing incentives underpinning the different versions of the trade-off thesis appear to be eminently plausible at the level of individual behavior. So why do we not observe any evidence of the disincentive effects of egalitarianism in aggregate cross-national data? Before turning to this question, let me briefly address some potential objections to Exhibits 1–6 as empirical evidence against different versions of the trade-off thesis.

The most obvious objection to the preceding discussion is that Exhibits 1–6 demonstrate only the absence of bivariate associations between inequality (or redistribution) and growth. Arguably, we must control for other factors that affect the rate of economic growth in order to observe the true effects of inequality (or redistribution) on growth. With such a small number of total observations, however, the room for multivariate regression analysis is limited. More importantly, it is not altogether obvious what factors other than initial levels of GDP per capita should be included in a regression model designed to assess the effects of inequality on growth in OECD countries.

Following conventional practice among economists, including initial levels of GDP per capita serves as a means to control for various catch-up effects—the basic hypothesis being that poor countries are able to import capital and borrow more advanced technology and therefore tend to grow faster than rich countries. In simple OLS regression equations with the growth of GDP per capita over 1994–2004 as the dependent variable and GDP per capita in 1994 along with some measure of inequality or redistribution in the early 1990s as the independent variables, the coefficient for GDP per capita is indeed negative, as the catch-up thesis predicts, but this coefficient becomes entirely insignificant (statistically as well as substantively) once we take Irish exceptionalism into account. Such regressions yield negative coefficients for wage inequality and household income inequality alike, but the coefficients do not come anywhere close to conventional criteria for statistical significance. In sum, controlling for initial levels of economic development does not alter the conclusion that there is no association between levels of inequality and rates of economic growth in OECD countries over the period 1994–2004.[18]

As everyone would agree, the rate of investment constitutes an important determinant of the rate of growth, but this variable is "endogenous" in the sense that the effects of inequality on the rate of growth should operate through its effects on the rate of investment (with higher inequality increasing the incentives to invest according to the standard argument). For this reason, neither Alesina and Rodrik nor Persson and Tabellini include the rate of investment in their multivariate tests. Indeed, their only control variables, other than initial levels of development, are primary school enrollment and democracy. Again, Exhibits 1–6 largely control for these variables by virtue of being restricted to OECD countries.

Related to the last point, I imagine that some skeptics might object to the fact that Exhibits 1–6 are restricted to OECD countries, suspecting that the trade-off thesis would fare better against data from a wider range of countries. To reiterate, my analysis is restricted to OECD countries because of the easy availability of reliable, comparable measures of inequality and redistribution and also because this serves as a way to control for potentially confounding variables. Furthermore, it should be noted that Alesina and Rodrik's and Persson and Tabellini's analyses, which include developing countries, yield results that indicate that countries with less inequality tend to grow faster (not slower) than countries with more inequality. There is no reason to believe that the simple version of the trade-off thesis would fare any better, but it is certainly possible that either or both modified versions would indeed fare better against data from a wider range of countries. Let me simply make one point on this score. The evidence against the argument that redistribution is harmful to growth presented in Exhibits 4–6 strikes me as quite compelling. If a more comprehensive analysis were to show that government social spending was associated with slower growth, it would remain an open question whether this association should be attributed to disincentives generated by redistribution, as opposed to corruption associated with redistributive government spending in developing countries.

Yet another set of potential objections has to do with the time period covered by Exhibits 1–6. Arguably, ten years is not a sufficiently long period for the growth-enhancing effects of inequality to manifest themselves. In a different vein, the skeptical reader might wonder whether the particular period 1994–2004 is somehow uniquely unfavorable to the trade-off thesis. Regarding the latter issue, it should be noted that Exhibits 1–6 favor the Nordic countries, especially Sweden and Finland, because they do not include the early 1990s, when these countries underwent deep recessions. If GDP-per-capita growth were measured over the period 1990–2004 rather than 1994–2004, the performance of the Nordic countries relative to other OECD countries would be less impressive. Still, plotting GDP growth 1990–2004 against various measures of income distribution and redistribution in the late 1980s produces overall patterns that are remarkably similar to those in Exhibits 1–6, failing to confirm the modified versions of the trade-off thesis as well as the original version.[19]

It deserves to be noted that the Anglophone liberal market economies, which have long been characterized by more unequal income distributions and relatively small welfare states, have performed much better relative to Japan and continental Europe since 1990 than they did during the "Golden Era" of postwar economic growth. For lack of data on income distribution and redistribution, it is not possible to repeat Exhibits 1–6 for earlier decades, but there is no reason to believe such an exercise would yield more support for the trade-off thesis. Quite the contrary, there are good reasons to believe that the 1994–2004 period is less unfavorable to the trade-off thesis than previous ten-year periods.[20] Likewise, the period since 2004 will be dominated by the complicated country-specific pattern of recession effects, a pattern that at least on the face of it wouldn't appear to be consistent with the trade-off thesis.

The conventional wisdom about egalitarianism having negative effects on growth does not rest on arguments that are particularly subtle or carefully circumscribed. Mainstream economists do not typically argue along the lines that "compressed income differentials can be expected to have negative consequences for efficiency and growth under the following conditions . . ." Quite the contrary, their claims about the disincentive effects that egalitarianism entails are strong and sweeping. These claims imply that we should observe at least some indication of an association between inequality and growth on a cross-national basis, for just about any set of countries and any time period, and without an elaborate battery of control variables. Why, then, do we not observe these effects in the data presented here?

ALTERNATIVE VIEWS OF INEQUALITY AND GROWTH

The point of this essay is not to disprove definitively the claim that egalitarianism is harmful to economic growth, but rather to argue that the misfit between the trade-off thesis and cross-national evidence represents a puzzle that deserves our attention. In this section, I propose a number of different arguments that might explain why we do not observe the patterns of association predicted by different versions of the trade-off thesis in aggregate data for the OECD countries. I shall not attempt to assess empirically the relative merits of these different arguments, as this would require a more systematic analysis than time or space permits. It should be noted at the outset, however, that several of the arguments elaborated here would, taken by themselves, lead us to expect a positive association between egalitarianism and growth. The cross-national evidence presented earlier is no more consistent with this expectation than with the expectation of a negative association between egalitarianism and growth. This suggests that we should think of the following arguments as identifying effects that offset the disincentive effects typically stressed by mainstream economists.

As noted earlier, with reference to Okun, the question of equality of opportunity introduces the possibility that egalitarianism might have positive consequences for efficiency and growth even within the framework of mainstream economics. For example, Henry Chiu develops a model of human capital accumulation that explains the negative association between inequality and growth documented by Alesina and Rodrik and Persson and Tabellini without resorting to their claim that inequality is harmful to growth because it promotes redistribution.[21] The key to Chiu's argumentation is the claim that a more equal distribution of income provides for a better match between natural talent and education. Crucially, redistributive measures themselves play a positive role in Chiu's model. In his words, "the rich who are made poorer [by redistribution] will stop sending the less talented sons [*sic*] to college and some of the poor who are more talented (than those who stop going) will find buying education justifiable as they are made richer."[22] Assuming that the more talented create more human capital with a given amount of education, the net result of this reallocation of education across households is to increase the total stock of human capital, which in turn should translate into a higher long-term rate of economic growth.

Chiu's line of argument resonates with broader claims in the comparative political economy literature to the effect that at least some redistributive social policies should be seen as a form of investment in human capital.[23] A great deal of comparative evidence indicates that universal health care, publicly financed child care, child allowances, and income support to low-income families improve the social and economic conditions of children in low-income families and thereby enable such children to do better in school. By Chiu's logic, this should provide for a better match between natural talent and tertiary education attendance. More generally, better socio-economic conditions for low-income families or, in other words, a smaller gap between the low-income and average-income families tends to be associated with better skills at the lower end of the income distribution, and there is every reason to believe that this too contributes to better economic performance—in particular, more broad-based and sustained productivity growth.

A different line of argument that also treats egalitarianism as a positive factor in economic growth focuses on the implications of wage compression for the incentives of firms to engage in productivity-enhancing technological and organizational changes. Working for the Swedish confederation of blue-collar unions (LO), economists Gösta Rehn and Rudolf Meidner developed this line of argument in the 1950s. Rehn and Meidner argued that a solidaristic approach to wage bargaining would be good not only for low-wage workers, but also for the Swedish economy. Wage compression, they argued, would boost productivity growth by squeezing corporate profits selectively. On the one hand, a concerted union effort to provide low-wage workers with higher increases than market forces dictated would squeeze the profits of less efficient firms (sectors) and force them either to rationalize production or go out of business. On the other hand, the wage restraint by well-paid workers implied by the principle of wage solidarity would promote the expansion of more efficient firms (sectors). The net effect of this differentiated pressure on firms would be to raise average productivity in the economy and thereby make it possible for average wages to rise without threatening macroeconomic stability.[24]

The core of the "Rehn-Meidner model" is the proposition that low wages represent a subsidy to inefficient capital. At the same time, Rehn and Meidner recognized that wage differentials were necessary as an incentive for workers to acquire skills and to take on more responsibility in the production process. The goal of union wage policy should be to eliminate differentials based on corporate profitability while maintaining differentials based on skill and performance. Advocating "equal pay for equal work," as distinct from "equal pay for everyone," Rehn and Meidner thus sought to distinguish between productive and nonproductive wage differentials— a point to which I shall return shortly.

Like Chiu's argument about human capital accumulation, the Rehn-Meidner argument posits that egalitarianism itself has positive consequences for efficiency and growth. This does not mean that the consequences of egalitarianism are entirely positive. Again, the cross-national evidence presented earlier might be taken to mean that positive and negative consequences essentially cancel each other.

In a different vein, one might argue that countries with more equal distributions of income have developed public policies that offset the disincentive effects of egalitarianism. This too would explain the absence of any association between egalitarianism and growth across the OECD countries. Public funding of tertiary education constitutes the most obvious example of such a compensatory policy. Everything else being equal, it stands to reason that smaller returns to education (i.e., smaller pay differentials between college graduates and high-school graduates) are needed to motivate people to get a college degree to the extent that the costs involved are subsidized by the government.

Several other arguments about positive economic effects of the public provision of social welfare should also be noted in this context. First, it is certainly plausible to argue that public monopolies provide for more effective cost containment, possibly also economies of scale, in the realm of health care and other social services, benefiting the economy as a whole. Second, one important justification for public provision of social insurance has always been that employer-provided social benefits represent an obstacle to labor mobility. Publicly provided unemployment, sickness, and retirement benefits should make workers more willing to move between firms and thereby provide for a more efficient allocation of labor. Finally, Katzenstein's interpretation of the historical association between economic openness and the size of the welfare state deserves to be noted here. Referring to the welfare state as a mechanism of "domestic compensation," Katzenstein conceives welfare benefits as side payments to losers from market-driven economic restructuring, financed out of the collective gains of trade. Put differently, Katzenstein argues that the public provision of social welfare is an important political lubricant promoting societal acceptance of free trade and market-driven restructuring.[25]

In Katzenstein's framework, social spending promotes growth by facilitating trade liberalization, not by redistributing income. Redistribution is a side benefit or perhaps a necessary "side cost" of the policy regime characteristic of Europe's small open economies. The key point here is that the public provision of social welfare may well have consequences for economic output that are independent of its consequences for income distribution and some of these consequences may be of a compensatory nature.

The arguments rehearsed so far are essentially political-economic arguments. Another way to address the puzzle of the misfit between the trade-off thesis and cross-national evidence is to probe the assumptions about individual motivations that underpin the trade-off thesis. The cross-national evidence might be taken to mean that material rewards are not as important in motivating individual behavior as mainstream economists commonly assume. As suggested by a great deal of theory and research in sociology and social psychology, perceptions of fairness are likely to affect worker motivation as well.[26] At the level of firms, Akerlof and Yellen argue that wage compression yields more harmonious labor relations and greater employee effort.[27] The issue of fairness is particularly pertinent to the extent that efficiency improvements depend on collective efforts by groups of workers. As Okun himself notes, "Production comes out of a complex, interdependent system and may not be neatly attributable to individual contributors."[28] To the extent that such a logic also operates at a societal level, government policies that redistribute income and thereby promote a sense of solidarity among workers may contribute indirectly to labor productivity and ultimately to GDP growth.

Alternatively, the cross-national evidence presented might be taken to mean that material incentives should not be conflated with inequality, as much of the literature on this topic seems to do. Björklund and Freeman rightly stress that the concept of "incentives" implies that individuals are able to adjust their behavior in response to observable differences in rewards. In their words, "all trends towards greater wage inequality do not necessarily lead to a more growth-promoting structure of incentives."[29] Most obviously, we should not expect inequality to promote growth to the extent that it results from the exercise of some form of "categorical discrimination"—for instance, discrimination against immigrants or women—or some form of monopoly power.[30] While rising pay differentials between college and high-school graduates might lead more individuals to opt for a college degree, rising pay differentials between men and women could not possibly have any behavioral effect. Strictly speaking, the trade-off thesis pertains only to "productive income differentials," but aggregate measures of inequality encompass a wide range of "non-productive income differentials" as well. Indeed, the cross-national evidence suggests that income differentials in countries with more equal distributions of income may be more productive than income differentials in countries with more unequal distributions of income.

Finally, we cannot avoid the question of the extent to which it is legitimate to generalize about the role of material incentives across countries or, in other words, across cultures. Standards of fairness are clearly embedded in a particular cultural context and will vary across countries and also over time. Arguably, the same holds for material incentives. Much of the economics literature on inequality and growth seems to assume not only that material incentives are necessary to elicit growth-generating behavior in all capitalist societies, but also that the size of incentives that are necessary to elicit some particular behavior is essentially the same. While the former assumption strikes me as very reasonable, the latter assumption does not seem reasonable at all. By all accounts, pay differentials within Japanese companies are much smaller than pay differentials within American companies, yet Japanese employees compete intensely for promotions and for differences in annual pay increases that are tiny by American standards.[31]

I do not want to argue that cultural differences are idiosyncratic. Quite the contrary, the Japanese example suggests, I think, that the incentives necessary to induce efficiency-enhancing investment and effort depend on the expectations of individuals and that individuals adjust their expectations to the existing structure of rewards. If Sweden's wage structure were suddenly imposed on the American labor force, labor productivity and economic growth would likely fall quite precipitously. But Sweden did not acquire its egalitarian wage distribution—or its redistributive welfare state—overnight. Rather, Sweden's current wage structure is the cumulative product of a developmental process that dates back to the 1960s, if not earlier.

Björklund and Freeman show that conceptions of what constitutes legitimate wage differentials tend to track perceptions of actual wage

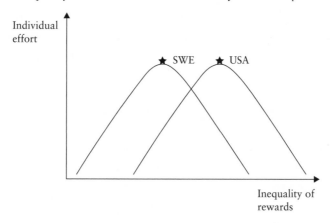

EXHIBIT 8   Illustration of modified optimal-inequality
thesis

differentials quite closely across countries and over time.[32] The evidence
they present indicates that individuals who live in countries with more compressed wages are generally aware of this and also consider large wage differentials to be less legitimate than individuals who live in more unequal
countries. In other words, "tastes for inequality" vary across countries.
Relatedly, I am suggesting that individuals who live in countries with more
compressed wages (incomes) may also value a certain amount of incentive
more highly than individuals who live in countries with less compressed
wages (incomes). Admittedly speculative, this argument brings us back
to Freeman's notion of optimal inequality. Rather than assuming that all
countries are located on the same hump-shaped curve, as in Exhibit 7, we
might imagine that there are several curves with a similar shape but differently located on the inequality continuum, as illustrated by Exhibit 8.
The fact that we do not observe any hump-shaped relationship between
inequality and growth in Exhibits 1–3 would seem to be more consistent
with Exhibit 8 than with Exhibit 7.

CONCLUSION

To sort out how inequality, redistribution, incentives, effort, and efficiency
relate to each other is a complicated matter. The discussion in the preceding
section raises more questions than it answers. Empirical research based on

micro evidence, pertaining to the behavior of individuals in different societies, is necessary to take this discussion further. For now, suffice it to say that the available macro evidence indicates that the efficiency and growth penalties associated with the egalitarian wage structures and redistributive welfare states are not nearly as large as conventional wisdom among mainstream economists and many other, more casual observers would have us believe. I hasten to add that this finding is based on cross-national differences that have persisted over long periods of time. For progressive forces in more inegalitarian countries, my final explanation for the absence of strong disincentive effects in the cross-national data—adaptation of reward expectations—amounts to a plea for a steadfast, but moderate (gradualist) approach to redistribution.

Part III

IS THERE A POLITICAL SOLUTION TO RISING INEQUALITY?

Rising Inequality and American Politics

John Ferejohn

Income inequality has increased sharply in the United States since the early 1970s, and there are no signs of any reversal in this trend even during the recent recession.[1] There is dispute about the extent of this increase, whether it is temporary (and even about whether it is real), and why it has occurred. Without being able to settle any of these disputes, it seems likely that political factors have played some kind of a role—possibly only a permissive one—and that we can choose policies that would limit the extent and nature of the inequality if we choose to. But, our capacity to make such choices is fragile and could be threatened by growing inequality itself.

It has often been thought that extreme inequality is dangerous to popular rule. Aristotle argued that should the poor or the rich monopolize power they would inevitably govern in their own (class) interest. He thought it wise, therefore, for a popular government to restrict the franchise in order to assure that authority will be exercised by the middle class—those be-

John Ferejohn is the Samuel Tilden Professor of Law at New York University, where he has been on the faculty since 2009. Prior to that he had been the Carolyn S. G. Munro Professor of Law at Stanford University. His publications include *Pork Barrel Politics: Rivers and Harbors Legislation, 1947–1968*; *The Personal Vote: Constituency Service and Electoral Independence*, with Bruce Cain and Morris Fiorina (winner of the 1988 Richard Fenno Prize for the best book in legislative politics during 1987); *Constitutional Culture and Democratic Rule*, coedited with Jack Rakove and Jonathan Riley; *A Republic of Statues*, with William Eskridge; and numerous articles in journals and collections. He was elected to the American Academy of Arts and Sciences in 1985 and to the National Academy of Sciences in 1988.

tween the poor and the rich—because their interests are a kind of compromise or balance between them. But, if the middle class is too small to rule effectively, he thought it would be desirable to devise other means of inducing moderate rule—specifically, institutions of mixed government (which he called "politeia")—to check the tendencies of either the rich or poor to corrupt the state.[2]

Rousseau worried that income/wealth inequalities would undermine conditions for republican government—which he thought required an element of direct democracy in deciding on the fundamental laws—by corrupting public norms and practices. Like Aristotle, he thought that this would work mostly by undermining or eroding the shared sense of a common good necessary to produce good legislation and to control magistrates, distorting the conditions for fair and honest deliberation. And the result would be laws that reflected not the general will but rather class or factional interests (which he called the "will of all").

The dangers of increases in inequality depend on whether it occurs mostly at the top or bottom of the income distribution. Inequality at the top raises the specter of certain kinds of social and political distortions whereby the wealthy separate themselves into a kind of separate society and erect protective barriers of various kinds. They may choose to live in gated communities, send their children to private schools, travel on private planes, frequent exclusive clubs, and otherwise make themselves a special and separate class. And some of the protections they may use are political: shielding themselves from view, criticism, and taxation by suborning public officials and parties. This is a kind of corruption of the political process where the rich people seek to capture parts of the legal/political system in order to protect their privileges. The means of capture could be direct and brutal or subtly legal, but the point is the creation and protection of special status and privilege. The capture of parts of the legal and political system within the United States has recently been described by Jacob Hacker.[3]

Inequality at the bottom, where a class of people is somehow left behind and impoverished, could lead to somewhat different problems but still can be characterized as producing a kind of corruption of popular rule. The impoverished might be alienated from the rest of society and might for that reason be easily swayed by demagogues to take actions inconsistent with the public or even with their own interests. This was certainly a common worry about wealth disparities in the classical republics (including both

Rome and Athens). It seems to be making a comeback in recent writings of both popular writers and academics.

While philosophers have worried about the political consequences of inequality, they have offered less cogent thought about its causes, at least little that seems to bear on current circumstances. Enlightenment-era writers like Locke, Rousseau, and various others presented a high-level claim that inequality was a kind of natural consequence of the creation of a state, which made possible the creation of institutions such as state-backed money, police, and a legal system for enforcing property rights. Such institutions permitted secure trade, a division of labor, and, as a result, high levels of wealth accumulation and investment. This was a commonplace view among classical political writers. But these ideas do not seem very helpful in examining recent developments that have been taking place within advanced states with already developed political institutions.

Economists have also tried to say something about both the causes and consequences of inequality, but much of their concern is for economic growth rather than political life. Economists have not always been so pessimistic either about the effects of inequality or about the pursuit of what might be called class interests as political philosophers have been. Many have seen the possibility that the effective pursuit of social wealth might depend on capital accumulation and investment and, of course, incentives, all of which may be associated with inequality. Kuznets long ago noted a U-shaped relation between inequality and growth: inequality first rises and then falls with growth.[4] There is a lot of disagreement as to why this happens, if there are genuine causal relations among these variables, and, if there are, how they work. But, the observed pattern has suggested to some that a minimum amount of inequality may be necessary for capital formation and be a precondition for or a facilitator of economic growth.[5] To others, inequality has seemed more of a necessary evil: providing appropriate incentives to work and invest may produce income inequality, but, in an ideal political economy, these would be taxed away in some nondistortionary way. To still others, inequality may simply be a consequence of rapid economic growth.

There is some empirical dispute about the nature of increasing inequality: whether the recent rise in inequality has occurred mostly at the top or bottom of the income distribution or both at the same time (so that income distribution has become polarized) or whether there is some time sequencing of the two processes.[6] I am less interested in characterizing the overall change than in picking out one part of it that seems very hard to deny. The work of Piketty and Saez, relying on very detailed tax records, has demonstrated the extraordinary increasing concentration of incomes in the top micro-fractiles of the income distribution: the 1 percent, .1 percent, and .01 percent of American households both over time and in comparison with France and the U.K. This increase seems both dramatic in magnitude, to have occurred quite recently, and to have reached the high concentrations of pre-Depression America. Changes in the middle and lower parts of the distribution seem to have moved more slowly, and more unevenly, and perhaps over a longer period of time.[7] So while I do not doubt that there has been some overall polarization of the U.S. income distribution, my reading of their data suggests that much of the change has happened in the upper (very long and growing) right tail of the distribution.

In any case, there is a question why it has happened. The upper tail of the income distribution, where most of the action has happened, is tiny by definition, and for everyone else incomes have been pretty flat or declining over time. Why would the average or median voter, or her representatives in government, have allowed this situation to happen and to persist? It is a puzzle.

IS RISING INEQUALITY AN EXCEPTIONAL AMERICAN PHENOMENON?

I should say at the start that there is much disagreement among experts on how to characterize and measure inequality and there are substantial differences among the data sets that permit measurement of inequality, both over time and within countries. So everything I say needs qualification (which I won't offer). There seems little dispute, however, that income inequality has risen substantially since the mid-1970s in most of the advanced democracies and elsewhere as well.[8] This suggests that its primary causes are probably rooted, at least in part, in changing technology and the changing nature of the world economy rather than in purely local circumstances.

However, while many of the advanced democracies have experienced rising pretax or market-driven inequality, most of them have taxed some of that increase away. That has not happened so much in the United States. For example, while Sweden has reduced the increase in pretax inequality each year by nearly 50 percent, Germany by 40 percent, and France by 35 percent, the U.S. reduction is typically around 23 percent, second lowest among advanced democracies in the Luxembourg Income Study (after Switzerland). Even the British, our partners in rising pretax inequality, have offset a substantial part of the increase through their tax and welfare systems.

By contrast, the United States has cut and flattened federal tax rates several times since the mid-1970s, thereby decreasing its capacity to limit inequality, and it has also shifted tax burdens to states and localities, which rely on comparatively regressive forms of taxation. At the same time, the United States has reduced at least some governmental income supports targeted to lower-income groups since the 1970s and has reduced requirements that employers provide job-related benefits for middle- and low-income employees. And at the very bottom, it has reduced the size, generosity, and reach of social programs that are aimed at poverty reduction for those outside the labor force.[9] Most importantly, it has lowered taxes on very high earners. It has not only reduced the progressivity of the tax code but also cut taxes on capital gains, and eliminated taxes on estates, at least for the present. Whatever the reasons for these developments, U.S. policy has been permissive of growing (post-fisc) inequality, both at the bottom and especially at the top of the income distribution.

So, based on available comparative data, it seems likely that rising post-fisc income inequality is most prominently an American (and Swiss) phenomenon. But, it should be emphasized that the Swiss experience a much lower level of pre-fisc inequality than the United States does and perhaps, for that reason, haven't as much of a reason to redistribute incomes. This is not to deny that more can be said to separate national responses to these trends. There is some reason to think that country-groups can be more or less ranked in terms of how much they redistribute incomes to correct market-driven inequality: the Scandinavian and small European states are on top; France, Germany, and Italy are in the middle; and the Anglo-Saxon countries are just below those, with the United States trailing behind.

In any case, it seems to me that the best account of this phenomenon probably centers on differences in the tax systems rather than on the expenditure side. This is partly a judgment that the big increases in U.S. inequality have been concentrated at the top of the income distribution, stretching out of the right-hand tail so to speak, and this is not likely to be very sensitive to expenditure programs of any kind. That is not to say that some people have not also been left behind or left out in some way, but there is simply not as much variation there; nor is there as much room for it. And, it is true that there has been a reduction in social welfare expenditures (in real terms) over this period. This is an older story and a mixed one since I am not sure that the decline in such programs has had a great net effect on the income levels of the lower fractiles of the income distribution.

Comparative studies of welfare states often conclude that cultural or institutional differences between the European and Anglo-American states account for much of the differences in the sizes and generosity of welfare systems. Some assert that different citizens in Scandinavia, for example, see the social welfare systems as a kind of insurance against risk that everyone faces, whereas the view in the United States is that welfare payments are directed to a specific class of people.[10] Other studies try to trace redistributive policies to the electoral system and party system with some success, arguing that the use of proportional representation rather than single member constituencies produces a bias in favor of governmental redistribution. Of course, cultural values do change somewhat over time and, within nations, political parties often differ not only in policy terms but also in which cultural features they try to appeal to, so it is probably impossible to separate cultural and political explanations very sharply. However, while political and policy variables can change quickly, there is some hope of getting some independent evidence as to whether they have changed. Doing this will help us to understand if rising inequality is a local American phenomenon or a broader one.

WHY WE NEED A POLITICAL EXPLANATION

Broadly speaking, there seem to be three kinds of causal theories that might explain increasing inequality, and each suggests a different answer to the political question posed earlier. The rise in inequality might be the result of forces exogenous to or external to the political system: it might, for example, be traced to transformations in productive technology or to declining technical impediments to global trade. New products and manufacturing or processes may increase the demand for capital and a motivation to accumulate funds. Globalization may also put downward pressures on wages either due to offshoring, imports, or freer immigration, and place limits on redistributional policies as well.[11] Perhaps, in these ways, the basic structure of the economy has changed in ways that advantage the skilled or highly skilled, or perhaps the advantage has shifted to high-level managers and entrepreneurs. Perhaps there has been a shift toward a knowledge/service economy or a shift of economic activity toward startups with flexible labor practices and away from large "Fordist" enterprises. A transition to a knowledge/service economy and away from industrial production may advantage entrepreneurs relative to other skilled people. And maybe all this is driving long-term deunionization, at least in the private sector.

If the technological account is right, inequality might have emerged more or less automatically from economic competition in a new technical/global environment, and it would take explicit political action either to regulate it or to counter its effects. The failure of such policies to emerge must be due to political facts: perhaps to popular attitudes toward inequality or to rigidities of the political system of one kind or another. Perhaps the parties—there being only two important ones in the United States—fail to represent the interests of the average voter for some reason or another, or perhaps they simply keep some relevant options off the political agenda. Incumbents may be too entrenched to need to pay much attention to the median voter, or perhaps the parties are overly polarized or overly dependent on campaign contributions. Or perhaps powerful interests can take advantage of the "veto structure" of American government to block legislative efforts to offset inequality. So, even if the fundamental causes of rising inequality are technical or in some other way exogenous to politics, there must be a political explanation for the fact that policies have not countered those tendencies.

Or, possibly the best explanation for rising inequality is cultural: are there some aspects of political morality or culture—the culture of liberalism or individualism—that provide the basis for the propagation and acceptance of growing inequalities? If so, this may explain why lower- and middle-class Americans seem to support tax cuts that do not seem plausibly to benefit them or their children, despite the fact that Americans do seem to think some kinds of inequality are unfair and even dangerous. If this is right, then an explanation would be found in the attitudes of average Americans toward taxation and redistribution. But if that is the best explanation, there is a puzzle: why did it take so long for inequality of the kind witnessed over the last quarter century to emerge? One would think that cultural beliefs would change very slowly, perhaps in tune with the replacement of generations. It seems to me therefore that either attitudes toward inequality have changed in a permissive direction, or else the explanation must be found elsewhere: perhaps in the changing operation of the political or electoral systems that respond to and express these attitudes in various ways by placing new options on the political agenda or keeping them off.

Perhaps rising inequality is rooted in or caused by the explicit operation of the political system itself. Perhaps new laws have been enacted that advantage those with high incomes so that state policy has played an explicit role in promoting rising inequality independently of technological developments.[12] Maybe there are distortions produced by recent changes in the campaign finance system or in the ways that candidates are nominated that have led the political system affirmatively to protect and promote high incomes or concentrated wealth.[13] These new policies, if there are any, may be a consequence of the recent successes of the Republicans following Ronald Reagan. Or maybe they are a result of an increased responsiveness of politicians of both parties to high-income constituents. Or perhaps the state's role is subtle and less direct. Certainly the system of property itself and the received distribution of property rights confer advantages on those who have wealth. Those advantages might naturally cumulate unless the state intervenes actively to regulate them. If this is right, we need to explain why it is that laws and policies facilitating growing inequality were enacted even if they were adverse to the interests of the average voter. This is a harder explanatory puzzle than the previous one since the average voter has been tricked into taking actions rather than just remaining inattentive.

INEQUALITY AND GROWTH

The rise in inequality and growth rates since the late 1970s poses a problem for the Kuznets hypothesis or at least for some interpretations of it. It no longer seems so plausible that late capitalism will more or less automatically see reductions in inequality. Or, perhaps Kuznets, writing in the 1960s, simply didn't anticipate that there could be more than one stage of explosive industrialization requiring the formation of new kinds of capital. Apparently the world has been experiencing a second wave of capitalism in the last thirty years or so and also increases in cross-border trade. If that is right, the relation between income and growth might be similar to what was observed at early stages—producing a U-shaped graph between inequality and growth—but the trend in inequality over time would no longer appear U-shaped.[14]

While some economists have thought that high levels of inequality might actually impede economic growth, this view is controversial within that profession.[15] The more standard views seem to hold that inequality does itself not necessarily threaten growth—indeed, it might be a cause of it or a "natural" consequence—but most policies that might be directed at limiting inequality tend to discourage investment and growth. So one account of the Kuznets curve is that rapid industrialization increases inequality but then the society is politically forced to adopt corrective policies, and those slow down growth. Recent developments call into question whether societies are politically forced to do any such things, or at least they raise the question of what kinds of societies (and political systems) are likely to adopt inequality-moderating policies.

The U.S. economy has experienced fairly robust economic growth rates since the late 1970s, with only temporary pauses (including of course the recent recession), and this is roughly the same period over which the increase in inequality has occurred. Moreover, compared with other advanced democracies, the growth of the American economy stands out. This pattern may be causally related to rising inequality, or inequality could be a consequence rather than a cause of growth. There are a number of policy changes or non-changes that may support either kind of relation. First, as mentioned, is the sequence of tax cuts dating from the early Reagan years. Second is the deregulation that has occurred in various parts of the economy, part of which is embodied in the abolition of federal agencies, and part in limitations on enforcement. And third is the permissive view that some administrations have taken toward large deficits that may have worked in favor of high growth rates. But other countries have not followed this model. Why? There are lots of possibilities to point to—the distinctive weakening of American labor unions, especially private sector unions; demographic differences; regulatory patterns.

POLITICS AND INEQUALITY

Perhaps part of the explanation is to be found in peculiarly American institutions such as federalism or the differences between American and

European parties or electoral systems. But, inequality is a recent phenomenon, and so I would look first to recent political developments for explanation. Coincidently or not, the modern campaign finance system—which facilitated contributions by businesses to politicians—was put in place in the mid-1970s, which marks more or less the start of the high-growth/rising-inequality era. The big tax cut of 1981 followed somewhat after that, and, while it was adjusted somewhat the next year, the flattening of the tax code has not really been reversed since. I am not suggesting that the new campaign finance system was introduced in order to permit lowering high-income tax rates, nor even that they were the major cause of it (though I think they probably played some role). Besides, even if the role of campaign finance were proven, there would be a need to explain why that happened, and when it did.

The sequence of political events suggests a hypothesis. The rise of inequality may be explained by developments within the political system. The most striking development, to a political scientist, is the sharp increase in party polarization and partisanship over the period from 1970 onward, at least among elected officials. There is of course much dispute about the causes of this increase and whether these changes have been accompanied by a deep polarization in mass attitudes, but I will not go into that.[16] But there are few questions, I think, about the proximate causes of party polarization: it is mostly to be understood as the effects of the Voting Rights Act (which led many rural and suburban southern districts to elect Republicans rather than conservative Democrats, and urban southern districts to return liberal Democrats). There is also little doubt about its correlation with the rise of income and wealth inequality.

But if increasing party polarization is the cause of rising post-fisc inequality, there are some puzzles to be addressed. First, while some analysts simply assume that the parties offer different policies, it is not at all clear how this is possible for players who are even roughly rational. Why wouldn't party competition drive candidates (and therefore parties) to converge on the position of the median voter? There are several possible answers to this. Some political scientists think that intraparty competition for nomination pulls candidates toward party medians, or selects noncentrist candidates, and away from the position of the median voter, and that post-nomination temptations for candidates to converge to the middle are limited by the prospect of losing support among contributors or activists. But it is not clear that such behavior can actually be sustained in a system of rational candidates and voters. A more satisfactory approach, advanced by John Roemer in a series of papers, is based on the recognition that political competition is not confined to the one-dimensional space envisioned by median voter theory, but involves multiple issues. In his framework, the parties compete by offering bundles of issue positions and may, in equilibrium, offer sharply different economic policies.[17]

In any event, there is the further question of how polarization works, specifically how it is connected to the other developments mentioned previously. Perhaps, as the parties separated from each other, external conditions were, at least until the Obama election, more favorable for the Republicans than the Democrats. The natural candidates for such an account are plentiful: the decline of unionization (a core part of the Democratic coalition), increasing tax aversion during the low-growth 1970s, perhaps the development of a more permissive system of campaign finance after 1974 (when Congress permitted the formation of business PACS) and the Buckley decision (which limited the degree to which contributions could be effectively regulated), or perhaps Republicans were simply blessed with more attractive candidates than the Democrats (who were tarred with defending policies that seemed no longer to work very well).

Or maybe one of the parties simply had an easier and more attractive story to sell to the electorate. The Republicans united behind an ideology of individual responsibility and traditional values, while the Democrats were left defending a disparate coalition of minorities and a complex set of paternalist state policies. Although the election of Obama might at first blush be taken to question the appeal of the Republican ideology, it's striking that this ideology resurged (via the Tea Party) rather quickly. There are certainly strains and cracks in the Republican coalition between the "values" people (the Christian coalition) and the "individualists" (libertarians). But this tension often plays out more at the practical level of policy-making rather than at the level of principle or narrative ideology. In any case, it is not so clear why the Republican story played better than the Democratic version: one could doubt that the Republicans would have gotten a favorable reception for individualist self-sufficiency during the 1930s or even the 1960s. Maybe this is just a kind of post hoc account for the fact that Republicans were winning more elections for various reasons.

Whatever the causes of the electoral outcomes, there is little question that when Republicans govern, their shared values and ideology direct them toward policies permitting widening inequality. One could also point to nefarious influences: that they have a large and growing fund-raising advantage, that their funds tend to come from those who are well off and their ideological supporters, and the development of an elaborate system of lobbyists that goes under the name of the K Street Project. Some of these developments are normal practices in American politics—natural incidents of the First Amendment (as emphasized by the Buckley decision)—and some are more unseemly (rapidly revolving doors) or even illegal (kickbacks and favors).[18]

Moreover, it is important to note, as Larry Bartels has (following the earlier work of Doug Hibbs), that inequality has increased mostly during periods of Republican government.[19] The Carter administration is a minor exception to this generalization, but otherwise the overall pattern seems clear enough. This may be due to the pro-employment and inflation-tolerant policies of Democrats, versus the pro-investment tax policies of the Republicans, or it may be due to policy differences that are unconnected with these propensities. So, maybe the answer is simple at one level. Most of the growth in posttax inequality is in the United States, and it is due to the fact that Republicans have tended to control the national government for most of the relevant period. To explain rising inequality, explain why people have come to elect Republican governments.

That raises the further question, of course: why would they do *that*, especially if Republican governments pursue economic policies that are bad for a majority of the people? There are several plausible answers: First, perhaps Republican policies tend to produce high growth rates, the benefits of which are widespread, so their policies are not really bad for the average person once these long-run effects are taken into account. Second, perhaps people are distributionally overoptimistic, irrationally so, about their chances, or those of their children, to attain to high incomes in the future. (So Republican policies don't *seem* so bad.) Or perhaps the answer is found (as Roemer thinks) in the fact that many or most people care more about religion or values issues than about economic policies.

And there is the further question: Why, when Democrats have governed lately—with Carter, Clinton, and now Obama—were these trends not reversed? Well, maybe they were, at least to a degree. Clinton did implement some (relatively small) tax increases at the beginning of his administration (when the Democrats controlled Congress), and Obama has, as of this writing, threatened to repeal the Bush tax cuts. But, on the whole, Democratic presidents have not done much to alleviate the increases in inequality that were being generated in the economy. Why is that? The answer may be that Americans have not merely been more willing to vote for Republicans but have also become more supportive of conservative policies in some broader sense—perhaps more averse to taxes or progressivity or perhaps more suspicious of government altogether—and that this has forced Democrats to shift their policy offerings in the same direction as the Republicans, although not quite as much.

These considerations all seem to push in more or less the same policy directions, it seems to me, and are, possibly, overdetermined as a causal explanation of rising inequality. I am not sure. Besides, I doubt that these things can be effectively changed in ways that would influence inequality trends. As it is understood by the current justices, the First Amendment stands in the way of any serious campaign finance reform, but even if that were not so strictly interpreted by the Supreme Court, it is not so clear how to have democracy without permitting quite a lot of political influence of this kind. If we want to reduce inequality, my guess is that we have to look to the people themselves.

PUBLIC OPINION AND INEQUALITY

There are some interesting findings from those who have looked into public attitudes toward inequality. First, at an abstract level, there is some popular awareness of increasing inequality expressed in survey responses, and most Americans seem to think that income gaps are too large. But only a small percentage of respondents seem to think this is important enough to adopt strong counteracting policies.

More concretely, when it comes to attitudes toward taxation, people seem to think they, and people like themselves, pay too much in taxes and that rich people pay too little. At the same time, however, people often express support for nonprogressive tax policies such as the flat tax. They may, of course, have other reasons for this: perhaps the desire to eliminate deadweight losses outweighs their concern with equality. I kind of doubt that. Interestingly, the support for the flat tax is largest among those who think the system is unfair (because too favorable to the rich). Ironic, no?

And, even more difficult to understand is the popular support for the elimination of the estate tax. Perhaps people are massively unperceptive about the likely incidence of that tax . . . or perhaps they have feelings of fairness that militate against taxing wealth as opposed to taxing income. I don't know. But it is a puzzle.

It seems to me that a potential explanation for these patterns of abstract and policy attitudes might draw on two kinds of optimism. Americans could tend to be macro-optimistic: to hold the belief that maintaining a system of inequality produces growth and so be willing to accept inequality as a price for prosperity. Or they could be micro-optimistic: to believe that they themselves or their children will likely get wealthier and therefore be vulnerable to higher taxes on wealth or income. There is the further question of whether sufficient optimism to explain popular attitudes toward tax policies could actually be justified rationally.

In any case, it is not so clear that public opinion as such has a direct policy effect. Leaving aside institutional mechanisms of influence transmission, it may be that certain publics are more influential than others. For example, some striking recent research suggests that policy-makers are relatively more responsive to those in the higher reaches of the income distribution. It is unclear why this is so: is it that policy-makers tend to listen to richer people or that they tend to agree with them for other reasons? Those who show up as "rich" in these public opinion studies are not especially wealthy after all and not different, in that respect, from policy-makers themselves. It is also unclear that this has changed much over time. But this work does suggest that one might want to address the "puzzling" public attitudes about tax policies in a more focused way that takes account of these possibilities.

These patterns are, at any rate, largely based on static snapshots, and it is not clear that opinion dynamics on these issues (income distribution and tax policy) can explain changing policy outcomes. We simply don't have the right information to answer that question. My guess is that these are probably fairly slow-moving attitudes that probably don't explain change very well. They might explain why there is no broad public reaction against increasing inequality, but I doubt that they could be a cause of it.

CONCLUSION

So here is the picture I see: Rising inequality is much more pronounced in the United States than in other advanced democracies, and it is most prominently concentrated at the very top of the income distribution. It is probably a consequence of a relatively long period of ascendancy by a fairly unified Republican party, a party able to formulate and implement ideologically coherent policies. And when the Democrats have held the presidency, they have slowed this trend somewhat but not really reversed it. The important policies seem mostly to be tax-related, at least as they permit growing inequality at the top. And, American public opinion toward rising inequality has been, on the whole (and for complex reasons), permissive of these developments.

The explanatory puzzle remains: Why have the Republicans continued to win elections, even as that party has become ever more permissive of income concentration at the top? Is this related to an increasing public belief that low taxes encourage growth? Is it due to an optimism among Americans about their own prospects of rising in the income or wealth distribution? Or have the Democrats in other ways made themselves a less attractive governing party and therefore left the field open to Republicans to establish policies that may lack deep support?

CAN ANYTHING BE DONE?

Let's focus first on the effective constraints. I don't think we are going to reverse the polarization of the parties any time soon. It seems to consist of two parts: With the collapse of Democratic control of the South, both parties have become more ideologically homogeneous. Second, the ideological "distance" between the party positions has increased, with the Republicans becoming homogeneously attached to popular low-tax policies.

And while it may be possible that certain public attitudes toward inequality could change, it seems less likely that tax attitudes would be as flexible. People have always thought that the rich pay too little in taxes, and they still do, but I am sure they are thinking of Donald Trump and not their own neighbors. In any case, they don't seem to connect that belief to specific kinds of taxing, and they don't seem to connect these things to inequality. It is unrealistic to think that ordinary people will ever have the same kinds of beliefs about the effects of taxes that policy experts have.

What about the system of political influence: campaign and party finance, lobbying regulation, etc.? As I have said, these practices are pretty close to the bone of democratic politics: petitioning leaders campaigning to defeat incumbents and other political activities are pretty well protected by current constitutional understandings. So, short of changing the makeup of the Supreme Court very substantially, I don't see a lot of room to maneuver here either. The wealthy will continue to enjoy great advantages in political influence, as they do now, and my guess is that those advantages will probably continue to increase.

So I am left with ordinary politics. If you want less inequality, or at least to slow its momentum, elect more Democrats to office. But that will probably have only a weak effect, unless the Democrats develop a coherent narrative embracing some kind of distributional objective that can direct and motivate redistributive (tax) policy-making when they are in office. The election of Obama has not, as I've mentioned, occasioned any such sea change, at least as yet. This is hard, of course: no one really knows how to make distributional politics a priority. And no one knows how to convince the public of the dangers of rising inequality or that tax increases are probably necessary to stop it.

But the stakes are high. I don't know firsthand how a prosperous and powerful republic begins to come apart, but I think it is at least plausible that a loss of commonality—a sense that we are in this together—is a part of it. There are disturbing signs of such losses already with the rise of gated communities, the growth of exurbs, the segmentation of media markets, and the polarization of our political elites. I think this worry is shared broadly across the ideological spectrum, though the remedies for it vary greatly. This is a worry that Aristotle and Rousseau and Cicero all shared, and I guess they were right to be concerned.

Unequal Democracy in America
The Long View

Jeff Manza

Modern democratic political systems claim that all citizens have equal opportunities to shape the composition of their elected governments (and hence
the policies those governments adopt). In the classical model of democracy,
governments are responsive to the mass public, making public policies favored by a majority of citizens while respecting the rights of minorities. In
such a world, participation is said to foster learning and engagement on the
part of all citizens such that compromise, reasoned debate, and consensus
would become possible.

Of course in the real world, no model of democracy has ever proved capable of achieving such a neat equality of representation and the balancing
of competing interests. Democracy in practice falls short, perhaps inevitably
so, of the ambitious theoretical goals associated with it for the past 2,500
years. For example, one person/one vote rules seem clear enough, but other
"inputs" besides votes inevitably influence the relative power of individuals
and groups. These "other" inputs—money, networks, media use, policy
ideas, social movements—are far less evenly distributed than the right of
each citizen to cast a single ballot. However representatives are chosen,
the resulting governing coalition inevitably privileges the wishes of some
voters over others. And even representative public opinion (derived from

Jeff Manza is a professor of sociology and department chair at New York
University. His research is in the area of social stratification, political sociology,
and public policy. He is the coauthor (with Clem Brooks) of *Social Cleavages
and Political Change* and (with Christopher Uggen) *Locked Out: Felon
Disenfranchisement and American Democracy*. He is finishing a book entitled
Whose Rights? Counterterrorism and the Dark Side of American Public Opinion.

polls of all citizens) provides uneven cues. Political leaders frequently make decisions on important issues on which the will of the public is unclear or unknowable, or the result of elite manipulation of one kind or another.

While all democratic polities exhibit shortcomings of one kind or another, the American political system is defined by a set of institutional rules and legacies of the past that enable some voices to be more readily heard than others. No other democratic country among the rich, affluent societies allows as much money into the political system, and while the rate of increase in the flow of political money in recent years has been shockingly high, this has always been an important feature of American politics. No other rich democracy has as low a rate of voter participation as the United States, or such large disparities in participation rates by income or class. And few other democratic countries have as decentralized a political system as the United States, giving powerful actors multiple opportunities to "veto" legislation they do not like. These institutional and political factors combine to make it very difficult for redistributive policies commonly found elsewhere to establish themselves in the United States. Political inequality is the normal condition of American politics.

In his essay on the sources of rising political inequality in this volume, John Ferejohn provides a broad overview of how *recent* trends in inequality in the United States have moved faster and with more consequences than in Western Europe. While recognizing there are important nonpolitical sources of rising inequality, Ferejohn notes that policy changes relating to fiscal policy (in particular, the important tax cuts enacted during the presidencies of Ronald Reagan and George W. Bush) have played an especially important role. Given this, he argues, it makes sense to look to recent political trends. Ferejohn fingers party polarization, and growing Republican Party control of national government, as the key proximate factors driving public policy to endorse economic inequality.

While these partisan political factors are unquestionably important, in this essay I want to offer a different interpretation than that of Ferejohn (and indeed, most other commentators on rising inequality). Ferejohn and many other writers on the new inequality sometimes imply the normal pattern in America is to move toward increasing equality, with the post-1970s period as the critical deviation.[1] But taking a longer-range perspective, it is now apparent that the period from the 1940s through the 1970s represents the truly significant departure from the normal pattern; it is the *exception* to the normal patterning of high inequality in the United States (especially when we focus on rising income and wealth inequality at the very top).[2] The underlying institutions, rules, and political economy are structured in ways that almost always facilitate inequality. The current period represents, in other words, a return to normalcy, not a departure from it.

In this essay, then, I develop a somewhat different argument about democracy and inequality in America than that of the more typical portrait represented in this volume by Ferejohn. I start with some basics: the right to vote and participate in elections, the institutionalization of a two-party system that discourages redistribution except under pressure from social movements from below, and the increasing openness of American democracy to political money and corporate bias. The inequalities embedded in some of these "fundamentals," and the institutions that create them, are well known (such as the role of money in politics), while others (like access to the vote in the first place) are more rarely discussed. Both are important to consider.

Institutional and political factors favoring inequality unfold over time. Understanding contemporary inequality is no different. I begin the second half of the essay with a brief discussion summarizing what should be viewed as the outlier period—from World War II to the 1970s—when a number of unique shifts (primarily having to do with changes in labor law and the regulatory regime during the New Deal, and rising racial and regional equality from the 1950s onward) combined to make possible *declining* political and economic inequality. I then turn more briefly to examine how some of the recent return to normalcy played itself out over the past twenty-five years, focusing on how some of the same developments Ferejohn highlights interacted with the underlying institutional inequalities. The cumulative portrait provides a related but somewhat different basis for understanding how and why American political dynamics reinforce social inequality than that suggested by Ferejohn. In the conclusion, I provide a brief speculation about what would be required for this state of affairs to shift back toward more equality, although I am doubtful that this is likely in the foreseeable future.

SOME FUNDAMENTALS OF AMERICAN DEMOCRACY

Political inequality has long been the subject of analysis by scholars and writers, but the intensity of concern has risen in recent years in the context of rising economic inequalities. This is so for two reasons. First, rising inequality has the potential to widen disparities in the "inputs" flowing into the political system. The example of political money is perhaps the most obvious. As the amounts and shares of income received by households at the top of the distribution have increased over the past three decades, the amount of money the rich have at their disposal to support political causes has increased dramatically. Although analysts have had trouble specifying the exact pathway through which money influences policy, there are nevertheless good reasons to think that there are links between the two.

Second, concern about inequalities in the political system may account, at least in part, for the failure of the American political system to effectively *respond* to rising inequality. The American welfare state stands out in the rich democracies for its low levels of public spending (with the United States currently devoting about 14 percent of its GDP to social spending programs, versus an average of 26.5 percent in the West European welfare state, and 18 percent in the other Anglo-American democracies frequently grouped together as "liberal" welfare states).[3] These figures are startling: even a 1 percent difference in government spending is enormous (translating to about $130 billion in public spending). To be sure, the United States does provide massive tax subsidies for private benefits, but these private benefits have a more limited redistributive impact.[4]

There are numerous other examples of the failure of the political system to respond to rising inequality: as Ferejohn has noted, repeated tax-cutting disproportionately benefiting the super-rich at a time when high-income households are already absorbing unprecedented shares of national income; or in the pointed refusal of Congress and the White House to adjust the federal minimum wage for a decade after 1997, leading to a 20 percent decline in real value (and the minimum wage has declined overall by some 36 percent in real value between 1979 and 2006).[5]

My argument is that understanding political inequality in the United States requires analysis of unique institutional arrangements and embedded practices. My focus here is on four critical "rules of the game": the right to vote, the patterning of participation, the nature of the party system, and the financing of elections. Each of these has played a significant role in enabling rising inequality to proceed largely unchecked by public policy. The constraints of the American political system in hindering the development of social democratic parties and strong unions have been a staple of political analysis since Werner Sombart's 1906 classic *Why Is There No Socialism in the United States?* It is important, however, to revisit the issue in light of new social and economic conditions. I begin with one of those fundamentals, the right to vote.

The Right to Vote

Democratic governance in the modern world is based, in part, on "universal" suffrage, at least the right of all citizens living within a political jurisdiction to have the right to cast one (and only one) ballot for all elected offices. Yet unlike virtually all other democratic constitutions around the world, the American constitution does not provide a guarantee that all citizens will be allowed to vote. When the framers met to draft the Constitution, there were no models of universal suffrage (at least for white men) to draw upon. Some participants floated ideas about declaring the vote a right, or even a "natural right." Such views were supported by radicals like Ethan Allen and Benjamin Franklin. Against these ideas were various conceptions of stakeholder democracy, in which only property owners or taxpayers would participate. The most commonly expressed justification was that only "stakeholders" had a material interest in the well-being of the community, and thus would exercise the franchise wisely.[6] In the end, however, the drafters compromised by delegating to the states the power to determine who could exercise the franchise. This power remains in the hands of the states, mediated by a series of constitutional amendments that later curtailed some of that power. As a result of these amendments, states can no longer discriminate based on race, sex, or age (for those over eighteen years old), nor can they impose poll taxes as a precondition of voting.[7]

In the first few decades after 1789, many states adopted rules that excluded many or all nonpropertied white men, as well as blacks and women. Throughout the first half of the nineteenth century, the nature and extent of the political exclusions against white men based on property ownership tended to fall, but barriers to participation for women, African Americans, and (increasingly) immigrants persisted. Women's suffrage arrived first at the state level, especially in the newer states in the West, and later nationally with the adoption of the Nineteenth Amendment in 1920. Despite the promise of the Fifteenth Amendment in 1870 (barring the states from explicit bans based on race), suffrage was not fully secured for

African Americans in the South until the adoption of the Voting Rights Act in 1965, a full century after the end of the Civil War. The exclusion of African Americans in the South is well chronicled, but it is important to note that not all measures adopted after the Civil War to restrict participation were limited to African Americans. All states began adopting registration requirements, some onerous, and a large number played with various kinds of literacy tests to fence out certain groups of voters (many of whom were poor whites or immigrants). The expansion of measures disenfranchising convicted felons after 1840 (and especially after the Civil War) constituted yet another type of restriction, one that remains in place to this day and that has become increasingly consequential as the felon population has grown dramatically in recent years.

Participatory Inequalities

In addition to the simple *right* to vote, there are large, persisting disparities in participation among the eligible electorate that have long been a defining feature of American political life. Here again, the character of American political institutions contributes to these disparities. Let's start with the class skew in voter turnout. Participation in American elections is far from universal; one recent international survey shows that turnout in U.S. national elections ranks only 138th highest among the 170 democratic countries surveyed, far lower than all similar rich, capitalist democracies except Switzerland (which ranked 137th).[8] The United States is further unusual for having a substantial cleavage-based skew in political participation: there is typically a turnout gap of some 25 percent or more between the high turnout groups versus low turnout groups (e.g., professionals versus unskilled workers, or whites and Hispanics in the case of race/ethnicity).[9] Such sharp socioeconomic-based cleavages are not generally found to the same degree in other countries.[10] In other words, in democracies where almost everyone votes, there are fewer group differences; as turnout falls, disparities in participation rise.

Why does the United States have such low levels of overall turnout, and why are the skews between groups so large? In the social science literatures on who votes, there are two broad streams of explanation: individual-level factors (generally focused on education level, race/ethnicity, class, religion, community, and knowledge/interest in politics), and political and institutional factors. Sociodemographic attributes of individuals, such as education level, are powerful predictors. For example, it is well established that people with more education vote at higher rates; but we cannot account for the relatively low rate of overall voter turnout in the United States inasmuch as most individual-level factors are similar in the rich democratic societies to-day. Political and institutional explanations, by contrast, point to the role of mobilizing activities by parties and political organizations, and institutional constraints such as voter registration requirements, the practice of holding elections on a working day, and the (limited) range of meaningful choices presented to voters in a two-party system. Here, there is much more variation across countries, and in combination these factors provide a useful understanding of the puzzle of low rate of participation in American elections.

Two critical institutional rules contribute to low turnout in the United States: (1) the difficulty of registering to vote, which is automatic in most other countries;[11] (2) the increased costs of voting as a result of holding national elections on working days, versus on either a weekend or national holiday in most other countries. Earlier estimates that the American system of voter registration pushed down turnout by 8–15 percent[12] likely over-estimate the impact today, as the difficulty of getting registered has been eased by the 1993 "motor voter" law that requires states to offer citizens voting registration materials through the Department of Motor Vehicles. And a number of states in recent years—eight at this writing—have moved to same-day registration systems, where voters can register at their polling place. Nevertheless, in a highly mobile society where registration is typically conducted at the county level, requiring voters to register (or reregister) before casting a ballot remains a significant barrier for many. Holding elections on a Tuesday, as mandated by the Constitution, further reduces turnout. Cross-national estimates of the negative impact of holding elections on a working day (versus a weekend) are around 5 percent,[13] with the penalty hurting turnout among workers with the least autonomy in their jobs or single parents (who have below-average incomes) the most.[14]

The level and type of mobilization efforts undertaken by political organizations of various kinds provide another set of explanations for why voter turnout is lower and the skew in participation higher in the United States.[15] Low-turnout groups are potentially subject to more influence by mobilization efforts than higher-turnout groups.[16] As with other participatory inequalities, the United States stands out for its lack of equalizing vehicles. In other democratic countries, the strength of unions and social democratic parties gives strong, systematic, and nationwide encouragement to poor and working-class voters to participate in elections. The United States, by contrast, has weak unions and completely lacks a social democratic or labor party. As a result, voter mobilization efforts aimed at working-class voters are much more of a patchwork, with social movement organizations playing a disproportionate role. While such organizations can have impacts,[17] they cannot substitute for the embedded organizational strength of strong unions and left parties.

The upshot of these dynamics has been that in the United States participation inequalities are far greater than in elections in other countries. Writing in 1949, V. O. Key asserted that "the blunt truth is that politicians are under no compulsion to pay much heed to classes and groups of citizens that do not vote,"[18] a conclusion that has been frequently reasserted. But the problem in American politics is even more dramatic than this implies. Other types of political engagement are even more unequal. Later in the essay, I will take up differences in donations to causes and candidates, which arguably are the most important source of participation inequality aside from voting itself. But it is worth noting that research on *all* forms of political participation—including working on a political campaign, participating in a protest event, writing a letter to an elected official, civic volunteerism of any kind—finds large inequalities between resource-rich groups and disadvantaged groups. The definitive study in this area remains that of Sidney Verba, Kay Lehman Scholzman, and Henry Brady, who find evidence of even larger disparities in other types of political activity than voting.[19] For example, while 17 percent of those earning over $75,000 a year (in 1989 dollars) reported working on a political campaign, only 4 percent of those earning under $15,000 did; 73 percent of the former report being a member of a political organization, but only 29 percent of the latter; 50 percent of the affluent group wrote to an elected official at least once in the previous year, while only 25 percent of the low-income group did.

The Party System and the Political Expression of Labor Interests

The institutional arrangements that shape and define political parties, along with their relative hostility toward organized labor, have combined to produce another key source of political inequality. American unions have, historically, been far weaker and represented fewer workers than in nearly all other rich democratic countries. Some part of the explanation stems from unique economic factors: American firms in the nineteenth century were big enough to successfully resist unions they did not want, setting in motion a limited style of "craft unionism" in which only a handful of American workers were organized.[20] A generation of scholarship has now shown that institutional and legal barriers to union growth made it impossible for unions to organize workers in the way that they were in Western Europe.[21] Union density in the late 1920s was under 10 percent of all private sector workers, a figure that put the United States at the bottom of the democratic world. American firms grew to dominate the global economy before the 1930s without having to battle organized labor.

Organized labor has generally had a relatively weak foothold in the workplace, but when we turn to political institutions the situation is even bleaker. The electoral system established by the Constitution—a "first-past-the-post" electoral system, in which the candidate (and party) winning the most votes in a single district wins the seat—makes it virtually impossible for third parties to gain traction. This has locked in place a party system in which socialist, Communist, social democratic, and labor parties have never been viable political contenders. The relentless logic of this "majoritarian" system has proved remarkably durable in enforcing major party hegemony. The reasons are not hard to fathom. While proportional representation systems allow minority parties to gain representation in legislative bodies with 5 percent of the vote or less, in the United States only the candidate/party winning the most votes in legislative districts wins the seat. A new party seeking to build support cannot do so gradually by electing a few representatives and building a reputation. Regional third-party efforts—most notably the Populists of the late nineteenth century and the Midwestern Progressives in the twentieth—have occasionally been viable for a period of time, but these efforts were easily parried by the major parties and their voters co-opted.[22]

The two-party system had become firmly established by 1840, and there has been only one successful example of a third party entering the political system and displacing one of the dominant parties since then—the Republican Party breakthrough in the intense conflicts of the pre–Civil War era in the 1850s and 1860 (when Abraham Lincoln won the presidency on a Republican ticket). American political history is littered with failed third-party efforts, many of which were launched by serious people with, in some cases, significant resources and/or apparent political opportunities.[23]

The stranglehold of the two-party system has had two major consequences. First, it has meant that both major parties are broad umbrella coalitions and winning elections always means winning a majority of votes in the center of the ideological spectrum. To be sure, egalitarian political ideas have not always been absent from American politics. The "radical Republicans" of the Reconstruction era, and in certain regions and historical moments the Democratic Party, have promoted egalitarian programs.[24] The Democrats have also, however, been far more strongly influenced by a broad coalition with heavy Southern representation. The Southern wing of the party was deeply hostile to any policies challenging the Jim Crow system, which greatly narrowed the range of acceptable possibilities for egalitarian public policies.[25] Egalitarian policies and reforms that impact the racial order were continually frustrated by Southerners until the final decades of the twentieth century.

Second, as we have noted, the two-party system has prevented a politically viable social democratic party from emerging. Even where socialism gained a partial foothold in American politics, it would eventually be strangled by the two-party system. The now vast "American exceptionalism" literature was first invented to capture this failure.[26] The absence of such a party is important for two reasons. A durable finding in the comparative politics literature is that strong left parties facilitate more generous welfare states.[27] The path to welfare state generosity through party strength is twofold: when left parties control governments, they can redirect taxing and spending policies toward redistributive outcomes; but even when out of government, strong left parties provide important electoral competition that can push centrist and conservative parties toward greater generosity.[28]

Powerful left parties are also important for shaping public discourses and keeping issues relating to poverty and inequality "on the policy agenda." Parties do more than just seek votes; they also organize voters and political ideologies into a coherent spectrum, providing citizens with inputs that remind them of egalitarian ideas and values, as the extensive literature on the cognitive bases of political beliefs suggests.[29] When the party system includes strong left parties, political debates in the media are much more likely to include pro-equality viewpoints, and media coverage of groups and individuals making egalitarian arguments grows. The narrower spectrum of ideological debate throughout most of American history has significantly reduced the visibility of egalitarian politics.

Perverse Openness: Corporate Influence and Political Money

The fourth institutional source of political inequality is the paradoxical "openness" of the American political system. Because of its uniquely fragmented and decentralized structure, with multiple powers devolved to states, counties, and local governments, with federal courts having significant veto power as well, there are numerous avenues for organized interests to express themselves (or block measures they oppose). While decentralization has on occasion meant that progressive states could innovate in new ways, the so-called "laboratories of democracy" have far more often meant that powerful actors have multiple "veto points" to defeat legislative initiatives they do not like in the courts or in state- and local-level governments.[30]

Tracing policy outcomes in almost any major policy domain inevitably leads to the conclusion that diverse veto points have hindered redistributive impulses. A few examples should suffice. Federal courts have notoriously frustrated progressive liberal designs at many points in American history; the Warren Court of the 1960s stands out as a remarkable exception to the general rule that the courts have limited the powers of the federal government to regulate economic activity or reduce the political power of influential interests.[31] Decentralized governance has similarly been impactful. The case of social welfare has been particularly well studied. Robert Lieberman and Jill Quadagno have shown how state-level implementation of social welfare programs foiled the universalist intentions of national reformers in the New Deal and Great Society eras, respectively.[32] As implementation devolved to state (or local) governments, holes were punctured in the programs to shift benefits away from African Americans (or to hold down benefits and make sure that they would not operate as alternatives to low-wage labor markets). Many other examples could be mentioned as well.[33]

Another key source of openness stems from the unique role of money in the financing of American politics. Compared to other democratic polities, the American system of campaign finance allows for an unprecedented role for external funds to flow into the system. American politics have always been awash with cash, as First Amendment principles have equated "free speech" with the right to invest in politics and permitted Congress relatively little scope for setting limits on political investment (with the Supreme Court's recent ruling that unrestricted "independent" corporate campaigns on behalf of political candidates cannot be limited by Congress merely the latest in a century-long struggle).[34]

The flow of money from businesses interests and the rich to candidates for political office in America is hardly a recent phenomenon. Opposition to big money in politics has been expressed in periodic muckraking journalism, Hollywood movies, and populist political rhetoric about the role of "big money" in politics. Fears that wealthy corporate and individual campaign donors were buying government influence were sufficiently pronounced early in the twentieth century that an early attempt at campaign finance reform, the Tillman Act of 1907, sought to ban all corporate contributions to federal campaigns. The effectiveness of this legislation, however, was limited by lack of enforcement and its susceptibility to loopholes and donations in the name of individuals. In her pioneering study of campaign contributions in the 1928 election, Louise Overacker found, for example, that nearly 70 percent of all money contributed came from donations of over $1,000 ($12,410 in 2009 dollars).[35] Similar limitations have characterized the numerous attempts at campaign finance reform right up to the present, including most recently the 2002 McCain-Feingold legislation, which has done virtually nothing to halt the flow of funds into the system.[36]

How and in what ways does political money matter? Theories of "investor" influence on the parties and legislation have proved difficult to definitively test and validate.[37] Much of the recent debate turns on complex methodological issues, producing what two leading analysts have characterized as "the statistical morass that surrounds the study of campaign finance."[38] We do not have the space here to discuss the debates over competing analytical approaches, but suffice it to say that scholarly consensus about the impact of money has proved elusive.[39] The complex array findings are more easily understood when broken down into four distinct outcomes: (1) who runs for political office (making a serious run for political office increasingly requires the capacity to raise huge amounts of money); (2) who wins (underfunded challengers have an almost impossible task against incumbents, although above a certain threshold the impact of resources on outcomes declines); (3) the voting patterns of legislators (who sometimes have to think about the needs of past and hoped-for future donors); and (4) other outcomes, such as facilitating access to legislators through the interest group process. At every stage of this process, there are compelling arguments and empirical evidence to suggest money skews outcomes, even if in no area is money alone plausibly viewed as a single decisive factor.[40]

Starting with the "who runs" question, there is good evidence that fund-raising requirements deter some kinds of potential candidates. Most dramatically, increasing numbers of super-rich individuals make runs for political office (or finance a favored ballot initiative campaign). A new personal spending record for political office was recorded in 2010 by Meg Whitman, former CEO of eBay, in her campaign for California governor; Whitman spent over $140 million. The previous record, just set in 2009, was the $108 million Michael Bloomberg spent to be reelected to a third term as mayor of New York.

Such dramatic examples aside, the routine requirement for being a "serious" candidate for elective office is the ability to tap a well-heeled network of affluent individuals and political action committees. The days of the "grassroots" campaign run by citizen-volunteers employing shoe leather and determination are largely over, except in small local electoral contexts. This is most problematic for candidates outside the political mainstream such as left-liberals and socialists, who want to advocate policies that would tax the rich—the very people they must raise money from—aggressively. The so-called "money primary" matters in particular because it shapes who gets media coverage.

At the same time, however, we should not overstate the point. There is evidence that in certain times and places, sophisticated, well-organized candidates with egalitarian views can package their positions appropriately and surmount the money hurdle effectively. Affluent egalitarians can be located and convinced to give; unions remain active political players (donating about $50 million in recent electoral cycles); and other sources of progressive financing from groups like environmentalists, feminists, anti-war and anti-nuclear groups, and others can come together in some cases. Every election cycle produces a few such candidates. But these counterexamples fly in the face of a much larger trend in the other direction.

Evidence of the impact of political money on who wins elections is notoriously more difficult to analyze. Republicans have for the most part since 1896 maintained a significant edge in support from large donors, and clear overall advantages in recent years where clear documentation is available (with overall marginal advantages of between 10 and 20 percent, higher when in control of both Congress and the White House).[41]

But both parties have long received enormous cash inputs from large do-nors, and it is rare in recent elections for serious Democratic candidates to lack sufficient resources. Strikingly, in recent years the Democrats have built a competitive donor base of business PACs that is somewhat dif-ferent than the Republicans, with huge shares coming from industries such as finance, trial lawyers, and the entertainment industry, while the Republicans receive disproportionately more from industries like oil and pharmaceuticals.

The research literature findings consistently show that well-funded challengers have, not surprisingly, a better chance to win. But whether incumbent spending influences reelection chances is harder to determine. Incumbents typically work harder to raise money (and receive more money from the national party) in close elections, thus making it appear as if money doesn't matter in analyzing the universe of cases.[42] In recent elec-toral cycles, the ability of both major parties to concentrate resources in a handful of close races with either an open seat or a threatened incumbent has meant that it is rare that lack of resources alone accounts for the out-comes of the most contested races. Nonetheless, rising rates of incumbent reelection in an era when politicians are increasingly unpopular suggest indirectly that the ability of incumbents to raise vast sums contributes to declining competitiveness.

The most important issues over political money, and its impacts on policy outcomes, however, ultimately concern whether politicians adjust their policy positions or votes to respond to the wishes of their largest do-nors. Evidence of outright vote selling or the creation of "spot" markets where elected officials exchange votes for future donations is rare, although when found such scandals typically generate lots of media attention. Yet it is rarely the case that the amount of money coming from any one donor is of sufficient magnitude to ensure a legislator's vote, especially as the totals being raised have grown so dramatically. Other factors—party member-ship, legislator's ideology and beliefs, public opinion (perceived or actual), or strategic calculations about how a vote will impact future elections and career prospects—have greater measurable impact on legislative behavior in the most serious research on the topic.[43]

Stronger arguments can be mounted for more subtle forms of influ-ence, such as "access" to elected officials that enables donors to press their case more effectively than those who do not give.[44] Such access, arguably a fourth type of impact, may shape legislation at the margins, for example, through the creation of special hidden tax breaks or exemptions inserted into legislation that can, in the aggregate, be quite expensive and deleterious to the overall purpose of a bill.[45] Access ensures that special interests are listened to, even if access alone does not drive the policy agenda.

INTERREGNUM: POLITICAL SOURCES OF DECLINING INEQUALITY IN AMERICA (CA. 1937–1975)

If political institutions have historically favored the powerful over the weak, there was one historical period in twentieth-century America in which inequality declined. The view propounded in this essay is that it is the era of declining inequality, not the current era of sharply rising inequality, that is the phenomena to be explained. Five unique forces combined in this era to produce declining inequality: (1) tax reforms, especially those adopted during World War II but largely maintained through the 1970s, which vastly increased income taxes on the highest earners; (2) changes in the regulatory regime during the New Deal, in particular those that set important limits on the financial sector, a key driver of wealth inequality in both the 1910s/1920s and again since the early 1980s; (3) New Deal labor law reforms, which initially worked to the advantage of unions and assisted in the rapid growth of private sector unions in the late 1930s and 1940s; (4) civil rights reform breakthroughs, which finally ended Jim Crow and extended full citizenship rights to African Americans, enabling the lowest-earning subgroup to make significant income gains (relative to whites) through the 1970s; (5) paralleling the end of Jim Crow, the South modernized, moving away from heavy reliance on agriculture toward industry, oil, real estate, and finance, raising incomes of all groups in the historically most impoverished region of the country.

Each of these dynamics has been widely explored elsewhere, although the role of the modernization of the South and its contribution to declining inequality through raising incomes in that part of the country has not routinely been included in much of the discussion of midcentury equality.[46] Marginal tax rates on high earners prior to 1981 were at levels that seem almost incomprehensibly high today. Raised to 90 percent during World War II, they remained at 70 percent all the way until 1981. Such rates dampened enthusiasm for high earners to seek outsized compensation packages. New

Deal regulatory changes that made "banking boring," as Simon Johnson and James Kwak put it in their fine analysis of the sources of the financial crisis of 2008,[47] provided steady profits but constrained the financial sector from the excesses that created super-wealth and ultimately financial collapse in the 1920s (and again in the 2000s). It was much more difficult for high earners to leverage exceptional returns in the market during this era. Unions also enjoyed their one period of ascendance in this era. During the New Deal, institutional reforms (first in the National Industrial Recovery Act of 1933, and then under the National Labor Relations Act of 1935) made it possible for unions to be organized on a broad basis, in some cases industry-wide (such as in steel, autos, and coal). Though it would take often heroic militance, union growth did happen. Union density—the percentage of all workers organized into unions—would reach over 35 percent by 1950. Finally, improving conditions for African Americans in the North (where industrial expansion opened decent-paying jobs from the 1950s onward), and civil rights legislation and Supreme Court rulings in the 1960s challenged the social and political exclusion of African Americans, while also generating unprecedented educational and labor market opportunities for a "new" black middle class. The rapid growth of the "New South" after 1970 benefited immensely from the region's grudging, uneven, but relatively rapid acceptance of the end of Jim Crow (with the region's other attractions, in particular its virulent antiunion environment, making it attractive to Northern capital and spurring rapid growth in the region). As incomes in the South (both black and white) moved closer to the national median, inequality declined.

Missing from this list are two other critical—albeit temporary—factors: the remarkable expansion of higher education, and American global economic dominance. Although the United States had long led the world in both the size and extent of its system of higher education and the scale and scope of its national economy, the comparative advantage skyrocketed after World War II as political coalitions across the country emerged that promoted educational opportunity. The rapid growth of higher education through the expansion of state universities from the 1950s through the 1970s significantly aided upward social mobility.[48] More recently, however, declining investment in higher education has halted the rise of an "educational meritocracy," and allowed several European countries to surpass the United States in terms of college graduation rates.[49] The global positioning of the United States in the world economy after World War II was also a unique but transient phenomenon. American economic dominance in the aftermath of World War II made it much easier for firms in key industries to be assured of relatively high profit margins and better positioned to compromise with their workers, especially when nudged by relatively strong unions.

The moderation of the classical sources of unequal democracy in the middle part of the twentieth century produced the "middle class America" now so cherished by many of the harshest critics of rising inequality ("Post-war America was, above all else, a middle-class society," writes Paul Krugman in the opening of his book on rising inequality[50]). Inequality declined. Political polarization was modest. Public policy moved left, especially in the 1960s; but it is striking to note that for all the talk of a conservative "Southern strategy," the rhetoric of the Nixon administration belied frequently liberal extensions of Great Society programs during the early 1970s.[51] Right up until the era of stagflation that followed the 1974–1975 recession, America enjoyed its one (and only) period of declining inequality since the Civil War. It would not last.

THE NEW POLITICAL INEQUALITY

Thus far we have discussed how American political institutions favor certain kinds of political disparities that favor those with more resources, and some of the resulting consequences (and how and why they abated in the middle part of the twentieth century). The contemporary era of rising inequality entailed not *only* the abating of each of the five factors identified earlier, but also a striking reassertion of the power of the institutions of unequal democracy. In this section, I turn to a brief survey of some of these developments.

With respect to the mid-century forces of equality noted in the previous discussion, each gave way beginning in the 1970s and 1980s. Policy changes have been widely noted. Marginal tax rates on high earners were cut in 1981, 1986, 1990, and 2001 (falling as low as 28 percent after the 1990 tax reform before stabilizing in a narrow range of 36–39 percent since 1993). Dramatic reductions in "capital gains" rates (just 15 percent since 2001) provide an especially useful source of tax avoidance for high earners at the top who enjoy significant capital earnings. Finally, steady union decline had, by the 1990s, left organized labor as but a shell of its former self, concentrated especially in the public sector (where its impact on wages was limited).

The most important shifts, however, came in the wake of financial sector deregulation and the resulting wave of financialization that transformed the American economy and society from the early 1980s onward.[52] "Boring" banking was transformed by the growth of a shadow banking sector, new financial instruments that went largely unregulated (and the profits under-taxed at the low capital gains rate), a bank merger movement, and eventually the wholesale shift of conventional savings banks into investment banks and fully integrated firms drawing fees across a range of financial transactions they historically were not involved in.[53] Super-profits, along with rapidly rising wages in the financial sector, soon followed.[54]

What factors brought about these changes? I would insist that any credible analysis must take the long view, conceptualizing the recent period as only the most recent manifestation of the regular rhythms of American political inequality. Each of the institutional underpinnings of unequal democracy reasserts itself. The right to vote began to decline, as a new wave of immigration after 1965 and rising rates of felony convictions left one in ten adults living in the United States unable to participate by 2008.[55] Among eligible voters, the participation skew between advantaged and disadvantaged voters and donors has widened. With respect to participation, the consensus view was that from the 1950s through the elections of the mid-1980s there was relatively little change in the patterning of postwar participation: the gap between workers and managers, or highly educated and poorly educated citizens, remained roughly constant.[56] But since the late 1980s, the most careful analyses suggest that there has been an increasing skew in participation.[57] Disparities in other kinds of political participation widened further, as rising inequality enabled the super-rich to increase their "investment" in politics. In recent decades, incentives for political candidates to seek funding have increased dramatically. Political strategists and campaign managers have reached consensus that high-spending media campaigns are the most efficient way to reach voters, and that "serious" candidates for office need to raise funds (with the "money primary" often signaling who is, or is not, a serious candidate). The consequences of this shift toward television-based campaigning are startling enough. Exhibit 1 suggests that since 1978, there has been a nearly tenfold increase in

EXHIBIT I
Trends in national election campaign finance, 1978–2006
(in millions of dollars, inflation adjusted)

Election Year	Total business	Total labor	Total ideological	Total individual
1978	66.5	31.8	8.3	NA
1980	93.4	35.3	13.1	NA
1982	106.7	43.2	22.9	NA
1984	122.4	48.4	28.3	NA
1986	111.4	54.2	34.0	NA
1988	152.3	58.0	32.9	NA
1990	139.4	52.7	22.4	NA
1992	263.1	62.4	26.7	459.8
1994	262.7	63.6	30.4	353.6
1996	407.7	71.8	33.5	536.5
1998	357.3	65.5	37.8	407.2
2000	669.7	104.7	54.0	817.6
2002	615.5	96.1	68.6	719.3
2004	769.4	101.6	77.1	1,014.2
2006	631.7	88.9	67.1	703.0
Δ1978–2006 (midterm elections)	950%	280%	810%	
Δ1980–2004 (presidential)	823%	288%	589%	
Δ1992–2004 (individual)				154%

SOURCES: 1978–1984: Corrado (1987); 1986–2000: Federal Election Commission Reports (www .fec.gov) and Center for Responsive Politics (www.opensecrets.org).

NOTES: All estimates shown in 2006 dollars. "Total" includes hard and soft (unregulated) contributions during 1992–2002 to all candidates for national office (U.S. House, Senate, and the presidency). After 2002, totals include hard and estimated 527 (ideological advocacy) contributions. Note that 1992/96/2000/04 are presidential years, and thus reflect higher overall contributions than in midterm Congressional elections without presidential ballot.

real dollars contributed by business interests to candidates for American national elections, as well as steady and seemingly inexorable growth in contributions from affluent individuals. One would be hard pressed to imagine that contributors give large amounts and get nothing in return, although (as noted above) the consequences are more subtle than is commonly understood.

Changes on the supply side have also influenced these trends: the vast increase in wealth at the top has expanded the resources available to "invest" in the political system.[58] And rising household affluence creates a similar dynamic. Giving among the wealthy for all purposes—civic, charitable, religious, as well as political—has increased in this era of rising inequality.

While much of this giving may have benign consequences, no such simple conclusions would be appropriate when it comes to political money.

Of perhaps equal or greater concern in recent years is the impact of political money in funding "agenda-setting" organizations. Increasingly centralized corporate control over the media undermines advocacy of progressive causes.[59] The rise of Internet-based media provides a potential but as yet largely unrealized counterweight. The remarkable growth in the resources flowing into conservative think tanks and foundations is especially significant. Starting in the 1970s, business organizations and conservative foundations began providing resources on a heretofore unprecedented scale in support of policy formation organizations inside the Beltway.[60] The considerable power of these policy organizations to intervene in political debates, get their representatives into the media, and provide policy advice to presidents and Congress is well established.[61] By all accounts, such organizations play a significant role in setting the policy agenda.[62] To the extent that the policy organizations with the greatest resources are disproportionately promoting a conservative policy agenda—as numerous studies have found[63]—they contribute to a larger environment in which many egalitarian policy ideas are simply "not on the agenda" for discussion.[64]

Recent Political Dynamics: Republicans Ascendant, Democrats in Disarray

Aside from the long-run dynamics, more proximate factors (including some of those discussed in the Ferejohn essay) merit brief attention. The rising political power of the business-oriented wing of the Republican Party, which has to a large extent set the national policy agenda from the early 1980s through at least 2006, is particularly important.[65] Republican political leaders from Ronald Reagan through George W. Bush, as well as a new generation of Republican politicians and party activists, have moved the party to the right. Although there is some disagreement over what impact this shift has had on public policy, it is certainly clear that Republican control over the policy agenda has moved tax policy, regulation, and foreign policy rightward in the past thirty years. Combined with high (and growing) rates of incumbent reelection, many very conservative and principled Republicans have persisted in office without serious challenge from Democratic opponents.[66]

The Republican majority between 1994 and 2006, and the conservative movement that fostered it, however, lost significant ground in the 2006 midterm elections. The decision of the Bush administration to start and sustain an increasingly unpopular war in Iraq backfired, as the party lost control of both houses of Congress and a majority of statehouses to the Democrats. The Republican majority that many observers thought had succeeded in consolidating power at the time of the 2004 presidential election has unraveled, at least for the time being.

Yet the election of Democrat Barack Obama in 2008, with a substantial Democratic majority in Congress, did little to produce a return to egalitarian policymaking of the post–World War II period. Against bitter opposition, the Obama administration has pushed through a national health plan that—if it is fully implemented—promises to provide health insurance coverage to about 95 percent of all Americans by the time it goes into effect in 2014. The administration's heavily compromised financial sector reform legislation partially reverses some of the massive deregulation of finance that underlay the financial crisis of 2008. But these modest legislative victories did little if anything to reverse the course of the past thirty years, and it strains credulity to think that under current conditions the Obama administration will be able to push policy much further.

The main reason for this stark conclusion is that the electoral bases of the major parties have shifted in important ways that discourage the parties—notably the Democrats—from pursuing an expansionary program of social provision. In the debate over trends in class voting in the United States, recent work has suggested two apparently contradictory findings. Income-based models have found persistence of the classical alignment, with lower-income voters remaining as Democratic as before.[67] To be sure, growing affluence (perceived or actual) has pushed all voters to the right,[68] but the relationship between *relative* income groups and vote choice has remained as strong as ever.[69]

However, an occupational-based model of class voting produces a more nuanced picture. Classes (as measured by occupational location[70]) have realigned politically. In our own six-class model distinguishing professional, managers, the self-employed, routine white-collar workers, skilled manual workers and supervisors, and nonskilled workers, we find that considerable realignment has indeed occurred. The results of our statistical analysis of class voting—originally presented in Hout, Brooks, and Manza,[71] and most recently updated and extended by Hout and Moody[72]—suggest a number of striking trends. Professionals had moved from being the second most

Republican class to the most *Democratic* class by the late 1980s. The self-employed moved from a centrist position to a strongly Republican bloc in recent elections. Skilled and nonskilled workers have shifted toward the center, although nonskilled workers remain in Democratic alignment.

The question of trends in class voting—and how they may be impacting elections more generally—has been reignited by the debate over the widely discussed best-selling book by Thomas Frank, *What's the Matter with Kansas?*[73] Frank argues that white working-class voters have defected to the Republicans, and into an alliance with affluent voters, creating a coalition "uniting business and blue collar" because of Republican inroads into the working-class electorate based on appeals to symbolic social issues and traditional family values. Our own investigation of these trends suggests a somewhat different picture.[74] We find evidence that social issues have become an important source of occupation-based class realignment, but *not* because conservative views on such issues have pushed working-class voters to the right. Rather, we find strong evidence that social-issue liberalism has pushed professionals toward the Democratic Party.[75] But while these professionals have changed their partisan identity, they have *not* become more supportive of social spending for the poor or other redistributive measures.

To chart the overall impact of change in the social bases of contemporary party coalitions, it is informative to focus on how the intersection of turnout, class-based voter alignments, and the size of groups combine to shape the Democratic and Republican parties' coalitions. In other words, by taking into account the relative *size* of social classes as well as their turnout and vote choice, we can obtain a better sense of the combined impact of class politics on the electoral strategies and policies that politicians and parties will ultimately pursue. Indeed, because processes such as manual workers' declining size and decreasing willingness to support Democratic candidates are difficult to reverse over short periods of time, they set in place powerful constraints that party officials cannot readily ignore.

How have class voters' turnout levels, alignments with parties, and relative size influenced the major parties' coalitions? In earlier work with Clem Brooks, I find that the Democratic Party experienced a major electoral shift from between the 1950s and the 1990s, moving from a party with far more working-class voters than professional and managerial voters to one with larger representation of the latter groups and a sharply diminished working-class electorate. We estimate the ratio of working-class to professional/managerial voters fell from almost 3:1 in 1960 to about 1:1 by 1992, and it has nudged even further in the direction of middle-class electorate since then.[76] In other words, while in 1960 there were three working-class voters for every professional/manager voter, by the 1990s the Democratic coalition had reached parity between working- and upper-middle-class voters.[77]

Decomposing this shift revealed several dynamics. Professionals have both grown in size and become significantly more Democratic. Both skilled and nonskilled workers have moved toward the center, although at different time periods. Skilled workers in the 1960s and early 1970s and non-skilled workers in the 1980s and 1990s moved toward the political center (although the latter remain in Democratic alignment, albeit not to the same extent as before 1980). Because both classes have declined in size, their relative contributions to the Democratic coalition have shrunk. This development only deepens when we consider a smaller but still significant increase in the share of votes coming from routine white-collar workers, which has also risen since the 1960s.

With such a significant shift in where the votes are now coming from, it is hardly surprising that Democratic strategists and politicians have faced less pressure to extend the economic and social policies of the New Deal. Indeed, it is precisely the growing prominence of middle-class voters within the Democratic coalition that provides party leaders with incentives to emphasize market-related and meritocratic policy ideas and arrangements. To be sure, there remain significant differences between the Democratic and Republican Parties. Political scientists Larry Bartels and Nathan Kelley have produced econometric evidence suggesting that since World War II inequality has grown significantly faster under Republican presidents.[78] Democrats in office have tended to slow the inequality express. But compared to their New Deal and Great Society predecessors, they have done nothing in recent decades to reverse it.

What about the Republican coalition? Has a similar shift occurred among the Republican electorate? In short, the answer is no. Like the Democratic coalition, the Republican coalition shows a marked increase in the representation of professionals and managers, although unlike the Democratic coalition it is managers rather than professionals who provide the bulk of the increased vote share from the educated middle classes.

The share of Republican votes coming from the working class has remained much steadier, as increased Republican voting among some segments of the working class has offset their declining size in the population as a whole. The most striking change, we believe, concerns not class but religion: the share of Republican votes coming from mainline Protestants has dropped precipitously. Once half of all Republican voters, mainline Protestants to-day provide less than one-fifth of all Republican votes.[79] This group once provided the electoral backbone of moderate and liberal Republicanism, supportive of civil rights and modest support programs for the poor. The mainline population, for various demographic and market factors, has hemorrhaged membership since World War II, while the increasing conservatism of the Republican Party on social issues has prompted them to move to the political center.[80] The loss of this moderate center has been, I believe, a critical but little-noticed source of the rightward shift of the Republican Party over the past fifty years.

Finally, we would be remiss if we did not mention enduring changes in public opinion that have, since the 1970s, made redistributive policy proposals difficult. From a comparative perspective, it is clear that Americans are dramatically less supportive of redistribution through the welfare state than citizens in other rich democracies.[81] But even within an already constrained political market for redistribution, some small but significant trends in public opinion have further tightened opportunities for redistribution. I have explored some of these shifts in a recent paper with my colleagues Brian McCabe and Jennifer Heerwig;[82] our key general conclusions are that declining confidence in government and rising conservative political ideological identity have offset Americans' persisting support for social spending programs across the liberal agenda.

A WAY OUT?

The interaction of longstanding American political institutions and recent political trends provides little evidence to suggest that public policy will contribute to reducing inequality for the foreseeable future. If the argument of this essay is correct, America will not be building a redistributive, European-style welfare state any time soon. For those concerned about rising inequality, this conclusion is a bleak one indeed.

Are there any forces that might nudge policy in another direction? History provides useful examples, even if mechanical application of lessons from the past is always problematic. These lessons suggest that the sources of any future reversal of inegalitarian policy trends lie not in a simple remaking of the electoral map, such as electing more Democrats to Congress or to the White House, but rather in challenges developing from outside the major political institutions. At key turning points in the history of the American welfare state, it has been challenger social movements that have shaken the political order in ways that have pushed complacent Democratic majorities to raise taxes on the wealthy and provide greater social supports for disadvantaged groups. This was true, most importantly, in the 1930s and again in the 1960s. In the 1930s, labor and social movement militance pushed the Roosevelt administration toward sweeping legislation that created, in the span of just a few years, the foundations of a national welfare state and strong unions capable of defending workers' interests across a range of industries. Franklin Roosevelt ran on a platform calling for a balanced budget and business-government collaboration. The "Second New Deal" policies adopted from 1935 through 1937—including the Social Security Act, the National Labor Relations Act, and the Fair Labor Standards Act— could hardly have been anticipated in 1932. But movement-driven events pushed FDR and the Democratic majority in Congress to contemplate, and ultimately adopt, policies that altered the course of inequality in America.

What happened in this critical period? One key factor was the backdrop of large, powerful social movement activity: the labor movement, unemployed workers' movements, the Townsend mobilization of the Aged—all contributed to disrupting the normal pattern of American politics, and gave the movements' allies in Congress and the administration unprecedented room to push for new policy reform. The scale of the upsurge in the 1930s is easily forgotten today. There were numerous takeovers of factories by workers engaged in sit-in strikes (over eighty in 1937 alone), a remarkable upsurge in successful organizing drives across a wide swath of industrial America, three large citywide general strikes in 1934 (in San Francisco, Minneapolis, and Toledo), and countless mass protests of unemployed workers and the poor.[83]

A similar dynamic erupted from the mid-1950s onward, when an increasingly militant civil rights movement challenged the previous subservience of the Democratic majority to the segregationist preferences of its Southern wing. As with the labor-based social movements of the 1930s, the remarkable mass mobilization of African Americans in the South forced (mostly Northern) politicians to confront an enduring set of inequalities. In the span of a less than two years, the social order of the Jim Crow South was swept away by federal legislation (with the adoption of the Civil Rights Act of 1964 and the Voting Rights Act of 1965). None of this could have been predicted in 1960, when John F. Kennedy narrowly won the White House on a platform with moderate positions on civil rights consistent with that of previous Democratic leaders. And the success of the civil rights mobilization created a space of other, related mobilizations to extend civil rights to women and ethnic minorities.

These historical examples suggest how a seemingly entrenched inegalitarian configuration of institutional and political forces can be forced to move toward greater equality. Yet while they provide hope, they also suggest just how daunting is the hurdle facing supporters of egalitarian politics. The labor and civil rights movements of the 1930s and 1950s/60s were remarkable movements that cannot simply be conjured up again. Any survey of the American movement landscape in the first decade of the twenty-first century can only conclude that while we may be in a "social movement society" on a small scale, with lots of single-issue advocacy groups claiming to be membership organizations, there are no large-scale egalitarian movements currently on the horizon of similar scope and power to those of the 1930s or 1960s.[84] Pessimism can only follow from this conclusion.[85]

The historical lessons of the 1930s and 1960s do, however, provide one powerful parallel for today. In both periods, massive migration (the external migration from Central and Southern Europe between the 1880s and 1920s, and the internal migration of African Americans from the 1920s to the 1960s) was slowly remaking the sociodemographic foundations of the American polity. The populations of America's cities and regions were shifting dramatically in both periods. In the first period, immigrant voters were slowly being incorporated into the political system. By the 1930s, under the leadership of Northern liberals inside the Democratic Party, these voters provided the difference in critical electoral contests. By the late 1950s, several decades of strong African-American migration from the South to the North transformed the social bases of the Democratic coalition, making

Northern politicians much more sensitive to the demands of their increasingly black constituents.

A similar dynamic is already well underway. Rising rates of immigration since 1965 are slowly changing the face of the American polity. Latino voters are approaching 10 percent of the electorate nationally, and in key states like California, Illinois, and Florida they have already begun to shift the political balance (with Texas and many other states likely to experience similar movement in the near future). Most projections have Latinos making up as much as a quarter of the total electorate by the middle of this century. Recent developments, including the tensions around immigration reform, may serve to keep Latino voters in an "aligned" position with the Democrats much the same way as Jewish voters entered an enduring alliance with the Democrats during the New Deal, an alignment that has largely persisted even in the face of growing wealth and status in the Jewish community. If Republican politicians continue to promote harsh anti-immigrant policies, a process that seems inexorable in the face of threatening political demography, one can envision an enduring alignment taking shape.

While a growing Latino electorate may benefit the electoral fortunes of the Democratic Party in the future, this does not in itself ensure more egalitarian public policies will emerge. But when combined with other emerging trends, the possibilities are intriguing. Because of a persistent gender gap ranging from 7 to 14 percent since 1980,[86] the overwhelming support of African-American voters for Democratic candidates, and the growing size of the Latino electorate, approximately three-quarters of the Democratic Party vote today comes from either women or racial and ethnic minorities. And that proportion will continue to grow in the future. This sociodemographic shift suggests the *potential* basis for pressure on Democratic politicians to respond in new and different ways to the emerging social problems of the twenty-first century.

Yet the ultimate lesson from American history is that electoral developments by themselves are unlikely to significantly reverse the inequality express of the past three decades. In some ways, the election of President Barack Obama represents the first successful expression of the new Democratic majority. But in the absence of large-scale pressure from new social movements from below, disrupting the balance of institutional and political forces, the Obama administration and the Democratic Congresses of 2006–2010 did little to initiate an assault on inegalitarian America. Key structural reforms that might shift the institutional context back closer to the environment of the late 1940s—for example, the passage of the so-called "card check" union legislation that would significantly alter the nearly impossible organizing obstacles unions currently face—will require a drastically different political environment than at present. Because it is difficult right now to envision where such pressure might emerge, one can conclude only that the political regime of inequality in America is likely to persist.

Part IV

WHY IS THERE
A GENDER GAP IN PAY?

A Human Capital Account
of the Gender Pay Gap[1]

Solomon Polachek

The October 14, 2002, issue of *Fortune* magazine features the fifty most powerful women in business. But the cover story, "The New Trophy Husband," seeks to find out who is "behind every powerful woman."[2] It argues that "increasingly it's a stay-at-home dad." The article depicts over a dozen successful women who attribute their accomplishments to an at-home husband managing the family. According to the article,

> At Ford, Xerox, Sun, Schwab, Verizon, J. P. Morgan Chase, Coca-Cola, almost everywhere you look in the upper ranks of the Fortune 500, it could be the woman wearing the pants and the man minding hearth and home. Call him what you will: househusband, stay-at-home-dad, domestic engineer. But credit him with setting aside his own career by dropping out, retiring early, or going part-time so that his wife's career might flourish and their family might thrive. Behind a great woman at work, there is often a great man at home. He is the new trophy husband.[3]

The *Fortune* article portrays atypical families. Although the trend is changing,[4] for most families the division of labor is the opposite. Husbands typically specialize in market work and *not* home management. In contrast,

Solomon Polachek is a distinguished professor at Binghamton University (SUNY), where he has taught since 1983. His research contributions include the book *The Economics of Earnings*, written with W. Stanley Siebert. He is currently editor of *Research in Labor Economics*. Polachek was elected president of the Peace Science Society (1999–2000), vice president of the Eastern Economic Association (2012–2013), and currently serves on editorial boards of *Conflict Management and Peace Science, Peace Economics, Peace Science and Public Policy,* and the *Review of Economics of the Household.*

wives are more likely than their husbands to dedicate themselves to home activities and forgo employment for pay. In this essay, I make the case that the household *division of labor* is of paramount importance in explaining social stratification and the resulting gender earnings inequality, and that increases in women's lifetime labor force participation relative to men's are responsible for the rise in women's wages relative to men's over the last century.

One other important point: *Fortune* had tried to write this "trophy husband" article five years earlier, but without success, not because the editors couldn't find enough women at the top, but because the women at the top believed it too great a stigma to depict their spouses as househusbands. And so, although *Fortune* attempted to do the article five years earlier, it simply could not find enough executive women who would talk about their husbands in *that* way, let alone get *that* kind of publicity.

I view this stigma to be one manifestation of what I call *societal* discrimination. I define societal discrimination to be non-corporate-instigated social processes leading to gender role differentiation, which I claim is mostly responsible for women's ultimate economic weakness. This role delineation may come about for several reasons. First, efficient behavior within the household leads household members to specialize. Why this specialization occurs is not completely understood; but perhaps it occurs because at the outset of marriage husbands command a higher wage, given they are on average over two years older and slightly more educated than their wives.[5] Second, social norms inherent in the culture make it difficult for women to take on work responsibilities.[6] Third, many past and present government labor market and tax policies blatantly favor men. The fact that men tend to be very reluctant to share household responsibilities, the fact that women acquiesce to taking on most of the household burdens, the fact that high school guidance counselors frequently discourage women from certain male-dominated courses, the fact that governments often impose hefty taxes on a wife's earnings (the marriage tax), and the fact that in the big scheme of things women got the right to vote only very recently are all symptoms of *societal discrimination*. I suggest that societal discrimination relates to the division of labor within the home.

A number of statistical "decomposition" analyses parcel the gender wage gap into two parts. One consists of that portion of the male–female wage gap that is explained by differences in such productivity-enhancing characteristics as education, labor market experience, occupation, industry, location, and other personal attributes that determine productivity at work (what economists call human capital variables). The second consists of that portion of the male–female wage gap unexplained by the statistical analysis. This latter "unexplained" portion is often taken to measure discrimination. Many adherents of these statistical approaches claim this latter measure represents blatant corporate discrimination in hiring, pay, and promotion practices. As will be explained later, mostly because human capital is not easy to measure and because societal discrimination can cause women to acquire less human capital than men, the statistical techniques used to apportion the wage gap are fraught with biases. Also, none of the currently used statistical techniques get at subtle discrimination in working conditions, such as sexual harassment, unless such harassment directly affects wages. Because of these biases, one does not get an accurate estimate of discrimination when using these decomposition techniques. Either one must be innovative in measuring human capital, or one must get at the effects of discrimination more directly.

In this essay, I make the case that the household *division of labor* is of paramount importance in explaining the social stratification that results in gender earnings inequality. The division of labor causes men to specialize in work more than women. As such, women spend less time in the labor force, invest less in marketable skills, do not achieve the same occupation or job status, and as a result earn less. Further, I claim decreases in societal discrimination diminish the divide between a husband's and wife's participation in the workforce. The trend of consistently rising female lifetime labor force participation, coupled with the trend of moderately decreasing male labor force participation, causes movements towards gender parity. I believe this relative increase in women's work compared to men's is why over the last century men's and women's wages got closer. Also, I believe this is in part the reason why *Fortune* could do its story in 2002, but not in 1997. And, I think that societal discrimination is far more important than corporate hiring and promotion discrimination in causing gender wage differences, in the first place. Surely, *societal discrimination* is a topic worth exploring further and debating scientifically with evidence.[7]

DIVISION OF LABOR IN THE HOME

Catalyst is a research organization designed to expand options for women in upper-level business jobs. Felice Schwartz, whose 1989 *Harvard Business Review* article spurred debate on the "mommy track," founded Catalyst in

1962. It is one of the leading nonprofit organizations focused on women's issues. Catalyst's original board of directors consisted of the presidents of Duke University, Mills College, Sarah Lawrence College, Smith College, and Wellesley College. Part of the organization's research concentrates on preparing a number of surveys on women's attitudes. In one recent survey of three thousand women in their mid-twenties to mid-thirties, the *biggest* barrier to women's advancement was personal and family responsibilities. Sixty-eight percent named this as their main problem.[8]

To illustrate this division of labor, one need only examine how lifetime labor force participation differs by gender and marital status. I do so with 1970 and 2004 data to show how the division of labor is changing. Exhibit 1 depicts gender and marital status labor force participation patterns for the United States in 1970 and 2004. On the horizontal axis is age. On the vertical axis are labor force participation rates. These rates indicate the proportion of each gender–marital status group in the labor force. Beginning with 1970, married men have the highest lifetime labor force participation. Married (spouse present) women have the lowest, peaking

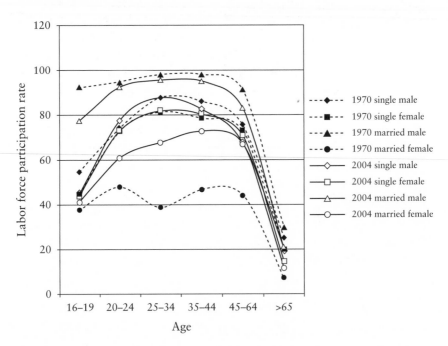

EXHIBIT 1   U.S. labor force participation by gender, marital status, and age

at about 43 percent between the ages of twenty-three and forty-eight. The drop around age thirty reflects intermittent labor force participation related to childbearing. The gap between single males and females is the narrowest. Single never-married men and women have roughly the same lifetime work patterns. By 2004, the differences are appreciably smaller. The biggest change is that married female labor force participation rose over the three decades. However, even in 2004, married women participate between one-fourth and one-third less than married men. Again in 2004, the labor force participation gap is miniscule for singles.

Although large marital status and gender differences in lifetime work still remain, these gender disparities are gradually diminishing. Female labor force participation is rising secularly and male participation is falling. However, in the 1990s, the growth in female labor force participation decelerated. Exhibit 2 emphasizes this recent deceleration in the growth of women's labor force participation during the 1990s. Women's lifetime labor force participation in 1990 is dramatically higher than in 1974, but women's lifetime labor force participation in 2005 is only marginally higher

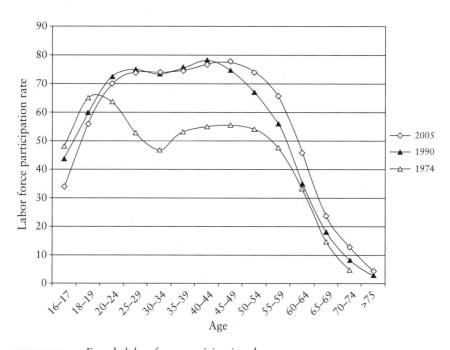

EXHIBIT 2   Female labor force participation, by age

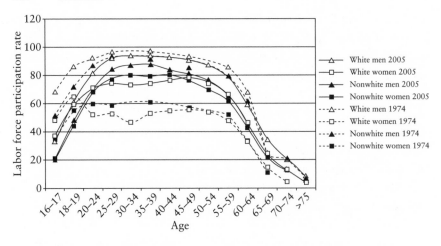

EXHIBIT 3   Labor force participation rates by race, gender, and age

than in 1990. As shall be illustrated later, I believe this deceleration explains why the gender gap narrowed less quickly in the 1990s than in the 1980s.[9]

Exhibit 3 emphasizes gender lifetime labor force participation differences by race. The same general pattern of high male-relative-to-female participation emerges. But interestingly, there is a somewhat larger gender difference in labor force participation rates for whites than for non-whites. To see this, note that white women participate less over their lifetimes than non-white women, whereas white men participate more than non-white men. As I shall show later in this essay, the bigger white male–female labor force participation gap suggests larger male–female wage differences for whites than for blacks.

One can examine these patterns from a slightly different perspective. Retrospective work history data (asking respondents about *their* past work patterns) as well as panel data (following respondents through time) illustrate the same patterns but do not rely on synthetic cohorts comprising individual respondents across various age groups. Given that synthetic cohorts compound cohort (generational) and lifecycle (aging) effects, one can argue that retrospective and panel data are superior. Exhibit 4 (based on Jacob Mincer's and my own 1974 study using the National Longitudinal Survey of Mature Women[10]) contrasts work patterns for married-once-spouse-present and never-married women. Never-married white women 30–44

EXHIBIT 4
Female work history data

Population group	Actual years worked	Years out of the labor force (home time)
WHITES		
Married once, spouse present, with children	6.4	10.4
Never married, no children	14.5	1.5
BLACKS		
Married once, spouse present, with children	9.1	10.3
Never married, no children	13.6	4.7

SOURCE: Mincer and Polachek (1974).

years old in 1967 (row 1 and row 2) worked 14.5 years out of a possible 16 years. In contrast, married-spouse-present women worked only 6.4 out of about 16.8 years. As before, similar patterns emerge for black women, but again the differences are more muted, with never-married black women having slightly less lifetime work and married-once-spouse-present black women a bit more lifetime work (9.1 years versus 6.4 years) than whites. Thus here too, being married greatly diminishes lifetime work, slightly more for whites than blacks.

While less stark, these same retrospective work history patterns emerge in more recent data. Using the 1980 Panel Study of Income Dynamics Data (PSID), Carole Miller finds that married women average 10.04 years out of the labor force.[11] Similarly, using a panel of 2,659 individuals from the 1976–87 PSID data, Moon-Kak Kim and I find that women averaged 9.62 years out of the labor force relative to men's 2.22 years.[12] Current data for foreign countries are comparable. Using Canadian data, Wayne Simpson finds that in 1993 married women with children averaged 7.6 years (or 36.4 percent of their work years) out of the labor force, whereas single women spent 1.5 (or 12.9 percent) of their work years out of the labor force. For men, this figure is 0.9 years (or 8.1 percent).[13] Data within narrow professions yield similar results. Catalyst finds that only 29 percent of women MBA graduates work full-time continuously after graduation compared to 69 percent for men, and similarly only 35 percent of women law graduates worked continuously since graduation compared to 61 percent for men.[14]

Children exacerbate these differences. For example, as illustrated in Exhibit 5, Susan Harkness and Jane Waldfogel find significantly lower labor force participation rates for women with children compared to women

EXHIBIT 5
*Men's and women's full-time employment status age 24–44—
an international comparison*

Full-time employment	AU 1995	CN 1994	UK 1995	US 1994	GE 1994	FI 1991	SW 1991
All men	.830	.762	.790	.844	.830	.777	.771
Women without children	.731	.677	.763	.731	.722	.851	.745
Women with children	.258	.469	.256	.495	.352	.710	.611

SOURCE: Harkness and Waldfogel (2003). Based on the Luxembourg Income Study data. Employment is defined as the share who have a job during the survey week. Full-time employment is defined as the share who have a job during the survey week and who work thirty or more hours per week.

without.[15] This is true not just in the United States, but in Australia, Canada, the United Kingdom, and Germany. In Finland and Sweden, the same result holds, but the pattern is mitigated given Sweden's and Finland's social policies promoting women's work. In virtually all cases (the exception is Finland), men's labor force participation exceeds women's, but the gap is exceptionally wide when comparing men to women with children.

HUMAN CAPITAL: THE LINK BETWEEN WORK AND WAGES

Why the concern with lifetime labor force participation? Economists such as Jacob Mincer[16] and Yoram Ben-Porath[17] showed how one's earnings are linked to "human capital" investments such as school and on-the-job training (obtained through seniority, networking, job mobility, and other post-school training). In turn, according to their lifecycle models, human capital investments mostly depend on expected lifetime labor force participation.

The theory is as follows: There are costs and benefits to acquiring marketable skills. The costs are direct (such as tuition and learning manuals) and indirect (mostly forgone wages during training). The benefits are higher lifetime earnings.[18] The more years one works, the greater the opportunity to reap the benefits of these higher earnings. So, for example, marketable human capital benefits would be zero were one never to work, independent of how many professional or PhD degrees one acquires. In a similar vein, dropping out of the labor force reduces lifetime work years, which according to the theory should decrease the potential rewards from investment in marketable skills. In contrast, those who expect to work long hours and those who foresee the greatest number of years at work should have the highest expected returns. Thus, all else constant, human capital theory postulates that the less one's lifetime labor force participation, the lower the benefits to investment, and hence the smaller one's incentives to invest in training. Since, on average, women work fewer hours throughout their lives, human capital theory predicts women to purchase less marketable investments than men. At the same time, statistical discrimination theory predicts firms likewise would invest less to train women.[19] In turn, lower rates of job training, relative to men, translate to lower per-hour relative women's wages, so that the male–female wage gap widens.[20] On the other hand, as women's lifetime labor force participation rises, and as men's lifetime labor force participation falls, the male–female wage gap narrows. Indeed, as I shall show, these trends are what the data indicate. But first, I mention a couple of other phenomena to bolster human capital theory's credibility.

First, as one gets older, earnings rise each year. The rate at which earnings increase varies over the life cycle. Young workers, below thirty-five, experience the most rapid per-year increases in earnings. Workers in their fifties find earnings growth to be relatively meager. For them, earnings rise hardly at all. Here again, the human capital model explains why earnings growth varies over the life cycle. Early in life (below age thirty-five), individuals have a whole work-life ahead. So with many years to work, training pays off big-time, since returns are reaped for numerous years to come. Later in life, the "present value" of training is smaller because there are fewer work years in which to accumulate the returns.[21] Accordingly, older individuals typically purchase less training, and concomitantly earnings rise less quickly. Of course, there are exceptions, such as in top executive positions, where pay increases markedly. Economists often view this phenomenon as a rank-order tournament paying large prizes to the "winner."[22] For a number of reasons, including "old boy" networks, these tournaments can be disadvantageous to women, which might explain aspects of the glass ceiling.

Second, a worker who anticipates discontinuous labor force participation obtains on-the-job training differently than the continuously employed worker.[23] Rather than begin one's work-life with large but diminishing amounts of training, the discontinuously employed worker initially obtains little training. However, the amount of training rises moderately after the worker permanently reenters the workforce, which for women usually occurs when childbearing is complete. As a result, women's earnings need not exhibit the usual concave age-earnings profiles characteristic of men. For this reason, women's lifecycle earnings profiles are flatter than men's and often exhibit a non-monotonic pattern (i.e., exhibit a midlife dip) depending on the degree of intermittent work behavior.[24]

EARNINGS PROFILES BY GENDER AND MARITAL STATUS:
MARRIED WOMEN WITH CHILDREN EARN THE LEAST

Earnings profiles depict what a specific worker or group of workers earn at various phases of their life cycle. For men, earnings profiles are concave, indicating that earnings rise relatively quickly at the beginning of men's working life, but that earnings growth tapers off by the time men achieve their fortieth birthday. Typically the greater the education of the group profiled, the higher the earnings profile. As an example, Exhibit 6 contains earnings profiles for males using 1990 U.S. Census data.[25] Successively higher profiles represent lifecycle earnings paths for individuals completing greater amounts of schooling.

Earnings profiles differ for men and women. As illustrated in Exhibit 7, male profiles are higher and steeper, indicating not only greater earnings but also quicker earnings growth, at least through most of the life cycle. This exhibit confirms the gender wage gap, but illustrates that the wage gap varies throughout the life cycle, being small initially, then widening,

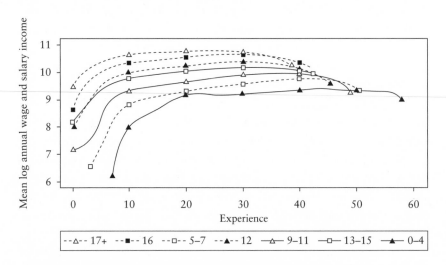

EXHIBIT 6   1990 Census-experience-earnings profile, white males
SOURCE: http://lily.src.uchicago.edu/econ350/mincer_graphs.pdf.

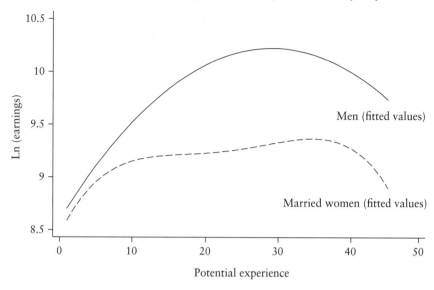

EXHIBIT 7   Earnings profiles by gender

NOTE: Computed from the 1990 U.S. Census of Population public use sample for men and married women with twelve years of school. (Upper profile represents men, and lower profile represents women.)

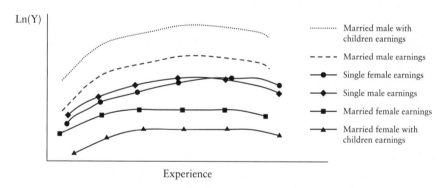

EXHIBIT 8   Typical earnings profiles by gender, marital status, and children

and eventually decreasing somewhat at older ages. Particularly interesting is why the gender wage gap varies over the life cycle. But before discussing that, let us examine the gender wage gap across demographic groups.

Exhibit 8 plots typical male and female age-earnings profiles for men and women, but now by marital status and whether they have children.

EXHIBIT 9

Female/male earnings ratios by country corrected for hours worked

Country	All workers	Married workers	Single workers
Germany (monthly)	0.688	0.573	1.027
United Kingdom (annual)	0.634	0.597	0.949
United States (annual)	0.685	0.594	0.955
Austria (monthly)	0.723	0.656	0.970
Switzerland (monthly)	0.617	0.578	0.945
Sweden (annual)	0.767	0.724	0.935
Norway (annual)	0.731	0.716	0.916
Australia (annual)	0.749	0.691	0.914

SOURCE: Blau and Kahn (1992).

NOTE: The earnings ratios were evaluated at forty hours. The earnings ratios for married workers are for married workers with one person other than spouse in the household (for Sweden, Norway, and Austria, one child); those for single workers are for non-married people with no other persons in the household.

EXHIBIT 10

Female/male earnings ratios by country for full-time workers (LIS data)

Country	Year	All workers	Married workers	Single workers
Germany	2000	0.691	0.662	0.852
United Kingdom	1995	0.757	0.690	0.996
United Kingdom	1999	0.783	0.736	0.977
United States	1997	0.713	0.635	0.972
United States	2000	0.716	0.635	0.966
Austria	1994	0.716	0.651	0.937
Austria	1997	0.771	0.754	0.911
Switzerland	1992	0.577	0.367	1.027
Sweden	1992	0.800	0.770	0.949
Australia	1989	0.738	0.696	0.906
Australia	1994	0.755	0.724	0.872

SOURCE: Luxembourg Income Study (LIS).

From these, a very interesting pattern emerges. Wage profiles for single males and females are very similar. The wage gap is narrow and in many data sets actually diminishes with age. In contrast, the married wage profiles differ dramatically. Married men have far higher and steeper profiles than married women. Children exacerbate these differences.

Francine Blau and Lawrence Kahn illustrate these patterns using international data.[26] Exhibit 9 contains their results and Exhibit 10 contains comparable results from the recently available Luxembourg Income Study (LIS). For single men and women, the wage gap is generally less than 10 percent. Single women on average earn over 90 percent of what men earn. But married women earn far less than married men. Here the wage ratio is typically in the 60 percent to 70 percent range.

Further deconstruction illustrates that children play a major role in the gender wage gap. Married women with children earn *less* than married women without children.[27] Married women who space their births widely apart receive even lower wages.[28] Opposite patterns hold for men: married men with children earn *more* than married men without children, and spacing children at wide intervals is associated with even higher male earnings.[29] Thus the gender wage gap varies by marital status, children, and spacing of children. Interestingly, the male–female wage gap among blacks is smaller than for whites. This is consistent with black women working relatively more over their lifetimes compared to black men than white women compared to white men. As it turns out, these demographic variables are more important predictors of the gender wage gap than any other explanatory factors.

Corporate discrimination cannot explain these wage patterns. Were discrimination the culprit, one would need an explanation as to why corporations hardly discriminate against single women, but discriminate enormously against married women—especially married women with children spaced widely apart. The truth is firms cannot even ask marital status in employment applications. But even if they could get this marital status information, they would hardly know anything about the number and spacing of one's fertility. On the other hand, given the close surroundings in a typical work environment, one might argue that an immediate supervisor actually is privy to an employee's marital status and number of children, even if corporations (or at least corporate human resources offices) do not know an employee's family history. And if so, this information can potentially influence employee performance evaluations. However, even if supervisors knew the number of children, they are far less cognizant of children's ages, and hence less likely to know much about child spacing.

Statistical discrimination models are equally impotent. Advocates of statistical discrimination argue that hiring and promotion decisions are based on corporate expectations. Companies expecting women to drop out of work frequently to fulfill familial responsibilities would refrain from hiring women in the first place. They would hire women in the more menial jobs and refuse to provide training. At best, there is only mixed evidence that this is the case. Audit studies (sometimes called "correspondence analysis") analyze firm hiring practices by sending "pseudo" job-seeking males and females with similar job résumés to respond to want ads.[30] There are problems with the approach because they neglect supply-side consider-ations.[31] For example, if a firm finds it costly to offer a job that is refused, the prudent employer will tend to offer jobs only to discernible groups that have a high probability of accepting the offer. If fewer female applicants (all else constant) signal low acceptance probabilities (perhaps because of higher commuting costs or the unavailability of day care), then firms can easily con-ceive the probability of an offer being accepted to be related to the proportion of female applicants. If the firm finds it costly to offer a job that is refused, a prudent employer will tend to offer fewer jobs to females. For this reason, audit studies need to incorporate the relative proportion of male-to-female job applicants to rectify this bias; but as far as I know, no studies do. Never-theless, whereas several studies find gender differences,[32] the very latest, most comprehensive analysis finds no gender difference in employers' proclivity to call back job applicants for an interview.[33] But even were corporations to discriminate in hiring and pay practices, women would counter by beginning their own businesses. However, we see little evidence of women initiating new business more frequently than men. Nor is there evidence that female-owned businesses hire more women than male-owned businesses.[34]

Hiring women disproportionately in low-paying jobs is a symptom of "occupational segregation."[35] But, as will be illustrated later, occupational segregation explains a relatively small portion of the gender wage gap.

Arguments that corporations refuse to train women turn out to be in-compatible with economic theory. Human capital theory shows that both employers and employees share training's costs as well as training's ben-efits. (Why sit through excruciatingly burdensome training sessions if one doesn't expect some type of reward on the job? Similarly, why pay for the training if productivity doesn't go up?) But according to the theory, the proportion of training costs paid by an employer exactly equals the pro-portion of productivity gains the company keeps. Similarly, the proportion paid by an employee exactly equals the proportion of increased productivity the employee gets through increased wages and job advancement. In short, the corporate share of the costs equals the corporate share of productivity gains; and the employee's share of the costs exactly equals the employee's share of the gains.[36] Were employers to misjudge an employee's work expec-tations, the employee would pay a larger part of the training costs, and as a result get a bigger share of the increased productivity. But we rarely observe women taking on a bigger share of training costs and benefits.

But even more important, government policies aimed directly at corporate discrimination haven't worked either. In the 1980s, under Reagan, affirmative action activities diminished. Just from 1980 to 1981, the Office of Federal Compliance dropped its budget from $48.2 million to $43.1 million.[37] Yet female wages grew 1.7 percent per annum faster than male wages in the 1980s than the 1970s. In the 1970s, enforcement of antidiscrimination laws increased twenty-fold.[38] Nevertheless, in the 1970s compared to the 1980s, female wages grew at a rate only 0.39 percent per year faster than male wages, resulting in very little narrowing of the gender wage gap.[39] According to Harry Holzer and David Neumark, whereas there is some evidence that "affirmative action programs redistribute employment . . . from white males to . . . women, . . . the extent of the redistribution may not be large."[40] In a six-country comparison of affirmative action, Jain et al. find mixed results of affirmative action–type programs and conclude that "there is no universal panacea . . . for resolving the employment problems of disadvantaged groups. . . . Cultural constraints . . . have an impact on the success of the programs."[41] This is confirmed by Blau, Ferber, and Winkler, who state that "a review of the trends in the male-female pay gap . . . gave no indication of a notable improvement in women's economic status . . . that might be attributable to the effects of the government's antidiscrimination effort, at least through the late 1970s or early 1980s."[42] In the 1990s, the number of class action lawsuits rose from 30 in 1992 to 68 in 1996, and the number of job bias lawsuits increased from 6,936 in 1990 to 21,540 in 1998,[43] but the rate of gender wage convergence slowed in the late 1990s.

Clearly something other than corporate discrimination must be at work.

HUMAN CAPITAL AND THE GENDER WAGE GAP

Recall that lifecycle human capital theory provides a cogent elucidation of how training influences earnings. The more education and on-the-job training one obtains (i.e., the more human capital one gets), the more one earns. But also according to the theory, incentives for acquiring job skills depend on how much one expects to work regardless of the reason for the differences in lifetime work behavior. Getting married, having children, and spacing children widely apart accentuate the division of labor within the family. For married men, this division of labor raises the amount of lifetime work. But conversely, the opposite is true for married women with children. Here the division of labor reduces lifetime work. As a result of this bifurcation, lifetime human capital theory predicts married men's incentives to invest in marketable skills increase, while married women's incentives decrease. According to the theory, these lifetime work differences should lead to higher married male wages and lower married female wages.

There is now ample evidence for these predictions. Aside from my study mentioned earlier,[44] recent research also finds a so-called "motherhood" penalty. For example, Korenman and Neumark find that cross-sectional ordinary-least-squares and first-difference estimates understate the negative effect of children on wages.[45] Waldfogel shows that having children lowers a women's pay by about 10 percent, after controlling for age, education, experience, race, ethnicity, and marital status.[46] Budig and England find about a 7 percent wage penalty per child.[47] Using the National Longitudinal Survey Panel, Baum confirms the finding that "interrupting work to give birth has a negative effect on wages" but that "this negative effect is at least partially eliminated when [controlling for] whether the mother returns to work at her pre-childbirth job."[48] Berger et al. find evidence that "the forces towards specialization become stronger as the number of children increase, so that the spouse specializing in childcare [has] some combination of lower wages, hours worked and fringe benefits."[49] Similarly, looking at British data, Joshi, Paci, and Waldfogel show that "women who broke their employment at childbirth were subsequently paid less pay than childless women [whereas] mothers who maintained their employment continuously were as well paid as childless women," though it should be noted that neither group was remunerated as well as men.[50]

Interestingly, as was already mentioned, gender differences are smaller among blacks than whites (Exhibit 11). In 2003 the gender earnings ratio (for full-time wage and salary workers) was 0.79 for whites and 0.88 for blacks. Recall from Exhibit 3 that non-white women, compared to non-white men, work relatively more over their lifetimes than white women compared to white men. As such the gender gap in labor force participation is smaller for blacks than for whites. According to the lifecycle human capital theory, a smaller lifetime labor force participation difference implies a smaller difference in investment incentives. For this reason, the gender wage gap for blacks should be smaller than the gender wage gap for whites. This is precisely what is observed.

EXHIBIT II
Median weekly earnings (full-time wage and salary workers)

	1990	1995	2000	2001	2003
White male	494	566	669	694	715
White female	353	415	500	521	567
Ratio	0.71	0.73	0.75	0.75	0.79
Black male	361	411	503	518	555
Black female	308	355	429	451	491
Ratio	0.85	0.86	0.85	0.87	0.88

SOURCES: U.S. Census Bureau, Statistical Abstract of the United States 2002 (Table No. 613, p. 403), 2004–5 (Table No. 623, p. 411).

Economists employ statistical decomposition techniques to measure lifetime labor force participation's role in explaining male–female wage differences. Essentially they estimate how much women would earn if women were to work as much as men over their lifetimes. They define discrimination to be women's predicted earnings shortfalls in this computation. Thus, discrimination is the extent to which women earn less than men, holding other demographic attributes constant. A number of statistical biases mar this computation.[51] One particularly relevant bias is the failure to account for the amount of job skills women would have sought had they expected to work continuously. Typical implementation of the decomposition adjusts for training received given *observed* work experience, but not the training one *would have received* had one intended to work continuously. By not including this extra training, these decompositions underestimate a discontinuous worker's potential wage. As such, discrimination is overestimated, given that discrimination is the difference between what the continuous worker actually earns and what one projects a discontinuous worker to earn were she to have continuous participation. Studies that appropriately incorporate the skills one would have obtained had one expected to work continuously explain up to 95 percent of the gender wage gap.[52]

Traditionally, the typical pattern of female lifetime labor force participation is illustrated in Exhibit 12. The point S reflects the year a typical woman graduates from school. After graduation, she enters the labor force for e_1 years. Following this, she drops out for H years to bear and raise children. When children enter school, she reenters the labor force for e_2 years to finish her career.[53] In 1967 the value of H was just over ten years.[54] In the 1985 National Longitudinal Survey, H was between

The life cycle

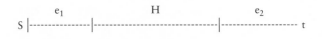

The earnings profile

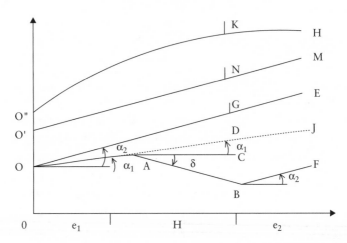

EXHIBIT 12   The effect of intermittent labor force participation on earnings

nine and fourteen years.[55] The typical man works each year, so that H approaches zero.[56]

Earnings profiles are illustrated in the bottom panel. They indicate how (the logarithm of) earnings change over the life cycle. The typical male earnings profile is O″KH. It illustrates that earnings rise (but at a diminishing rate) throughout the continuous worker's lifetime, possibly tapering off and even declining close to retirement. On the other hand, intermittent workers exhibit a different earnings profile. First, initial earnings (the y-intercept) are lower (point O). Second, the slope of the earnings profile (α_1) is initially smaller, rising to A. This lower slope indicates that the percentage increase in wages per year of experience is smaller than for the continuous worker. Third, earnings are essentially zero during the "home-time" period (H), but earnings potential (were one to work) diminishes by an "atrophy" rate δ percent per year out of the workforce. Fourth, the reentry wage after dropping out is lower than when one left (B is lower than A in real terms). Finally, after reentering the labor force, earnings grow at a rate α_2 (which is slightly higher in magnitude than α_1) from B to F.

Typically, the α_1 and α_2 coefficients range from 1.2 percent to 4.0 percent, depending on the population subgroup studied and on one's level of education. The δ coefficient ranges from −4.5 percent to −0.5 percent depending on the respondent's amount and type of education. In general, the higher one's education and the more skilled one's job, the greater the magnitude of these coefficients. As mentioned earlier, α_2 exceeds α_1 because upon reentering the labor force one has a greater commitment to working more continuously.[57]

How would a woman's earnings profile look if she worked continuously, instead of dropping out?[58] Standard decomposition projects the discontinuous worker's earnings profile along OA to D (and finally to J). As such, earnings would grow at α_1 per year. However, another possibility is that the profile is steeper initially, rising from O at rate α_2. This steeper profile reflects a greater rate of human capital investment, given greater expected lifetime work expectations now that home time is zero. Still another possibility is a higher profile. This higher profile accounts for more market-oriented subjects a person would take in school given greater lifetime work expectations. This third alternative leads to profile O′M. As mentioned, the typical decomposition study adopts the first (and simplest) approach. But as we shall see, this simple first approach leads to an overestimate of discrimination.

The earnings gap between a male (usually a married man with children) working continuously and a female intermittent worker reentering the labor market after dropping out H years can be expressed as segment BK. This is the difference between the man's wage (K) and the intermittent worker's reentry wage (B). This gap can be divided into three segments: (1) BC is the direct depreciation of skills caused by atrophy. Distance BC amounts to the product of the number of years out of the labor force (H) and the per-year depreciation of earnings power measured by atrophy rate δ. (2) CD is the forgone wage growth caused by lost seniority, assuming one's earnings rise from A at rate α_1. And (3) DK is the earnings gap between a male's earnings and the earnings a female would have, should she work continuously.

According to the standard decomposition, DK depicts discrimination. It measures the male–female earnings gap, assuming women have men's labor market characteristics (e.g., worked as many years as men $(e_1 + H)$).[59]

However, this latter gap (DK) misstates the amount of discrimination. To see this, decompose DK into three parts: DG, GN, and NK. The gap DG reflects the additional earnings growth (α_2 per annum compared to α_1) attributable to extra on-the-job training arising from expecting greater labor market continuity. (Recall that projecting earnings according to α_1 does not take account of the extra on-the-job training incumbents would obtain given that they gain more from human capital investment now that they are expected to work continuously.) The gap GN reflects additional earnings levels attributable to the more market-oriented schooling one obtains when one is in the labor market a greater number of years over one's lifetime. Finally, this leaves NK. This "new" unexplained gender wage differential better reflects discrimination because it accounts for the extra human capital investments women would make if they expect to work more years over their lifetimes. Failing to take account of how female earnings projections change when lifetime work expectations increase biases upward the typical estimate of discrimination (DK).[60] Thus failure to adequately adjust for expectations overstates discrimination. I provide more on this in the next section, when I mention the several studies that appropriately get at this bias.

Another major flaw with this decomposition is its failure to attribute the lower female levels of lifetime work to discrimination. In particular, the approach legitimizes gender differences in lifetime work because it seeks to determine what female wages would be had women the same lifetime work patterns as men. But the very fact that women work less than men may itself reflect discrimination. After all, is it not possible that *society* discriminates by shackling women with home responsibilities, thereby forcing them to drop out of the labor market to raise their children? Isn't it possible that this division of labor is exacerbated by the unavailability of day care, not to mention hefty taxes on wives' "secondary" earnings? Also, is it not possible that guidance counselors discriminate by advising female students against market-oriented fields of study, such as science and engineering? If so, male and female differences in work history (as well as other differences) also constitute discrimination. Yet the decomposition approach does not treat these lifetime labor market differences as constituting discrimination. Neglecting these societal forces causing women to work less over their lifetimes leads one employing the decomposition approach to underestimate discrimination.

To recapitulate, the statistical decomposition approach hinders one from accurately measuring discrimination.[61] There are two major biases. The first results from ignoring legitimate reasons why men and women have different lifetime wage trajectories. This bias yields overestimates of discrimination. The second results from adjusting for gender differences in lifetime work, when these lifetime work differences can be caused by discrimination. This bias yields underestimates of discrimination. Because of these potential biases, researchers and policy-makers would be better served to use the decomposition approach to answer specific questions regarding the gender wage gap, rather than to estimate discrimination. This is the approach I adopt here. I now use the decomposition approach to explore the importance of the human capital model in explaining the gender wage gap.

HOW IMPORTANT IS THE HUMAN CAPITAL MODEL IN EXPLAINING THE WAGE GAP?

At least in the past, the typical woman dropped out of the labor force for more than ten years. With this information one can go back to Exhibit 12 to compute the proportion of the wage gap explained by discontinuous labor force participation. As indicated earlier, BD is a lower-bound estimate of the human capital model's importance (in explaining the earnings difference between the intermittent and continuously employed worker). The typical depreciation of skills (δ) is about 0.5 percent, but is as large as 4.5 percent for highly educated workers. Multiplying δ by the ten years out of the workforce yields a 5 percent atrophy of earnings power. This 5 percent is the direct earnings power loss caused by dropping out. The typical α_1 coefficient is 1.5–2.0 percent. Multiplying α_1 by the ten years out of the workforce yields a further potential earnings loss of 15–20 percent. This 15–20 percent is a lower-bound estimate of how much earnings would have risen had one remained in the labor force. Summing these two implies that a worker would earn 20–25 percent more were she to remain in the workforce continuously. This means that about 50–62.5 percent of the gender wage gap is explained, given the 40 percent male–female wage differential.[62] However, as indicated earlier, this simple computation is biased. While it accounts only for direct depreciation of skills, it underestimates the steeper wage growth (DG) that would have been achieved, as well as the effects of more market-oriented schooling (GN) that would come about were one to anticipate greater lifetime work activity. The few studies that incorporate DG and GN explain up to 95 percent of the wage gap.[63]

THE NEGLIGIBLE EXPLANATORY POWER
OF CORPORATE-BASED OCCUPATIONAL SEGREGATION

In contrast to the human capital approach, feminist economists originally led by Barbara Bergmann espoused "segmented" labor market theories to explain gender wage differences. These economists believed that the economy was divided into "good" and "bad" jobs. Either implicit or explicit corporate discrimination policies prevented women from getting the good jobs, thus leading to "occupational segregation." Although this theory rings true (given the vastly different male and female occupational distributions), statistical analysis reveals that occupational segregation explains very little of the male–female wage gap. For example, Chiswick et al. explain 28 percent of the wage gap when using the 1970 U.S. Census.[64] However, they find that single women's wages would fall, had they the male occupational distribution. Using the same approach, Treiman and Hartmann explain between 11 and 18 percent of the gender earnings differential when using data on 222 U.S. Census occupations and 35–39 percent using 495 occupations.[65]

One problem is that these studies do not hold constant demographic characteristics. Thus they do not account for how much human capital one might have acquired. In particular, men may achieve higher-paying occupations because their greater lifetime work led them to invest more. As such, the studies mentioned earlier likely overestimate occupational segregation's importance because lower levels of human capital, rather than discrimination, might instigate women to be in lower-paying occupations.[66] Some studies remedy this defect by incorporating a multivariate approach. When adjusting for worker demographic characteristics, occupational segregation explains less than 7 percent. For example, Johnson and Solon get an explanatory power of 3 percent,[67] Paula England less than 5 percent,[68] and Victor Fuchs between 0 and 6 percent.[69] A later, more comprehensive study by MacPherson and Barry Hirsch also finds that occupational segregation explains less than 7 percent of the male–female wage gap.[70] Finally, a recent study by Aisenbrey and Bruckner likewise indicates that occupational segregation accounts for a small and declining proportion of the male–female wage gap.[71]

HUMAN CAPITAL AND SECULAR CHANGES IN THE WAGE GAP

If human capital theory carries weight, as I have argued, then the gender wage gap should narrow as women's lifetime labor force participation increases. As I now show, this is exactly what one finds.

Exhibit 13 examines wage ratio data for the United States compiled from Goldin[72] and O'Neill.[73] The vertical axis depicts the female-to-male earnings ratio and the horizontal axis represents the year. In all, five sets of data are plotted. Three cover the period from 1815 to just prior to 1940, one covers the time period from 1955 to 1987, and finally one covers 1979 to 2001. The early data clearly trend upward. Similarly, the latter period

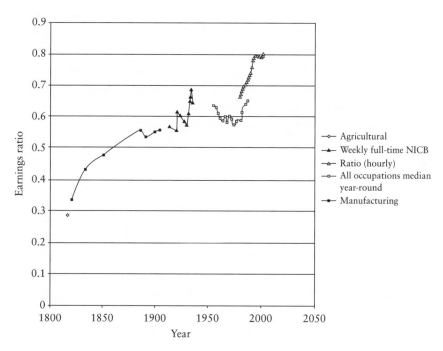

EXHIBIT 13   Ratio of female-to-male earnings

SOURCES: First four series obtained from Goldin (1990), Table 3.1, pp. 60–61. Hourly wage ratios based on CPS outgoing rotation groups computed by June O'Neill (2003).

from the mid-1970s does as well, with the possible exception of 1994–2000 (though the data again rebound in 2001).[74] Only the data from about 1935 to around the early 1980s are flat, showing virtually no increase in female relative to male economic success, but these latter decades are anomalous.

By comparing the 1970s and 1980s, my own research with John Robst[75] offers an explanation of why the 1970s (and probably the 1960s) might be anomalous. We show that the wage gap beginning in 1980 narrowed 1.7 percent more quickly than in the 1970s. In a sense, this more rapid convergence is strange because female labor force participation rose a bit faster in the 1970s than the 1980s.[76] However, the reasons for these exceedingly paradoxical trends are consistent with the lifecycle human capital model. The rapidly rising female labor force participation in the 1960s and 1970s actually brought down female wages because the new, inexperienced entrants earned less than the older, more senior employees, thereby making female wage growth appear less rapid. The decline diminished in importance during the 1980s as the relative growth in new female entrants declined, and as the proportion of years actually worked by women increased. If one were to adjust for labor market joiners (and labor market leavers), the male–female wage convergence is actually very similar for both decades.[77] Indeed, the findings by Blau and Kahn indicate the current research understates male–female wage convergence in the 1980s, as well.[78] Using statistical techniques that account for changes in the earnings structure, they find that women's progress is considerably greater than previously thought. June O'Neill uses NLSY data to find that the adjusted female-to-male wage ratio in 2000 was over 95 percent.[79] This certainly corroborates the convergence.

But similar trends are also observed for other nations. The Luxembourg Income Study (LIS) is a collection of household data compiled from ongoing statistical surveys in twenty-six countries. The database provides statistics on demographic, income, and expenditure variables on three levels: households, persons, and children. I concentrate on extracting education, age, and earnings data for white males and females from the person files of the countries, at least half of which contain information on hourly earnings.[80] Of those, I present plots (Exhibit 14) of female-to-male earnings ratios adjusted by education, potential labor market experience, and marital status (when available). For each country, the ratios were computed from at least three cross-sectional wage regressions. Most countries exhibit

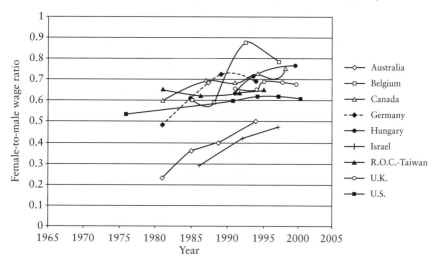

EXHIBIT 14   Female-to-male wage ratio trends by country (adjusted for education, potential experience, and marital status)

SOURCE: Computed from Luxembourg Income Study (LIS) data.

increasing female wage ratios. For example, in Exhibit 14, Australia, Belgium, Canada, Germany, Hungary, and Israel exhibit greater gender wage convergence than the United States. Given rising female labor market participation in these countries, this convergence is consistent with the human lifecycle capital model's predictions.

In the United States, the rate of gender wage convergence moderated somewhat in the 1990s. This weakening of women's relative wage gain is apparent in Exhibit 15. The hourly wage series, which rose so precipitously from 1980, becomes relatively flat from 1993 through 2001. During this seven-year period, women's wages rose just 0.1 percentage point per year, compared to 1.0 percentage point per year from 1980 to 1993. What brought about this reversal is the obvious interesting question.

The latest research on this argues that changes in the labor force selectivity (the difference in unmeasured qualities between working and non-working women), changes in discrimination, and shifts in supply and demand may have caused the convergence of the gender pay gap to wane.[81] I take a simpler, more straightforward approach. Human capital theory argues that wages rise in conjunction with human capital investments. But, as I have shown earlier in this essay, the prime impetus for human capital

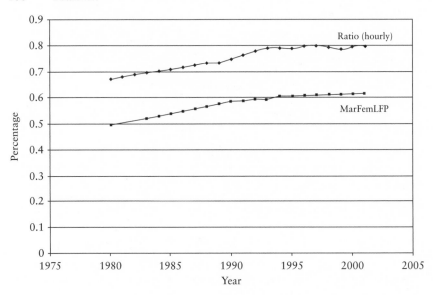

EXHIBIT 15   Female wage ratios and married female labor force participation

SOURCES: Hourly wage ratios are based on O'Neil's (2003) computations from the CPS Outgoing Rotation Groups. Married women's labor force participation is obtained from Table 569 of the 2002 Statistical Abstract of the United States.

investments is a strong lifetime work commitment. As already noted, women's (especially married women's) lifetime work expectations rose dramatically at least from 1980. (The trend from 1980 is shown in Exhibit 15.) But, in the mid-1990s, something different seems to have happened to married women's labor force participation. The upward trend moderated radically. Whereas married women's labor force participation rose almost 1 percent per year from 1970 to 1990, growth in women's participation nose-dived to 0.5 percent per year from 1990 to 1995. It declined even further to just 0.1 percent from 1995 to 2001.

One can employ the same logic that explains why a rising female labor force participation rate boosts women's earnings to account for how a *decreasing* labor force participation *reduces* women's earnings growth. Recall that earnings power depends on human capital training investments. In turn, training depends on lifetime labor force participation. The more one works, the greater one's incentive to get trained. And the more sizeable one's training, the more one earns. Concomitantly, the less one works, the smaller the incentive to acquire training. The less one trains, the smaller one's marketable skills, and the less one earns.

As female labor force participation rose throughout the century, women undertook more schooling and other complementary on-the-job post-school training. On the other hand, incentives to continue investing more precipitously fall as labor activities begin to hold steady, so that women's human capital investments cease to grow. Apparently, such is the case from 1993. The fervor of human capital investment intensity ceased, and hence wage growth dropped virtually to zero as women's labor force participation growth dwindled. This relationship is evident in Exhibit 15. The relative female-to-male wage ratio virtually parallels the married female labor force participation rate. As this female participation rose from 1980 to 1993, so did relative female wages. As the growth in this female participation tapered off beginning in 1993, so did relative female wages. These are just the patterns the lifecycle human capital model predicts.

What about the future? Is the slowing simply an aberration or will the gender gap again begin to narrow? Current projections indicate a slight acceleration of women's labor force participation for all age groups with the exception of those aged 35–44. If these projections are accurate, then theory predicts trends in women's investments in marketable skills should again increase. As such the wage gap should continue to narrow, perhaps even at an accelerated rate.

CONCLUDING THOUGHTS

Over the last century, the gender wage gap narrowed substantially. Women's wages went from about 48 cents on the dollar in 1850 to almost 80 cents on the dollar in 2001. However, despite this narrowing, women still earn 20 percent less than men, and there is evidence of a subsequent slowing in the trend.[82] But interestingly, men's advantage is not uniform across the population. Single women almost achieve parity, while married women, especially those with children, have very far to go. Were corporate discrimination the prime reason for the gap, one would need an explanation of why such discrimination differs not just by marital status, but also by the number and spacing of children.

Professor Blau argues that corporate discrimination in hiring, pay, and promotion practices predominates in explaining the gender pay differences.

Whereas I acknowledge corporate discrimination, particularly in noncompetitive institutions or in government employment, where some even argue discrimination occurs against men, I believe this type of discrimination to be relatively unimportant in explaining the overall gender pay differential. Instead, my research shows that the main reason for the gender wage gap is the division of labor in the home. The division of labor causes women to work less over their lifetimes. As a result, women invest less in marketable skills. I denote societal discrimination to describe the process that brings about this division of labor. I do so because many sociological and economic forces hinder women's ability to work as much as men over their lives. These include social norms, government tax policies, and inadequate day care.

Over the century, fertility rates declined, divorce rates increased, and women's lifetime labor force participation rose. At the same time, men's lifetime labor force participation fell. I argue that this increase in women's lifetime work relative to men's caused women to invest more in work skills, such as professional education and on-the-job training. As a consequence, women's wages grew relative to men's.

I claim that anyone who believes the human capital theory to be of secondary importance in explaining the gender wage gap will have to answer at least the following five questions:

1. If corporate discrimination were a major factor, how would one explain wage comparability between single males and females?
2. If division of labor within the household were not important, how else would one explain the *opposite* effects of marital status, children, and the spacing of children on male and female wages?
3. If human capital is not an important cause of male–female wage differentials, then why does it have so much explanatory power?
4. If factors other than human capital are so important, then why don't they explain a greater proportion of the wage gap compared to human capital?
5. If corporate discrimination were so important, how would one explain why during the 1980s the male–female wage gap shrunk at unprecedented rates, when government affirmative action activity dramatically decreased?

The Sources of the Gender Pay Gap

Francine D. Blau

The sources of the gender pay gap can usefully be divided into two broad sets of causes directly related to gender: gender differences in qualifications and labor market discrimination against women. Based on the available evidence, my own view is that both of these factors play a role in producing a gender pay gap. And, changes in each dimension—that is, in the extent of gender differences in qualifications and in the extent of labor market discrimination—have played a role in the decrease in the gender pay gap we have observed over time. In this essay, I shall lay out the reasoning and evidence behind this conclusion. I shall particularly emphasize the major point of disagreement between myself and Professor Polachek—that is, the importance I ascribe to labor market discrimination. How women fare in the labor market may also be affected by broader economy-wide or labor market–wide forces, such as the relative demand for workers in various occupations and industries. While

Francine D. Blau is the Frances Perkins Professor of Industrial and Labor Relations and professor of economics at Cornell University and a research associate of the National Bureau of Economic Research. She is the author of *Equal Pay in the Office* and, with Lawrence Kahn, of *At Home and Abroad: U.S. Labor Market Performance in International Perspective*. She is the editor, with David Grusky and Mary Brinton, of *The Declining Significance of Gender?*, and, with Ronald Ehrenberg, of *Gender and Family Issues in the Workplace*. She received the Carolyn Shaw Bell Award for furthering the status of women in the economics profession from the American Economic Association Committee on the Status of Women in the Economics Profession in 2001 and the IZA Prize for outstanding academic achievement in the field of labor economics in 2010.

such factors can be quite important, I give them less emphasis here, given my primary focus on the role of labor market discrimination.

According to published government statistics, in 2010, women full-time workers earned about 81 percent of what men earned, still a substantial gender gap in pay. Nonetheless, this represents a large increase over the 64 percent of men's pay that women full-time workers earned in 1980.[1] In this essay, I first describe the potential sources of the gender pay gap that economists have identified. I then consider the empirical evidence on the role that each has played in producing the gender pay gap and in explaining the substantial increase in women's relative pay that has occurred in recent decades. The sharpest increase occurred over the 1980s, and I will also consider what we know about why the pace of change slowed in the 1990s.

THE SOURCES OF THE GENDER WAGE GAP

There are many possible concepts that can measure pay. When economists consider pay, they generally focus on wages, or pay per hour. This differentiates the pay measure from how many hours an individual worked. This is always important but may be especially so for gender comparisons since women tend to work fewer hours than men. Thus, my focus here is on wages and the gender wage gap.

Gender Differences in Qualifications

One of the major gender differences in qualifications, and the one that has received the most attention from economists, is the gender difference in the amount and type of human capital investments. Jacob Mincer and Solomon Polachek have done especially important work in highlighting the role of labor market experience in explaining the gender wage gap.[2] Given the traditional division of labor by gender in the family, in which men have primary responsibility for earning the income and women have primary responsibility for homemaking and child care, women tend to accumulate less labor market experience than men. Further, because women anticipate shorter and more discontinuous work lives, they have lower incentives to invest in market-oriented formal education and on-the-job training. Their resulting smaller human capital investments lower their earnings relative to those of men. The traditional division of labor may also disadvantage women if the longer hours women spend on housework decrease the effort they put into their market jobs compared to men, controlling for hours worked, and hence also reduce their productivity and wages.[3] The traditional division of labor could potentially lower the income of women relative to men in a variety of other ways by impacting women's hours worked, commitment to their jobs, willingness to undertake job-related travel, etc.

To the extent that women choose occupations for which on-the-job training is less important, gender differences in occupations are also expected. Women may especially avoid jobs requiring large investments in skills that are unique to a particular enterprise, because the returns to such investments are reaped only as long as one remains with that employer. At the same time, employers may be reluctant to hire women for such jobs because the firm bears some of the costs of such firm-specific training, and fears not getting a full return on that investment.[4]

Labor Market Discrimination

I have no doubt that human capital is indeed important in explaining the gender wage gap, and that changes in gender differences in human capital have played an important role in explaining trends over time in the gap. (I review some evidence on this later.) However, in my view: (i) Labor market discrimination against women has also played an important role in causing the gender wage gap. So, it is not an either/or situation, but rather both have played a part. (ii) Decreases in discrimination against women have likely played a role and contributed to the decline in the gender wage gap, including over the 1980s when the largest declines occurred. (iii) Even though there have been important and significant decreases in the extent of discrimination, discrimination against women still exists and is perhaps all the more difficult to combat because the remaining discrimination is likely to be less overt and more subtle than in the past. Indeed, there is growing evidence from social psychologists that suggests discriminatory attitudes and stereotyping may even be unconscious on the part of those who perpetrate it.[5]

A useful place to begin the consideration of labor market discrimination is with a definition: labor market discrimination exists when there are wage or occupational differences between men and women that are not accounted for by productivity differences.[6] One important point here and elsewhere is my reference is to "labor market" discrimination. Other processes may exist within the family, in educational institutions, and even as a result of the impact of broader cultural forces conveyed by the media or advertising, for example, that discourage women's human capital investments or shape their preferences in ways that result in their faring less well in the labor market. Such processes are sometimes called "premarket" or "societal" discrimination. They may in and of themselves be worthy of study and policy intervention. However, they are distinguished from labor market discrimination in that the behavior that produces them and the policies relevant to addressing them differ from those related to labor market discrimination.

It is also important to emphasize that, in defining labor market discrimination, it is not a question of whether men and women in the labor market are equally well qualified, on average, but rather whether the wage gap that we observe between them exceeds what could be expected based on any gender differences in qualifications. Such "unexplained" gender differences in wages are a departure from what would be expected from the operation of a purely competitive labor market with no discrimination. In such a competitive labor market, employers would, in their hiring, promotion, training, and wage decisions, care about nothing other than the qualifications of workers.

Why might labor market discrimination exist? There are a number of interesting models developed by economists that analyze the reasons for and the consequences of such discrimination. I do not have space to go into them in detail, but I would like to give a flavor of such models to suggest some of the reasons that labor market discrimination might exist. Economic modeling in this area was spearheaded by the pathbreaking work of Gary Becker, who received a Nobel Prize in economics, in part for his theory of discrimination. In the Becker model, discrimination is due to what he terms "tastes for discrimination"[7] and what Ronald G. Ehrenberg and Robert S. Smith have expressed in more everyday language as "personal prejudices" against a particular group;[8] in this case, it would be prejudices against women.

Becker postulated that discrimination was rooted in the desire to maintain social distance from the group. He originally developed his model to explain race differences in labor market outcomes, but these ideas are readily applicable to women (as well as to other groups potentially facing discrimination). It might seem odd to allege that males in the labor force would be prejudiced against women since men and women often live together in the same families. But I think the issue here is one of socially appropriate roles. A male manager might be delighted to have a female secretary but object to having to deal with a software engineer who is a woman. The members of a construction crew might be perfectly happy to have a woman bring them their food during the lunch break, but not if she stood next to them doing wiring or plumbing.

Becker postulated that discrimination could be due to such prejudices on the part of employers, in which case employers engage in hiring or wage discrimination because of their own disutility of employing women. But it could also be coworkers who have such prejudices, as my construction example implies. Perhaps male coworkers do not want to work with women; here again I would say most likely in roles that do not seem to be gender-appropriate or perhaps as peers or superiors.[9] And the Becker model postulates that it could also be customers or clients who have such prejudices. For example, customers might not want to buy a car from a woman salesperson or see a woman doctor or a woman lawyer. In the case of coworker or customer discrimination, employers discriminate against women due to the higher costs or lower revenues associated with hiring them.

One problem that economists have identified with the model of employer discrimination based on personal prejudices is that discrimination is not costless to the employer who forgoes the opportunity to hire more of the lower-priced female labor and less of the higher-priced male labor. Therefore, less discriminatory firms should have lower costs of production. Such a competitive advantage would enable them to expand and drive the more discriminatory firms out of business in the long run. As the less discriminatory firms expand, the demand for female labor would be increased and the male–female wage gap would be reduced. If there were enough *entirely* nondiscriminatory firms to absorb all the women workers, the discriminatory wage gap would be eliminated. Hence, the question is how discrimination, which represents a departure from profit-maximizing behavior, can withstand the impact of competitive pressures.

One answer to this question is that discrimination may simply result from a lack of such competitive pressures in the economy. Becker hypothesized that, on average, employer discrimination would be less severe in competitive than in monopolistic industries, and there is some empirical support for this prediction, which I discuss later. It has also been suggested that *monopsony* power by employers in the labor market plays a role in producing and perpetuating the gender pay differential.

One way in which firms may gain monopsony power over workers is due to workers' imperfect information about job opportunities and the resulting necessity for workers to engage in job search. In a competitive labor market with perfect information, even a slightly higher wage at another firm will induce workers to move to that better opportunity. However, when information is imperfect, workers must search among employers for a good job match, thus incurring "search costs." Since search is costly, workers will be less mobile across firms than they would be if information was perfectly and costlessly available, and it will take larger wage premiums at other firms to bid them away. Thus, the presence of search costs can give employers a degree of monopsony power over workers. A model developed by Dan A. Black shows how such monopsony power could result in the persistence of discrimination over time.[10] If we assume that some employers discriminate against women and are not willing to hire them, we see that women will have higher search costs than men. As a consequence, employers will exploit this greater monopsony power over women and offer them lower wages than men. Thus, when information is imperfect and there are search costs, it is more credible that employer discrimination can persist in the long run.[11]

An effort to understand the persistence of discrimination in the face of competitive forces was also a motivation behind the development of models of statistical discrimination. Such models assume a world of uncertainty and imperfect information for employers; thus differences between groups in the expected value of productivity are expected to result in differences in the treatment of members of each group. So, for example, employers may believe that women are more likely to quit their jobs or to put their families ahead of their work responsibilities than men with similar observed characteristics (education, experience, etc.). As a consequence, they may pay women less, exclude them from jobs requiring substantial firm-specific training, or deny them promotions.[12] They will discriminate against all women because they cannot easily distinguish the more from the less career-oriented women. Since the real or perceived average gender differences that underlie statistical discrimination against women in the labor market tend to stem from the traditional division of labor in the family, this constitutes another route by which traditional gender roles within the family adversely affect women's labor market outcomes.

It has been argued that such statistical discrimination, making decisions on the basis of the average characteristics of the group, is consistent with profit maximization and can thus persist in the face of competitive forces. However, Dennis J. Aigner and Glen G. Cain contend that such models are no more convincing in explaining the *persistence* of discrimination than models based on employers' tastes for discrimination.[13] To the extent that employers' views are accurate, the lower expected productivity of women will reduce their wages, but women as a group will be paid their expected productivity. This does not constitute labor market discrimination as economists define it, that is, pay differences that are not accounted for by productivity differences. Presumably they would make a similar argument regarding hiring and promotion decisions. Moreover, they note that when employer beliefs regarding average differences are false or erroneous, economic discrimination clearly exists, but in their view discrimination based on such misperceptions is even less likely to persist in the long run than discrimination based on tastes.

However, such models may have greater usefulness in explaining the persistence of gender differentials in wage than Aigner and Cain suggest. Consider first the situation where employer perceptions are correct. In this case, the concept of statistical discrimination provides a plausible reason for the existence and persistence of wage and occupational differences between men and women with similar measured characteristics; this is in itself a useful contribution even if it does not shed light on the persistence of economic discrimination in the long run. But if the employer views are correct, is it appropriate to consider this a form of "discrimination" in any sense? From a normative perspective, the answer may be yes, to the extent that basing employment decisions on a characteristic like sex—a characteristic that the individual cannot change—could be viewed as inequitable. Indeed, the practice of judging an individual on the basis of group characteristics rather than upon his or her own merits seems the very essence of stereotyping or discrimination. Such behavior is certainly not legal under the antidiscrimination laws and regulations, for example.

Now consider the situation where employer perceptions are incorrect. If statistical discrimination is accompanied by feedback effects (discussed further later), this may indeed be a credible source of persistent discriminatory wage differences between men and women. For example, if employers incorrectly expect that women are more likely to quit their jobs, they may respond by giving women less firm-specific training or assigning them to dead-end jobs. Faced with few incentives to remain on the job, women may respond by exhibiting exactly the higher turnover that employers expect.

Although the foregoing considerations help to shed light on the persistence of employer discrimination in the long run, it should be acknowledged that there is probably no simple answer to the question of why competitive forces have not entirely eliminated discrimination against women and other groups. This has led some economists to doubt that labor market discrimination is responsible, in whole or part, for gender inequality in economic rewards. Yet it is important to recognize that the phenomenon that we seek to understand is intrinsically complex. Further, the various models of discrimination, each emphasizing different motivations and different sources of this behavior, need not be viewed as alternatives. Rather, each may serve to illuminate different aspects of this complex reality.

Feedback Effects

So far I have for the most part considered gender differences in human capital and discrimination as if they are two completely distinct sources of the wage gap. However, the case is more complicated than that. These two sources of the wage gap can reinforce each other and this is important because it may make it difficult to separate the impact of these two components when we look at the empirical evidence. On the one hand, the gender division of labor in the family may result in women investing less in human capital, thereby lowering their wages and adversely affecting their occupations in the labor market. The statistical discrimination theory fits in well here too, with employers treating all women as if they were pursuing a traditional division of labor in the family; this generates discrimination against women as a group in the labor market.

On the other hand, there is also an effect in the opposing direction. This is sometimes called a feedback effect, where gender differences in labor market outcomes caused by discrimination *feed back* onto the gender division of labor in the family and reinforce it. Thus, it has been pointed out that even a small amount of discrimination at the beginning of the career can accumulate to have a large impact on the gender wage gap as this initial discrimination influences the division of labor in the family. For example, if couples feel that one partner needs to drop out of the labor force for a while when the children are small or that one partner should be the secondary worker, that is, give priority to the other partner's career, then it makes sense for the low-wage partner to be the one to drop out or to be the secondary worker. Thus, if labor market discrimination lowers the wages of women relative to their husbands, this works to reinforce the traditional division of labor in the family. I am not going so far as to suggest that the division of labor in the family is solely due to discrimination in the labor market, but I am arguing that the traditional division of labor in the family is reinforced by gender inequities in the labor market.[14]

Another example I would give of feedback effects relates to occupational choice. The first two women to serve on the U.S. Supreme Court, Sandra Day O'Connor and Ruth Bader Ginsburg, graduated from law school in the 1950s. They both graduated at or near the top of their class. However, neither was able to obtain a clerkship with a justice of the Supreme Court or with a distinguished judge at another level of the judiciary, and neither was able to obtain a job at a major law firm. They both pursued stopgap approaches for a while and eventually did succeed. But the women of that time were likely aware of these sorts of difficulties, and hence many might not have gone to law school at least partly for that reason. Then when we analyze the sources of their wage gap, we would attribute some of it to women not having the same advanced training as men. Yet some of the causation may go in the opposite direction: anticipating labor market discrimination, women may be less likely to invest in their human capital than men—particularly training to enter predominately male fields.

Wage Structure

Both the human capital and discrimination explanations for the gender pay gap might be considered "gender-specific" in nature—that is, focused on gender differences in either qualifications or treatment. Analyses of gender differentials have traditionally tended to emphasize these types of gender-specific factors. However, important work by Chinhui Juhn, Kevin M. Murphy, and Brooks Pierce on trends in the race pay gap over time in the United States has highlighted an additional factor, overall wage structure, which is also relevant to analyzing gender differences in wages.[15] Wage structure is the array of prices determined for labor market skills and the rewards to employment in particular sectors. This insight has been applied by Lawrence M. Kahn and me to analyze international differences and changes over time in the gender wage gap.[16]

The human capital model suggests that men and women tend to have different levels of labor market qualifications (especially work experience) and to be employed in different occupations and perhaps in different industries. Discrimination models too suggest that women may be segregated into different sectors of the labor market. This implies that the returns to skills and the size of the wage premiums that workers receive for employment in high-wage occupations and industries potentially play an important role in determining the gender wage gap. All else equal, the larger the returns to skills and the larger the rewards received by individuals in predominantly male occupations and industries, the larger will be the gender wage gap.

While gender-specific factors and wage structure each potentially play a distinct role in affecting the gender wage gap, they are likely to interact. For example, since the 1970s, the labor market returns to skills such as education, specialized training, and experience have risen in the United States and in many other countries, likely due in part to technological change, including computerization. To the extent that the prices of skills for which women have a relative deficit have risen, such changes in wage structure will raise the gender wage gap. However, technological change itself is not likely to have gender neutral effects on labor demand, given occupational and industrial segregation patterns by gender. So, for example, it is likely that computerization has reduced the demand for blue-collar production labor and therefore lowered the relative demand for sectors where men are disproportionately represented.[17]

Thus, changes in wage structure and in the favorableness of demand and supply for women workers are factors affecting trends over time in the gender wage gap. To the extent possible, their effects, along with changes in the relative qualifications of men and women, must be netted out in order to infer changes in the extent of discrimination against women.

EMPIRICAL EVIDENCE OF DISCRIMINATION

Evidence from Statistical Analyses

Now let us turn to empirical estimates of discrimination. How do we generally measure discrimination and how good are such estimates? The typical approach to analyzing the sources of the gender wage gap is to estimate the statistical relationship between wages and qualifications or productivity-related characteristics for men and women. The gender wage gap can then be statistically decomposed into two components: one that is due to gender differences in measured characteristics and the other that is unexplained and potentially due to discrimination. My reading of such empirical studies is that they provide evidence consistent with both human capital differences and labor market discrimination in explaining the gender wage gap and actually give a bit of a quantitative edge to discrimination rather than human capital.

Before considering specific estimates, it is useful to address the accuracy of such estimates. Ideally when one seeks to measure something—discrimination in this case—one would like to measure it directly. With the traditional statistical approach, we measure discrimination indirectly—that is, as the portion of the wage gap that cannot be explained by measured qualifications. That gives rise to two possible types of opposing errors.

On the one hand, discrimination could be overestimated if there are important productivity-related differences between men and women that cannot be measured and men are more highly endowed with respect to these unmeasured characteristics. So, for example, men might have specialized in more lucrative fields of study in college or graduate school, and that information may not be available in the particular data set that is being analyzed. Or, men might be more motivated and committed to their jobs than women, a factor that is intrinsically difficult to measure. In these cases, part of the gender wage gap that would be classified as "unexplained" and attributable to discrimination would in fact be due to men's higher unmeasured qualifications. A caveat to be noted here is that women may be better endowed, on average, with some unmeasured factors—interpersonal skills, for example.[18] Further, some of the included variables may be correlated with unmeasured factors (e.g., more highly educated people may be more highly motivated) and hence their inclusion may at least in part adjust for the effects of the omitted variables. Nonetheless, the point is well taken and concern about omitted variable bias in estimates of discrimination is fully appropriate.

On the other hand, there are factors that could lead us to underestimate discrimination. This is because some of the included variables may reflect the direct effects of discrimination. For example, occupation and industry—essentially what jobs people are in—are influenced by the hiring and promotion decisions of employers, as well as by the preferences and job choices of individual workers. In addition, feedback effects, which were discussed earlier, could have caused or at least contributed to the gender differences in many of the human capital variables that are often used as controls in analyses of this type.

Accepting for now that traditional statistical estimates of discrimination are imperfect, it is nonetheless of interest to see what can be learned from them. After discussing results from one study that is typical of this kind of work, based on research that I did with Lawrence Kahn,[19] I will then consider information from alternative approaches, which tend to support the central conclusion from the statistical analyses: there is evidence of discrimination against women in the labor market.

The study that Kahn and I did is based on data from the Panel Study of Income Dynamics (PSID), a large, nationally representative data set that includes information on actual labor market experience, which, as suggested by my discussion of the human capital explanation, is a crucial variable in analyzing the gender wage gap. The sample is restricted to full-time workers in order to focus on women and men whose commitment to employment is as similar as possible. Exhibit 1 shows three measures of the female-male

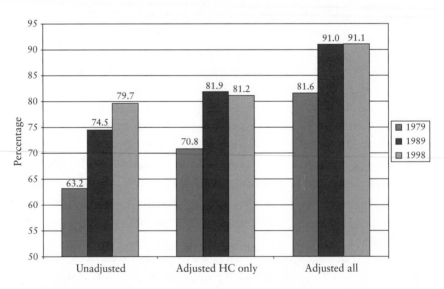

EXHIBIT I   Unadjusted and adjusted female-male wage ratios, full-time workers, 1979–1998

SOURCE: Constructed from data presented in Francine D. Blau and Lawrence M. Kahn, "The US Gender Pay Gap in the 1990s: Slowing Convergence," *Industrial and Labor Relations Review* 60, no. 1 (2006).

wage ratio for each of three years: 1979, 1989, and 1998. The "unadjusted" ratio is based on the observed mean wages for each group. The ratio "adjusted for human capital only" controls for gender differences in actual labor market experience, education in years, and whether the individual has a college diploma or an advanced degree. The ratio "adjusted for all variables" additionally controls for gender differences in occupation (nineteen categories), industry (twenty-six categories), and unionization. The "unexplained gap" from each of the latter two estimates provides suggestive information about the extent of labor market discrimination.

To establish a baseline and illustrate the findings of this type of analysis, let us begin by looking at the ratios for 1979. We see that the unadjusted wage ratio is 63.2 percent, meaning that the wages of women full-time workers were about 63 percent of male full-time workers' wages in that year. Controlling for the human capital variables only, the gender wage ratio rose to 70.8 percent. This shows that gender differences in human capital were indeed quite important. However, women still earned 29.2 (= 100 − 70.8) percent less than men when we control for the human capital variables. Further adjusting for occupation, industry, and union membership, in addition to human capital, raises the gender ratio to 81.6 percent. However, I would again point out there is still a sizeable remaining gap—18.4 percent, despite fairly detailed controls for industry and occupation. Moreover, as our foregoing discussion suggests, it may not be appropriate to control for these additional variables in testing for discrimination, although omitting them likely discards some relevant information on productivity-related differences between men and women. Hence I provide both sets of estimates.

Exhibit 1 indicates that the unadjusted wage ratio increased over time, particularly over the 1980s when it rose by over 11 percentage points to 74.5 percent, with a smaller further rise of 5 percentage points to 79.7 percent in 1998.[20] First, I shall consider how the determinants of the gender wage gap differed between the most recent year, 1998, and 1979 and then look at the question of the determinants of the changes in the gender wage gap over the 1979 to 1998 period, focusing particularly on the reasons for and significance of the slowing convergence in the gender gap over the 1990s compared to the 1980s.

A striking difference between 1979 and 1998 is that, in the latter year, adjusting for gender differences in the human capital variables does not increase the gender ratio by very much: the unadjusted ratio of 79.7 percent increases only slightly, to 81.9 percent, when we control for human capital. Kahn and my detailed analyses indicate that one reason for the smaller role played by measured human capital in 1998 is that women narrowed the gap in prior full-time experience from 6.6 years in 1979 to 3.5 years in 1998.[21] The remaining male advantage in experience was largely offset by a female advantage in education. Although men had an edge in the incidence of college degrees in the earlier years, by 1998 the incidence of college degrees was slightly (1.2 percentage points) higher among women than men in our sample of full-time workers. This in turn reflects faster increases in female than in male educational attainment in the population as a whole, such that, among younger cohorts, women are now more likely to be college graduates than men. Another factor contributing to the female advantage in educational attainment in our sample is the positive selection on education of women into employment in general and into full-time employment in particular. In contrast, when we add controls for industry, occupation, and unionism, the gender ratio increases substantially to 91.1 percent. This indicates that gender differences in these variables, particularly industry and occupation, remained a substantial source of gender differences in wages in the late 1990s.

In terms of the unexplained gap, we find that it fell over the 1979-to-1998 period as a whole. The unexplained gap fell from 29.2 percent in 1979 to 18.8 percent in 1998, adjusting for human capital variables only, and from 18.4 percent to 8.9 percent, when all variables are controlled for. This may correspond to a reduction in discrimination over this period, though, as we have seen, the unexplained gap can reflect other factors, and we shall note some of them in greater detail ahead. In both 1979 and 1998, the contribution of the unexplained gap to the gender differential was far more important that the human capital variables, suggesting at least the possibility that discrimination was a more important factor than differences in human capital in accounting for the gender wage gap.

How do we explain the decrease in the gender gap between 1979 and 1998, and why was convergence slower in the 1990s than the 1980s? Kahn and I found that convergence in men's and women's human capital was an important factor in the narrowing of the gender wage gap, and that such improvements had a comparable effect in both the 1980s and the 1990s.[22] In the 1980s, women's human capital upgrading consisted entirely of rising experience. In the 1990s, decreases in the gender gap in experience contributed considerably less to wage convergence, but rising relative educational attainment of women played a much larger role.

Occupational upgrading of women also contributed to women's relative wage gains in both decades, as women moved out of clerical and service jobs and into professional and managerial employments, and as men moved out of (or lost) craft and operator jobs, particularly in the 1980s. Deunionization, or a decline in the share of the labor force that is unionized, reduced the gender wage gap in both decades as well, because men, who are more likely than women to be unionized, lost union jobs at a faster pace than women. The impact of these factors—occupational gains for women and deunionization—was greater in the 1980s than in the 1990s. Thus, slowing convergence in sectoral location in the 1990s is part of the explanation for the slowdown in wage convergence.

However, the main reason for the slower convergence in the gender gap in the 1990s than in the 1980s (at least in an accounting sense) is that the "unexplained gap" decreased by much less in the 1980s than in the 1990s. This may readily be seen in Exhibit 1, which shows that the adjusted wage ratio increased substantially over the 1980s, but remained roughly constant over the 1990s.

What is the significance of this change? Perhaps a reasonable starting point is to inquire about the reasons for a decline in the unexplained gender wage gap in general. Such a shift may reflect a decrease in labor market discrimination against women, but also an upgrading of women's *unmeasured* labor market skills, or a shift in labor market demand favoring women over men. This implies that slower convergence in the unexplained gap in the 1990s than in the 1980s could be due to a smaller decline in discrimination against women in the 1990s; a slower improvement in women's unmeasured qualifications relative to men's in the 1990s; or less favorable demand shifts for women in the 1990s. Kahn and I present evidence that each of these factors appear to have played a role in explaining the observed trends, although it is not possible to specifically apportion a share to each factor.[23] This suggests that the entire difference between the two decades is not necessarily due to trends in the extent of discrimination against women, but that this factor did play a role.

It might at first appear unlikely that labor market discrimination against women decreased by more in the 1980s than in the 1990s because civil rights legislation passed in 1991 made the legal environment more favorable toward antidiscrimination lawsuits in the 1990s than it was in the 1980s, by making it more profitable for private law firms operating on a contingency fee basis to represent defendants in job bias lawsuits. This contributed to a more rapid growth in such lawsuits over the 1990s.[24] Nonetheless, if women's labor force commitment changed more dramatically in the 1980s, and we find some evidence consistent with this, it is possible that employers' *perceptions* of women's labor force commitment also changed more dramatically in the 1980s. If so, one of the possible bases for statistical discrimination against women may have eroded faster in the 1980s than in the 1990s.

An additional scenario whereby discrimination could have narrowed more slowly in the 1990s is related to the glass ceiling hypothesis. The so-called glass ceiling problem refers to the explicit or, more likely, subtle barriers that inhibit women's progress at the highest echelons. If there is indeed such a problem, it may have had a greater negative impact on women in the 1990s than in the 1980s, as women's 1980s gains placed more of them into the higher-level positions where glass ceiling barriers might hinder their further upward progression. If women are indeed increasingly constrained by glass ceilings, then one might expect to find less wage convergence with men at the top of the distribution than at other points. We find some evidence that this is the case.

Other Evidence of Discrimination

Given the problems with traditional statistical studies of discrimination, some economists have taken different approaches to the question. First, let me consider two studies that have applied traditional statistical techniques to especially homogeneous groups and employed extensive controls for qualifications, thus minimizing the effect of gender differences in unmeasured productivity characteristics. Mary C. Noonan, Mary E. Corcoran, and Paul Courant studied two cohorts of graduates of the University of Michigan Law School, five and fifteen years after graduation; the first graduated between 1972 and 1978 and the second between 1979 and 1985. The results for the two cohorts were quite similar. The gap in pay between women and men was relatively small at the outset of their careers, but fifteen years later, women graduates earned only about 60 percent as much as men. Some of this difference reflected choices that workers had made, including the propensity of women lawyers to work shorter hours. But, even controlling for current hours worked, as well as an extensive list of worker qualifications and other covariates, including grades while in law school, and detailed work history data, such as years practiced law, months of part-time work, and type and size of employer, a male advantage of 11 percent remained.[25] In a similar vein, Catherine J. Weinberger examined wage differences among recent college graduates in 1985. Her controls included narrowly defined college major, college grade point average, and specific educational institution attended. She found an unexplained pay gap of 10 to 15 percent between men and women.[26] While one must be cautious in interpreting the unexplained gaps identified in these two studies as entirely due to discrimination, for the reasons we discussed previously, these findings are consistent with discrimination against highly educated women.

A second set of studies used an experimental approach. David M. Neumark analyzed the results of a hiring "audit" in which male and female pseudo–job seekers were given similar résumés and sent to apply for jobs waiting on tables at the same set of Philadelphia restaurants.[27] In highpriced restaurants, a female applicant's probability of getting an interview was 40 percentage points lower than a male's and her probability of getting an offer was 50 percentage points lower. A second study examined the impact of the adoption of "blind" auditions by symphony orchestras in which a screen is used to conceal the identity of the candidate.[28] The screen substantially increased the probability that a woman would advance out of preliminary rounds and be the winner in the final round. The switch to blind auditions was found to explain 25 percent of the increase in the share of musicians in the top five symphony orchestras in the United States who were women, from less than 5 percent of all musicians in 1970 to 25 percent in 1996.[29]

Third, several studies have examined predictions of Becker's discrimination model.[30] As we have seen, Becker and others have pointed out that competitive forces should reduce or eliminate discrimination in the long run because the least discriminatory firms, which hire more lower-priced female labor, would have lower costs of production and should drive the more discriminatory firms out of business. For this reason, Becker suggested that discrimination would be more severe in firms or sectors that are shielded to some extent from competitive pressures. Consistent with this reasoning, Judith K. Hellerstein, David Neumark, and Kenneth Troske found that, among plants with high levels of product market power, those employing relatively more women were more profitable.[31] In a similar vein,

Sandra E. Black and Philip E. Strahan report that, with the deregulation of the banking industry beginning in the mid-1970s, the gender pay gap in banking declined as men's wages fell by considerably more than women's (12 percent vs. 3 percent).[32] This suggests that during the period of regulation, banks shared the added profits fostered by regulation primarily with men. It was thus men who lost the most in the shift to deregulation. And, Black and Elizabeth Brainerd find that increasing vulnerability to international trade reduced estimated gender wage discrimination in concentrated industries, again as predicted by Becker's model.[33]

Finally, additional evidence on discrimination comes from court cases. A number of employment practices that explicitly discriminated against women used to be quite prevalent, including marriage bars restricting the employment of married women[34] and the intentional segregation of men and women into separate job categories with associated separate and lower pay scales for women (e.g., Bowe v. Colgate-Palmolive Co., 416 F.2d 711 [7th Cir. 1969]; IUE v. Westinghouse Electric Co., 631 F.2d 1094 [3rd Cir. 1980]). While many such overt practices have disappeared, court cases suggest that employment practices still exist that produce discriminatory outcomes for women.

One high-profile case is the $54 million settlement of a sex discrimination lawsuit against Morgan Stanley in 2004, in which plaintiffs claimed that the firm underpaid and did not promote women. Allegations of sexist practices reportedly included claims that Morgan Stanley withheld raises and desirable assignments from women who took maternity leave, and that it condoned a hostile workplace where men made sexist comments and organized trips to topless bars and strip clubs.[35] Another example of a major case was the $31 million settlement in 2002 of sex bias charges against American Express Financial Advisors, where it was also claimed that female employees were underpaid and given fewer job opportunities. According to the plaintiffs, the company steered the most profitable accounts to male financial advisers and, corporate-wide, men were given preferential treatment in training, mentoring, and promotion. It was alleged that this was "the product of a stereotype—pervasive both inside Amex and throughout the industry—that women do not have what it takes to succeed in the financial planning business and that only young males have the temperament and the ability to achieve aggressive sales."[36] As another example, in 2000, the U.S. Information Agency agreed to pay $508 million to settle a case in which the Voice of America rejected women who applied for high-paying positions in the communications field. A lawyer representing the plaintiffs said that the women were told things like, "These jobs are only for men," or "We're looking for a male voice."[37]

A number of sex discrimination suits have been filed against grocery chains as well. In 1994, Lucky Stores, a major chain, agreed to a settlement of $107 million after the judge found that "sex discrimination was the standard operating procedure at Lucky with respect to placement, promotion, movement to full-time positions, and the allocation of additional hours" (Stender v. Lucky Stores, Inc., 803 F. Supp. 259; [N.D. Cal. 1992]). Similar lawsuits against several other grocery chains have also ended in settlements, including Publix Super Markets Inc. of Florida, which, in 1997, agreed to pay $81.5 million to settle a sex discrimination lawsuit that accused the chain of keeping women in dead-end, low-wage jobs. Although women made up half the company's workforce, less than 5 percent of its 535 store managers were women.[38]

Some insight into the underrepresentation of women in higher-level positions found in the cases cited previously is provided by a recent study of eight years of data from an unidentified regional grocery chain on gender differences in job titles and wage rates.[39] The authors find a pattern of gender differences in initial job assignment and upward mobility within the firm that "generally penalized women, even when the analysis account[ed] for individuals' characteristics."[40] While one might dispute the reason for these differences, the authors found that job segregation of women and men was dramatically lower in the period after the company lost a discrimination suit (1984) and reached a settlement (1986) in which it initiated affirmative action policies. This implies that it was possible to find women interested in higher-level jobs, leading one to doubt that such segregation was entirely voluntary.

CONCLUSION

The past thirty years have been a period of enormous change in the status and achievements of women in the labor market. I have focused here on one specific measure of outcomes, the gender wage gap. There is no doubt that the relative earnings of women have increased dramatically during this period, with particularly sharp gains in the 1980s. This development is extremely important, not only because of the improvement it indicates in women's labor market outcomes, but also because higher wages for women encourage greater investment in human capital and higher levels of commitment to the labor market, paving the way for further increases in their wages in the future.

While the gains are important and dramatic, they are not an invitation to complacency. Women still earn less than their male counterparts with similar measured characteristics. This "unexplained gap," which is potentially due at least in part to labor market discrimination against women, has been diminished but by no means eliminated. Moreover, while the decline in the unexplained gap was particularly pronounced during the 1980s, there was no evidence of a further decline in the 1990s. To the extent that this reflects slower decreases in the extent of labor market discrimination during the 1990s, it means that we must continue to be concerned with inequitable treatment of women in the labor market.

Professor Polachek and I differ in our assessment of the importance of labor market discrimination in influencing the magnitude and trends in the gender wage gap. While I would place a greater emphasis on discrimination as being a highly significant factor, we are in agreement that the qualifications of women compared to men also play an important role. Further, we agree that to the extent that the qualifications of men and women differ, gender differences in the roles of women and women within the family are a fundamental determinant. This means that further change in the gender wage gap in the future also requires that we address the issue of work–family conflict and continue to seek ways that allow both women and men to successfully combine challenging careers with their family responsibilities.

Part V

THE FUTURE OF RACE AND ETHNICITY

A Dream Deferred
Toward the U.S. Racial Future

Howard Winant

In his epoch-making study of U.S. racial dynamics, *An American Dilemma: The Negro Problem and Modern Democracy*, Gunnar Myrdal introduced a theory of "cumulative and cyclical development" to explain the fitful but in his view inevitable progress of U.S. "race relations" toward more democratic and egalitarian conditions.[1] The account of "development" Myrdal offered was tentative; the book's purposes were never primarily theoretical and only in the most general sense political. As is well known, the author and his collaborators argued in favor of the extension of democratic principles to include "race relations," notably black–white relations, in the context of the battle for democracy that was World War II. They contrasted U.S. national goals and aspirations in the war effort with the racial despotism of the country as a whole, particularly (though not only) the states of the U.S. South. Myrdal linked his idealized concept of a democratic "American creed" with an assimilationist vision of racial progress, an idea of racial "development" that was still very much oriented to the white liberal outlook, as his critics, most notably Ralph Ellison,[2] were quick to point out.

Howard Winant is a professor of sociology at the University of California, Santa Barbara, where he is also affiliated with the Black Studies and Chicana/o Studies departments. He founded and directs the University of California Center for New Racial Studies. He is the author of *The New Politics of Race: Globalism, Difference, Justice*; *The World Is a Ghetto: Race and Democracy Since World War II*; *Racial Conditions: Politics, Theory, Comparisons*; *Racial Formation in the United States: From the 1960s to the 1990s* (coauthored with Michael Omi); and *Stalemate: Political Economic Origins of Supply-Side Policy*.

211

In some respects, the war against Nazi totalitarianism was the engine that Myrdal thought would drag the Jim Crow South—still mired in the quasi-colonial and agrarian backwardness to which it had been relegated after the abandonment of Reconstruction in 1877 and the ratification of a renewed racial despotism in the *Plessy* decision—into the modern world. In later work, Myrdal extended his theory of "cumulative and cyclical development" to the global stage, stressing the interdependent dimensions of the world economy and the deleterious consequences of global poverty, not only—obviously enough—for the poor regions of the planet, but also for the rich countries. The challenge of achieving racial democracy in the United States—the key theme in *An American Dilemma*—was now linked to problems of economic development and self-determination in the emerging postcolonial world.[3]

Half a century or so later, what has survived, what has been vindicated, and what discarded, of Myrdal's vision? In many ways, he was prescient: the connection between planetary anticolonial impulses and struggles for racial democracy "in the belly of the beast" has now been widely acknowledged, and a substantial literature has arisen to document these correspondences and associations.[4] While Myrdal's assimilationism and relative imperviousness to nationalism and racial collectivity earned him many critical barbs, the age of racial nationalism seems now to have receded, and a new "neo-assimilationist" account of racial development across generations (aka "segmented assimilation) has gained ground.[5] Myrdal's "cumulative" and "cyclical" dimensions of racial "development" can be confirmed: the partial but still vital successes of the civil rights era certainly mark a ruptural moment, a "break" with the explicitly racist past whose dimensions were not only national but also worldwide.[6]

At the same time, the containment of the movement's radical potential and its relegation to relative quiescence and incorporation into the "normal politics" of the post–civil rights era testify to the cyclical dimension of development Myrdal stressed. The U.S. racial regime charged a high price for its concession of "moderate" reforms: in many ways, these reforms ratified the old racial inequalities as much as they altered them.[7] Reform vitiated the underlying radical agenda of redistribution and inclusion that had animated the movement at its apogee. Reform was far from the whole story: the "velvet glove" of enhanced civil rights was accompanied by the "iron fist" of repression, particularly by imprisonment, which multiplied more than tenfold (!) between the mid-1960s and the end of the century.[8] Perhaps most perniciously, civil rights reform institutionalized a new ideology of racial aversion or colorblindness that was sustained by an unprecedented, indeed quite mindboggling, disjuncture between racial fiction and fact. Colorblindness constituted the "official story" that racism and indeed racialization itself were now artifacts of the past, relics of the bad old days that had finally been overcome. This account ramped up a great deal when Barack Obama was elected president and simplistic references to a "postracial order" became fashionable. Obama himself largely deploys colorblind racial ideology, although he also occasionally critiques it as well.[9] Beneath this ostensibly postracial view, of course, the palpable and quite ubiquitous system of racial distinction and inequality remained entrenched. Though modernized and "moderated," structural racism was actually fortified by civil rights reform. Ironically and bitterly, it was validated more deeply than ever before by its official denial and repudiation in the "post–civil rights" racial regime.

What to make of this new set of racial conditions in the twenty-first century? What can be said about trends toward the racial future? Social scientists and social theorists can never claim to predict the future. Still, some observations can be ventured: at the least, trying to imagine the U.S. racial future will impel us to reassess the recent racial past.

In pursuit of clues about the contours of the racial future, I propose to examine three aspects of present-day U.S. racial conditions: (1) demographic shifts and their political implications; (2) colorblind racial ideology and its discontents; and (3) the post–civil rights era crisis of the U.S. racial state. Still guided by the model of "cumulative and cyclical development," my idea here is to consider some key trends and tendencies, some emergent new patterns in U.S. racial dynamics, which I suggest will shape twenty-first-century U.S. politics, operating across all three areas of my discussion. Although half a century after Myrdal's analyses we remain confined by the weight of a despotic racial regime, today we can also detect the emergence of new democratic prospects in the vicissitudes and contradictions of twenty-first-century racial politics.

DEMOGRAPHIC SHIFTS AND THEIR POLITICAL IMPLICATIONS

Demographically, the country is becoming a lot less white. This reflects immigration rates and fertility rates, considered as racial matters. As a destination for immigration, the United States perpetuates its heritage as a "settler nation," but it does this in a way quite different from earlier patterns of conquest, settlement, coerced extraction of mass labor, and outright extirpation. Patterns of immigration retain their deeply structured features: political-economic factors shape them, and migrant networks operate them, speaking very generally. But the very volume of immigration, the social forces that drive it, and the pressing economic needs it fulfills both for immigrants and their employers combine to give immigrants a role in reshaping U.S. society that recalls earlier great waves of immigration, notably those at the turn of the twentieth century.

The racial dimension of immigration, and of the growing immigrant population, gives new meaning to the term "settler nation." For example, due to its extensive incorporation of migrants from the global South and East especially, the United States can exercise a sort of "domestic foreign policy." "Islamophobia" and new waves of nativism represent current manifestations of a familiar pattern by which the United States as a nation has internalized its foreign conflicts, both employing racist scapegoating of immigrants from countries it seeks to control, and adjusting its outlook and policies toward those countries as it learns from (and sometimes assimilates) their emigrants (or their emigrants' descendants) within its own borders.

To be sure, nativist politics remain strong. The white (or "Anglo-Saxon") nation is beginning to encounter its own population in the same way that Europe and, more broadly, the global North and West confront the rest of the world. The vast majority of the world's population is dark-skinned; those considered to be "white" people are less than one-fifth of the world's people.

The trend toward a "majority-minority" demographic is advancing in the United States. In other words, a situation is emerging in which no single racially defined group, including those considered white, will be a majority in the country. Although we are still at quite some distance from that pattern nationally, major regions and cities are already majority-minority: California became an M-M state in 2000; New Mexico attained M-M status in 2002; Texas became M-M in 2005; and Hawaii and the District of Columbia have long been M-M.[10] Arizona, Florida, New York, Nevada, New Jersey, and Maryland are projected to lose their white majorities around 2025. The three most significant cities—New York, Los

Angeles, and Chicago—are either already M-M or are very close to being so. Across the entire country, whites are poised to become one racially defined minority group among others, probably at some point in the middle of this century.[11]

These tendencies have extensive political implications at every level of the public sphere, in every state agency, and also in civil society and private life. Here I will address only a few issues.

The Racial Future of Voting Behavior

Today, with minor discrepancies, U.S. political parties are divided along racial lines. The Republicans are the white party. In U.S. history, there has generally been one political party that took charge of racial rule. This has been especially true vis-à-vis black/white demarcations—for example, the organization by the Democratic Party of white supremacist rule in the Jim Crow era.

But rapid swings are possible. After the critical election of 1932, U.S. blacks (those who could vote) shifted their loyalties away from the "party of Lincoln."[12] This occurred even though Roosevelt's New Deal coalition effectively delegated control of the South (where most blacks still lived) to the plantocratic/agrarian/racist/"Dixiecrat" wing of his party. The South was essentially a one-party state, a racially despotic regional regime, whose rulers continued to function as the quasi-colonial administrators they had become after Reconstruction. Although the Republicans maintained a "liberal" position on race as long as the Democrats/Dixiecrats retained power, when the Democrats endorsed civil rights reform in 1964, this set off a white shift to the Republican Party, decidedly in the South and to some extent nationally.

This is the most familiar pattern of racial voting, but it is not the only such case. Consider the Anglo/Latino (white/brown) divide in Texas, Arizona, California, and elsewhere in the Southwest. Since Proposition 187 passed in California in 1994, debate about major racial vote swings has come to focus on Latino voting. But numerous cases of voting rights discrimination against Mexican Americans, along with other civil rights cases involving Latinos (school segregation, jury selection, etc.), have occurred since World War II.[13] Indeed, the current wave of Latino protest activity—focused on immigrants' rights—further opens wedges in the Republican Party that Proposition 187 first dramatized.[14]

In the future, battles for Latino votes can be expected to increase in intensity. This voting bloc appears at present to have consolidated within the Democratic Party, although, as noted, swings in voting behavior cannot be ruled out. Increased Latino electoral clout will make itself felt most notably in the M-M or near M-M states of the Southwest, but notable increases in the Midwest and South can also be predicted.[15] Immigration can be expected to remain a central factor in electoral contests during the next decades, driven by shifting demographics, the unease generated by globalization ("outsourcing," labor market competition, etc.), and the deep nativist tendencies—fundamentally racially based in my view—that resurface periodically in U.S. political culture.

In this context, it is fruitful to consider dynamics of *panethnicity*, notably Latino varieties of the phenomenon. Recent research on attitudes toward immigration and immigrants, as well as studies of "segmented" processes of immigrant assimilation and mobility (notably work focused on transgenerational acculturation, educational achievement, and status attainment), has highlighted contrasting tendencies in immigrant racial formation processes. Focusing most notably on Latino immigrants but also on Asians, Middle Easterners, and others, we see the patterns of uneven racialization and deracialization that panethnicity theory would predict.[16] *Centripetal* pressures generate panethnic (i.e., racial) community ties, as well as sympathy and solidarity with new arrivals; racial/ethnic enclaves develop around religious, cultural, and economic institutions; racially/ethnically demarcated occupational niches are forged both within and outside the community; and parallelisms emerge in political and cultural attitudes, both fostered within ethnic communities and imposed from without by discrimination and prejudice. Simultaneously, however, *centrifugal* tendencies make themselves felt as immigrant languages fall into disuse and English comes to predominate; as disdain is expressed for more recent arrivals ("Fresh Off the Boat" or FOB); as the desire for assimilation takes hold; and as racial/ethnic elites urge conformity with host-nation customs and practices.[17] Although external pressures (discrimination, harassment, violence) can sometimes become serious enough to provide grounds for panethnic solidarity, ethnic/national differences and divergences frequently reassert themselves where racial ties remain tenuous.

This range of cross-cutting potentialities and pressures (of course treated very schematically here) can be predicted to generate a variety of political currents—and notably electoral strategies—in the years ahead as demographic trends toward greater racial/ethnic diversity continue, and M-M conditions become more common. The demographic shifts noted here may well limit the intensity of contemporary nativist mobilization in comparison to the strong anti-immigrant upsurges seen in the past.[18] Past pressures for "anglo-conformity"[19] or virulent nativist appeals such as the anti-Irish movements of the 1840s (the "Know-Nothings"), the assaults on West Coast Asian communities from the 1870s onward,[20] and the 1930s' mass deportations of Mexicans from Southern California[21] would be considerably harder to stage today. In the past, nativism could draw upon solid white majorities, less differentiated by class, and unschooled by the civil rights movement and its allies. Barring further catastrophic events of the order of the 9/11 tragedy, occurrences that are susceptible to racialization and xenophobic fearmongering, the traditional U.S. recourse to a "domestic foreign policy" that addresses global conflicts by recourse to racist domestic practices (think of the World War II internment of Japanese and Japanese Americans, the Palmer raids on Eastern and Southern Europeans in the 1920s, and the upsurge of Islamophobia that followed the 1979 Iranian hostage crisis, not to mention 9/11) is probably out of reach for the present racial regime. In the absence of such developments, the electoral effect of an increasingly immigrant-derived, M-M national demographic appears to trend Democratic. Explaining this tendency is beyond my present scope: it is clearly due more to the rampant nativism of the Republicans than to significant Democratic efforts—as of mid-2011—to woo Latino voters. Indeed, Obama's immigration policies have not improved on those of his predecessor.

The Racial Future of the Welfare State

The shifting demographics of race are turning out to matter as well in other key political and policy arenas. In education, health care, and criminal justice, to name but a few, racial dynamics remain crucial. The rise of neoliberalism, which began under Reagan but continued under Clinton and Bush II, meant the vitiation of an already beleaguered welfare state: notably in the 1996 welfare "reforms" that abandoned AFDC in favor of the draconian policies of TANF.[22] By shredding the "safety net" that had been established in the 1930s and only belatedly and grudgingly extended to racial minorities in the 1960s, the U.S. racial regime greatly widened the gap between the formal ("visible"), largely white economy and the informal ("invisible"), largely non-white economy. This trend also increased the distance between city and suburb, reinforced segregation in schooling and residential patterns—vis-à-vis both Blacks and Latinos,[23] and significantly hardened policing and criminal "justice" patterns.[24] The privatization and outright withdrawal of welfare state programs of social investment and collective consumption,[25] combined with repressive policies in policing, incarceration, and immigration, amount to classic neoliberal social policy, a domestic "structural adjustment program." In the U.S. context, such a recipe must rely upon such "fear factors" as national security and law and order. In other words, it must be framed racially.

To obtain some preliminary sense of these shifts, it is worthwhile to consider the changing dynamics of educational and occupational patterns in the United States. The student body in the public education system is moving toward majority-minority status, though it is still some decades away from that. Census Bureau estimates of that transition locate it around the year 2025.[26] What are the implications of this trend for re-segregation (already well under way), economic mobility, and generalized racial conflict? Who will teach these students? What career prospects will they have? If, as Robert Rubin and others have argued, the U.S. economy will become increasingly centered in the "knowledge industries," this will require major investments in public education and far more effective integration of schooling with shifting patterns of employment. Current trends in educational policy are headed in precisely the opposite direction: disinvesting, relying on mechanistic and formulaic testing of basic skills rather than teaching adaptive and creative thought processes ("intelligence" in the Deweyan use of the term), and abandoning large numbers of low-income children (disproportionately black and brown) to permanent subemployment.

A closely related question is the composition of the U.S. workforce. It is becoming darker in parallel with the trend toward a majority-minority society. As informal labor markets grow in size and importance,[27] it becomes more difficult to assess employment patterns with specificity.[28] Consider the Social Security system, perhaps the most durable element of the New Deal–based welfare state. Already there are fewer white workers paying the FICA taxes to support Social Security payments to white baby boomers like me when we retire (I was born in 1946). The Social Security system—forced savings through regressive payroll taxation, pay-as-you-go financing—has long been seen both as a powerful guarantor of political legitimacy and as a "third rail" of the welfare state: a New Deal achievement that worked to curtail and regulate excessive and highly ideological "free market" pressures from the political right. Bush II's blundering campaign for Social Security "privatization" was but the first assault on the system from the headquarters of reaction.[29] The 2011 Republican program for stepwise reprivatization of Medicare and reductions in Social Security benefits (led by Representative Paul Ryan of Wisconsin) continues this trend.

But by the mid-twenty-first century, a majority of U.S. workers will be non-white. To the extent that they are employed in the formal economy, they will be paying their FICA/payroll taxes (organized regressively: exempting annual incomes above $106,800) to support those largely white retirees born in the mid-twentieth century and later. Well before 2050, in short, the calculus of cost and benefit in the Social Security system will shift: it will no longer afford political legitimacy or constitute an unshakeable pillar of support to many working people—the ones with darker skins. We may very well see revolts against this remaining bastion of the welfare state (or against its inadequacy) on the part of people of color. Opposition to Social Security from the "left"? There's something new![30]

Affirmative action represents another such issue, that is, a policy subject to unanticipated trends toward rearticulation. As of now, affirmative action in education or employment is on life support at best, as a combination of biased jurisprudence and store-bought referenda (California Prop. 209 [1996]; Michigan Proposal 2 [2006]) has challenged it across the country. The Supreme Court has proved unwilling, in case after case, to tackle the ongoing dynamics of racial discrimination, unless that discrimination is construed to harm the interests of white people.[31] As employment trends continue, as whites in some states (e.g., California) are outcompeted by Asians for desirable university slots, and as whites feel more and more beleaguered,[32] the United States may well experience demands for affirmative action *for whites*, as has occurred in South Africa.

Indeed, there may be pressures for a *de facto* regression to an *apartheid* society like South Africa was (and in many ways still is). Imagine an ever-darker United States, shorn of its unquestioning commitment to WASP culture and elite leadership . . .[33] Hollywood frequently presents this vision of the American future as nightmarish and dystopic. In such films as

Blade Runner and *Escape from New York*, the United States is depicted as a society in which an isolated white elite live behind gates and in fortified high-rises, while private armies (or public ones) guard them from the hungry and enraged dark-skinned mobs of the excluded, the marginalized, the wretched of the earth.[34] While I wouldn't want to go too far with this comparison, it does bear some resemblance to the segregated societies of the present: the French *banlieues*, the ongoing disparities of South Africa, the shantytowns and *favelas*, miscegenated as they may be, of Lima or São Paulo. Incorporation, inclusion, and the defusing of racial tensions may well be structural imperatives in the "post–civil rights era," requirements for hegemonic rule and social stability. But at the moment these needs for social integration are hardly being met. The ghettos and barrios of North America endure.

COLORBLIND RACIAL IDEOLOGY AND ITS DISCONTENTS

The reigning racial ideology in our country today is that of "colorblindness."[35] There is a pervasive belief that the most effective anti-racist action is simply to ignore race. Adherents of this colorblind perspective deny that skin color informs our perceptions, shapes our attitudes, or influences our individual, collective, and institutional practices. Of course, such sweeping claims of transcendence are often hard to sustain, so if colorblindness advocates can't deny all that, they argue that at least individuals and institutions *should* follow colorblind norms, exerting a maximum effort to make race "a thing of the past."

   This denial of race draws upon a range of arguments: chief among these is the gradual abandonment of biologistic conceptions of race that began at the beginning of the twentieth century and culminated in the idea that race is a "social construct."[36] Other claims for colorblindness are grounded in prevailing scientific critiques of the concept of race. These initially emerged at the close of World War II as a response to the eugenicist ideologies and practices of Nazi Germany (and the United States as well). Today a new scientific approach—based in genomics—seeks to substitute for the concept of race a view that human corporeal differences are the outcomes of genetic/ evolutionary factors that have been concentrated in certain geographical areas. Building on these sorts of views, those adhering to the colorblind view of race advance the following claim: having been thoroughly discredited as a biological or genetic category, race should now be regarded as a questionable *social* category as well.

Colorblindness both reflects and subverts the legacy of civil rights and other racial justice movements of the 1950s and 1960s. At one point, it provided the general framework for anti-racist movement goals, a moment most familiar from the famous passage in Dr. King's 1963 "I Have a Dream" speech:

> I have a dream that my four children will one day live in a nation where they will not be judged by the color of their skin but by the content of their character.[37]

But colorblindness represented something very different in the last years of Jim Crow segregation than it does in the twenty-first century. In August 1963, as the marchers converged on the Lincoln Memorial and Dr. King's and other civil rights leaders' voices rang out across the capital,[38] overt racism, the U.S. version of *apartheid*, was still the law of the land. Desperate public officials and private citizens, many of them avowed white supremacists, were struggling to preserve it at all costs from the growing popular consensus that sought its destruction.

Contrast this with the situation in the twenty-first century. Today racism is tacit. Although explicitly racial laws are frowned upon, courts wink at implicitly discriminatory measures and indeed preoccupy themselves with supposed discrimination against whites. The reforms of the civil rights era seem increasingly ineffective against an ongoing structural racism that sees, hears, and says no evil. To ignore ongoing racial inequality, racial violence, racial disenfranchisement, racial "profiling," quasi-official resegregation of schools and neighborhoods, and rising anti-immigrant racism—it's a long list—under the banner of colorblindness is to indulge in a thought process composed in equal parts of disingenuousness and wishful thinking. This is the environment in which colorblindness is portrayed as the racial *desideratum* of our time, and enforced as the law of the land.

Indeed, by almost every conceivable indicator researchers can bring forward, the same racial inequalities—the same "structural racism"—that existed in the past continues today: modified here and there perhaps, but hardly eliminated and not even much reduced in scope—for example, in terms of U.S. black-white disparities, or in terms of anti-immigrant nativism. This is not the place to inventory the data, but whether we look at wealth/income (in)equality, health, access to/returns to education, segregation by residence or occupation, rates of surveillance or punishment by the criminal "justice" system, or many other indicators that compare racial "life-chances," we find strikingly persistent patterns.[39]

Can we really embrace a colorblind approach to race in the face of persistent nativism? Can we ignore the existence of a prison system whose highly disproportionate confinement of black and brown people is a national scandal? Can we even begin to understand U.S. racial dynamics through a colorblind perspective when virtually every facet of U.S. economic life, every aspect of U.S. governance, and every artifact of U.S. culture is organized along racial lines? Can we accept claims that racism is "a thing of the past" when, as Melvin Oliver and Thomas Shapiro report, median white net worth in the United States is as much as *eight times* greater than median black net worth?[40] Can we agree with the colorblind approach to race when, as Gary Orfield and John T. Yun document, school segregation not only has persisted but also has been both exacerbated and normalized in the United States, gaining acceptance from the public, from education officials, and from the judiciary's wholesale abandonment of *Brown v. Board of Education* (1954) and other desegregation-oriented decisions of the 1960s?[41] Can we even take seriously professions of belief in colorblind attitudes when those who claim to hold such views have simultaneously proposed laws that would criminalize all undocumented immigrants—largely Latinos and overwhelmingly people of color—as well as anyone who assists them?[42] Can we use a colorblind analytical approach to understand the Bush administration's response to Hurricane Katrina, which destroyed New Orleans (67 percent black) in September 2005? What if Katrina had hit, say, Greenwich, Connecticut (90 percent white) with equal force?

But such examples of the inadequacy of colorblind racial ideology do not tell the whole story. In the long term, colorblind racial ideology can "work" only to the extent that it reflects the successes of the post–civil rights era in ameliorating racial injustice and inequality. A purely fabricated, mythical colorblindness could hardly be sustained either intellectually or in the interactions of everyday life. Whether framed in scholarly, political, jurisprudential, or commonsense discourse, the effectiveness of colorblind ideology depends on its verisimilitude[43] and the credibility of its claim that U.S. racial conditions have improved: more equality, more inclusion, less discrimination, less racial violence and racial repression. These demands were on hand in the 1960s. Today, the democratizing and egalitarian accomplishments of the civil rights upsurge appear attenuated at best, and largely unrealized at worst.[44] What happens to a dream deferred?

Still, we won't succeed in understanding colorblindness if we see it as simply erroneous or deceptive, merely a hoax or a matter of wishful thinking. Indeed, it is precisely because the old U.S. *apartheid* system was formally dismantled, and because the new racial dynamic that was substituted for it was more open and fluid, that it became possible to advance the colorblind position. By exaggerating the accomplishments of the civil rights reforms, by repudiating U.S. white supremacism as a "thing of the past," by providing a facile means for whites (and not only whites) to denounce racist practices and beliefs of a certain type (overt, explicit, etc.), colorblindness enables officials, intellectuals, pundits, and ordinary folk to engage in a kind of *anti-racism lite*.

As a racial project, indeed as the *hegemonic*[45] racial project in the United States today, colorblindness is a rude beast: ineffective, uneven, ungainly, deceptive, contradictory. But since hegemony is about the incorporation of opposition, is it really such a surprise that there are contradictions in its logic? The inconsistencies and inaccuracies of colorblindness have been extensively discussed. But what has not been sufficiently emphasized is the incomplete and unconsolidated status of the colorblind racial project and the implicit limits of its bid for hegemony at the turn of the twenty-first century.

From a colorblind perspective, one has not to "notice" race, not to see it. Or one wouldn't be "blind" to it, right? But what happens to *race-consciousness* under conditions of colorblind hegemony? Quite clearly, awareness of raciality does not dry up like a raisin in the sun. Just as colorblind racial ideology serves as a means to occlude recognition of race beneath the veneer of a supposedly already-accomplished universality, race-consciousness works to highlight racial differences and particularities. Race-consciousness involves *noticing* the ongoing presence and significance of racial identity, racial inequality, and racial injustice. To experience race-consciousness in the post–civil rights era is to pay heed to the unfulfilled social justice agendas that remain from the era of civil rights (and of course from the more remote past).[46] It is to understand at least in part the power plays of race and racism: the vast fabric of inclusion and exclusion, advantage and disadvantage, solidarity (tacit or explicit) imposed on individuals and groups[47] by a social system committed to racial classification *in practice* (even if it often denies what it's doing).

Although drawing attention to race—racial identity and difference, racial inequality and oppression, racial exclusion and violence—allows me to question the depth and seriousness of the colorblind racial ideology, I want also to recognize that race-consciousness exhibits certain contradictions as well. It is easy to mischaracterize race or misinterpret the significance of racial identity. Just when does race matter, anyway? Always? Sometimes? If the answer is "sometimes," what about those situations when race "doesn't matter"? Are there conditions under which we should *not* notice race? Is not racial identity often ambiguous and contradictory? What is the significance for the meaning of race of transracial solidarity and alliance? What is the significance for the meaning of race of transracial friendship, or transracial identity, or indeed love across the color line? These old themes no doubt retain something of their transgressive and unsettling character, but they are also increasingly normal, regular, and unremarkable.[48] Can trust and solidarity exist across racial lines? Is it possible either in individual or collective social practice to "get beyond" race? If so, how definitive is racial identity? If not, what are the implications for multiculturalism, democracy, humanism?

This is a bigger set of issues than I can effectively address in the present space, so I shall simply summarize the dilemmas involved. There is always a risk of authoritarianism behind race consciousness—not only in the obvious authoritarianism of white supremacy, *apartheid*, and colonialism, but also in movements of resistance to these regimes. This sort of problem has characterized many resistance movements: in Marxism, for example, democratic practices have given way to Stalinism and other forms of repression; anticolonial movements have spawned dictatorships; religious movements against persecution have persecuted their own dissenters. Race consciousness, though an obviously indispensable rejoinder to the "cheap trick" of colorblindness, cannot deny the inherent fluidity and sociohistorical situatedness of racial identity and racial difference without risking a collapse into a despotism of its own.[49]

Consider this: If after the 1960s, the neoconservatives[50] appropriated the ideal of colorblindness—which had been a radical movement ideal—thereby turning it into a cheap and ineffective form of anti-racism, was that then the end of the story? Was that the only time that such a bold political move could be pulled off? Or can that appropriation, that theft of a demo-cratic ideal, be *re*appropriated, such that a new ideal based *both* on dif-ference and solidarity, *both* on particularity and equality, might emerge? I would certainly not want to call such an ideal "colorblind," but I would expect it to include the possibility of overcoming racial difference, at least in part, through a creative type of consciousness and action, a *radical racial pragmatism*. An emphasis on "self-reflective action," to invoke a term from John Dewey by way of Hans Joas,[51] is at the heart of the new racial politics needed in the twenty-first century.

Not only among the talking heads at Fox News or in the far-fetched racial jurisprudence that dominates the present period, but also in everyday life today, we are often exposed to the putative common sense of "post–civil rights era" colorblindness. Many students tell me, for example, that they "don't see race," that "a person is just a person," and that they seek "to treat everyone as an individual." Mostly of course it is white students who say this, but by no means do these expressions come only from the lips of whites.

For a long time, I argued with such claims: "You don't see race? Have you had your eyes checked lately?" But in recent years, I have come to see that response as counterproductive, tending to validate the self-righteous-ness that frames colorblindness, whether willfully or naively.

I am now taking a new approach in my effort to counter the "anti-racism lite" that such positions entail. Rather than arguing directly against colorblindness, I want to recognize the unresolved dimensions, the contra-dictions that necessarily follow from the civil rights movement's (and its al-lies') combined historico-political accomplishments: its incomplete but real successes, its tentative visions of a solidaristic and "beloved" community, as well as its mistakes and limits, its necessary compromises, and its repression at the hands of a state committed to racial despotism. If the post–civil rights era is characterized by anything, it is the experience of tension between col-orblindness and race consciousness. Rather than denying that race matters, rather than arguing that nothing has changed, we should go deeper into the contrarieties of race. We can recognize, we can understand, how race still shapes social and political life in both small-scale and large-scale ways, while also acknowledging that today we can sometimes "bracket" race, as a phenomenologist might say: we can sometimes emphasize it, and some-times barely notice it. This is itself an achievement of movements for racial freedom. Such a perspective demands a radical racial pragmatism: some-thing very democratic, something based in *self-reflective action*. Pragmatism is all about that: checking yourself, looking at the practical consequences of a social practice, legal decision, or political action.

Colorblind ideology usually serves to mask racism, particularly the social structural racism that, underneath the mask of tolerance and inclu-sion, remains rampant. But sometimes, standing on the shoulders of the movements that have gone before us, we can ally across racial lines, work with or love someone of a different race, assume the place of the "racialized other."[52] People of color have always had to do that vis-à-vis whites; cannot whites learn to do that as well?

THE POST–CIVIL RIGHTS ERA CRISIS OF THE U.S. RACIAL STATE

Because the U.S. state remains a racial state, its efforts to adopt the color-blind racial ideology remain partial, incomplete, and contradictory. Col-orblindness cannot become fully hegemonic. It has had a good run as an attempt to "get beyond" racial conflict and outflank anti-racist opposition, but it is encountering powerful and in some ways unanticipated obstacles. The limits to colorblindness are developing both as the result of the continu-ing injustice and suffering brought about by racism,[53] and as the product of internal contradictions in the racial regime itself.

The chief irony of the post–civil rights era is that while formal legal equality has been significantly achieved in many institutional arenas, sub-stantive racial inequality remains, and in many cases has deepened. The ideology and language of colorblindness have worked to render persistent (structural) forms of racial inequality less visible. But there is a fundamental instability to "colorblindness." Challenges to it have therefore steadily come from the progressive left and from communities of color, an opposition bloc that sometimes overlaps and is sometimes itself fissured by racism. At some fundamental level—and of course there are exceptions—colorblindness im-plies a white standpoint. Go ahead, ask the person of color standing nearest to you how colorblind s/he thinks the United States is . . .

Despite neoconservatism, despite the concerted drive to institutionalize the colorblind paradigm that has been in operation since the 1970s, race-consciousness remains. Opposition calls for redistribution, for legalization of the undocumented, for jobs for those hit especially hard by the recession and the ongoing restructuring of the U.S. economy, for renewed commitments to egalitarianism and the reconstruction of the welfare state, and for the revival of affirmative action policies, represent the political horizon of anti-racist politics at present. It is unlikely that an increasingly non-white electoral base will vote against public schools, health care, union rights, or immigrant rights. The prospect of a majority-minority society, no longer constrained by a taken-for-granted Anglo-conformism and no longer embracing the colorblind paradigm, represents a significant threat to the present racial regime.

But a second and more volatile set of challenges to colorblind racial ideology is emerging from the ongoing instabilities and conflicts of the "post–civil rights" era, indeed from *within the racial state itself*. As a practical matter, the "post–civil rights era" racial regime must frequently negate its own insistence on "colorblindness." It can't help violating its own ideology of "colorblindness"; its managers and theorists have to think racially in order to rule. It currently demonstrates this in numerous policy arenas: in its reliance upon profiling as a tactic of generalized social control—in everyday policing as much as in the "war on terror"; in its abandonment of its responsibilities for rebuilding New Orleans; in its recourse to race-based voting-suppression tactics in electoral contests; in its assaults on the welfare state and its insistence on a privatized "ownership society" that calls into question even such basic New Deal measures as Social Security; in its revival of the nativist framework through its drive for "immigration reform" on the Mexican border and beyond; and in the racial dimensions of its neoimperial foreign and war policies in the Middle East and elsewhere.[54]

Even in such areas as science policy, schooling, and environmental regulation, the racial regime maintains commitments to racial practices that contradict or undermine its official colorblindness. Both private firms (notably big pharmaceuticals but others as well) and the state (acting through the National Institutes of Health and the National Science Foundation) have made substantial investments in the new racial genomics, which is now a big scientific enterprise as well as a developing system for social control.[55] Resegregation and disinvestment in public education is a species of reverse social engineering. Of a piece with the social entropy of current incarceration practices, the "savage inequalities" it creates constitute nearly impenetrable patterns of structural racism.[56] Environmental racism presents a similar pattern. Although toxic assaults upon communities of color continue to receive little attention in mainstream political forums or media, they represent an ongoing denial of the colorblind story, one whose consequences—like those of the exploding prison population or the abandonment of public education—are already spilling over into more prosperous and whiter communities.[57]

THE DREAM LIVES ON

The contradiction between these practical commitments and the official ideology of colorblindness seems unsustainable. The post–civil rights era formula of colorblindness cannot succeed in dissipating racial conflicts; only an overarching effort at social reconstruction could even begin to tackle such a task.

Confronted with the limits of "colorblindness," daunted by the enormity of structural racism, we could easily succumb to despair. But my argument here leads in the opposite direction: racial hegemony has not been achieved; the current "post–civil rights era" racial regime is beset by contradictions. To recognize the many obstacles that still confront the "dream" of racial democracy, equality, and justice is also to recognize the enormous achievements of the movement for racial justice over the latter half of the twentieth century: the movement made race and racism a public matter, a "social fact" in the Durkheimian sense. The beleaguered and in many ways absurd state of colorblind racial ideology is a result of those movement achievements as well. Movements may experience setbacks, the reforms for which they fought may be revealed as inadequate, and indeed many of their leaders may be co-opted or eliminated, but racial subjectivity and self-awareness, unresolved and conflictual both within the individual psyche and the body politic, abide. The dream lives on.

In this essay, I have hinted at the political potential of *radical racial pragmatism*. Such a viewpoint suggests that we see politics as an everyday creative practice, that we understand "self-reflective action" as an everyday matter. Such an approach enables a new interpretation of race and racism. Let us, then, think about race and racism, as well as a wide range of other political themes, as *everyday encounters between despotic and democratic practices*, in which individuals and groups, confronted by state power and entrenched privilege but not entirely limited by those obstacles, make choices and locate themselves over and over in a constant "reconstruction" of everyday life.

Not only because it has failed to fulfill the promise of racial equality and justice, but also because it defaults, so to speak, to racial rule as a key component of hegemonic rule, the contemporary U.S. state *must violate its own racial norms*, norms that are themselves the products of post–World War II civil rights and anti-imperial political struggles. Because of this, and because people continue to struggle with issues of race in their own lives—pragmatic, self-reflective action once again—there is still room to create a more egalitarian, racially just, and democratic future.

Or does it explode?

Racial and Ethnic Diversity and Public Policy

Mary C. Waters

A humbling exercise for anyone attempting to predict the future of American racial and ethnic inequality is the following. Imagine that it is 1910 and you are asked to predict the patterns of inequality in 2010. There are 92 million Americans, 10.2 million or 9 percent of whom are non-white. Of the non-whites, 9.8 million are blacks, another 266,000 are American Indians, and 114,000 are Japanese and Chinese. Immigration is at an all-time high—15 percent of the population is foreign-born, and in the nation's largest cities the percentages are much higher. It has been forty-five years since the end of the Civil War, and the situation of African Americans has improved, but is still quite dire. Non-white illiteracy has fallen from 80 percent in 1870 to 30 percent by 1910, but African Americans remain very poor, 85–90 percent concentrated in the rural south, where Jim Crow racism is gaining rather than declining and much of the political and educational progress blacks made in the Reconstruction period after the Civil War has been rolled back. World War I, World War II, the Depression, and the Civil Rights movement, as well as the immigration restrictions put in

Mary C. Waters is the M. E. Zukerman Professor of Sociology at Harvard University, where she has taught since 1986. Recent books include *Coming of Age in America: The Transition to Adulthood in the 21st Century* and *The Next Generation: The Children of Immigrants in Europe and North America*. Her study of the children of immigrants in New York, *Inheriting the City: The Children of Immigrants Come of Age*, won several awards, including the American Sociological Association 2010 Distinguished Contribution to Scholarship.

place in the 1920s, are all unimagined. The sweep of the twentieth century changes would have been impossible to predict, and yet given the preoccupation of Americans with racial matters, future inequality would have been a natural question for a social scientist to ponder.

Social scientists of the time were concerned about the future of American race relations, and of course they could not foresee many of the major historical events of the twentieth century that would affect patterns of American racial and ethnic inequality. But it is instructive to note that social scientists in 1910 were concerned with "races" from Southern and Central Europe whom we now see as "whites," and would not have predicted the variety of non-white, non-black peoples who have come to the United States in large numbers since 1965. Predictions at the beginning of the twentieth century would have categorized the American population in ways we now see were very historically specific. Thus Harvard economist William Z. Ripley, writing in the December 1908 *Atlantic Monthly* on "Races in the US," worried about the degrading effects on the American population of races such as Jews, Italians, and Poles.[1] Another Harvard professor and leader of an immigrant restrictionist league, Henry Cabot Lodge, stressed in 1896 that the differences among European groups were as large as the differences between Europeans and Africans, and that Southern and Central Europeans were decidedly inferior to Northern and Western Europeans.[2]

Indeed, a whole area of scholarly research has developed in the last few decades investigating the ways in which European immigrants who came to the United States between 1880 and 1920 (about twenty-three million people) were racialized. People at the time used the word "race" to describe national origin groups such as the Irish, the Italians, and the Greeks. The federal government developed a "list of races or peoples" for use in classifying immigrants and their descendants. Historians have now been debating in their scholarship whether these immigrants and their children were seen as "white," as "non-white," or as "in between peoples." This literature, collectively referred to as the "whiteness literature," debates the degree to which these European groups were excluded or included in the category "white" and debates how, over time, they came to be seen as indistinguishable from Northern and Western European whites.[3] While the debate about where racial lines were drawn and what processes led to their diminishment is still vibrant, scholars do agree about the outcome. By the late twentieth century, white ethnic groups descended from these European immigrants intermarried at very high rates, expressed symbolic attraction to their ethnic identities, and generally were considered indistinguishable as white Americans.[4]

In this essay, I certainly don't aspire to predict patterns of American racial and ethnic inequality over the next one hundred years. Yet I do think that the historical lesson of changing patterns of categorization and changing demographics is important and relevant for even short-term predictions about patterns of American race and ethnic relations. In thinking about the near-term patterns of racial and ethnic inequality, I think it is very important to recognize the shifting meaning of racial and ethnic categories, the rapid demographic changes that immigration has brought to our population. I will argue that too much of our scholarly research and our public policy for the twenty-first century is still using categories and concepts from the twentieth century. While I agree with many of the points made by Howard Winant in his essay on the U.S. racial future, I do not agree with the way in which he frames his discussion of race, or with the choice of categories he makes. Winant uses a frame of race relations that contrasts "whites" and "people of color." I do not think this division captures the important dynamics in American race and ethnic relations.

My argument is that we are in the midst of demographic and social changes that are shifting the boundaries and meanings of race and ethnicity in the United States. The demographic transformation of our population through immigration along with rising intermarriage and growing recognition of multiracial ancestries both by individuals and by the state are blurring the boundaries between traditional racial/ethnic groups. At the same time, growing income inequality, declining wages for those with the least education, and the historical legacies of slavery and racism create economic and social conditions that disproportionately affect African Americans. Our public policies designed to address historical injustices to African Americans and the ongoing discrimination that they face— race-based policies such as affirmative action—are poorly equipped to address these issues. This is because categorization by race increasingly combines immigrants and natives who have very different needs and strengths, and also because such policies do not differentiate within racial groups based on social class. Race-based policies are also bound to become increasingly precarious as the boundaries between races become increasingly porous and fuzzy. Enforcement of the Voting Rights Act, which involves the drawing of election districts based on race, will become increasingly problematic as these categories become more ambiguous.

I do not argue that this means American society has abolished discrimination, nor that we should have only colorblind public policy. Specifically I argue that dealing with twenty-first century inequalities requires that we let go of twentieth-century categorizations of the population. I do not think that the major axis of difference in the United States in the coming decades will be between whites and non-whites as Winant (this volume) suggests. A more likely scenario is that many "non-white" Hispanic and Asian groups will have a great deal of economic success and social inclusion, while poor African Americans, reservation-based American Indians, and dark-skinned, poorly educated immigrants and their children are left behind. I think we should have policies directed toward diversity, which include new immigrants and their offspring, as well as policies directed toward racial justice, which target native-born African Americans of low social class. Above all we should also have policies designed to help those at the bottom of the income distribution—policies that address the economic problems of the working poor. This would go a long way toward addressing issues of racial and ethnic inequality. (Although in the case of poor African Americans, I will also argue that race-based social justice policies are needed.) Thus I disagree with Winant's division of policy options into colorblind versus color-conscious. I think we need *both* universal social policies to help all poor Americans regardless of race, as well as targeted policies toward African Americans in particular.

DEMOGRAPHICS

In 1965, Congress passed the Hart-Celler Immigration Act, which repealed the restrictionist admissions system based on discriminatory nationality quotas that had severely limited immigration to the United States since the 1920s. This act installed a new global admissions system under which immigration reached all-time high levels by the end of the twentieth century. It also put numerical limits on immigration from the Western Hemisphere for the first time—limits that would lead to growing undocumented or illegal immigration in the coming decades. At the same time, worldwide demographic and political changes, often referred to collectively as globalization, created a number of conditions that encouraged international migration.

From 1971 to 2000, 19.9 million legal immigrants arrived in the United States, along with millions more undocumented, eclipsing the 18.2 million immigrants who came in the thirty-year period from 1891 to 1920 (once remembered as the high-water mark in American immigration). Between 2000 and 2005, an estimated 7.9 million immigrants arrived, the largest number arriving in a five-year period in the nation's history. As a result, the foreign-born population has steadily increased since 1960, rising from 9.7 million in that year to 35.2 million in 2005. The foreign-born of the early twenty-first century are more numerous than ever before, but at 12.1 percent of the population, they constitute a smaller proportion of the total population than they did a century ago, when they were 14.7 percent.

Another 10 percent of the U.S. population are the children of immigrants—referred to by scholars as the second generation. So, currently, at least one in five Americans are first- or second-generation. Only 14 percent of the foreign-born in the United States are from Europe. The largest group (43 percent) are from Latin America (including Central America, South America, and the Caribbean), while 25 percent are from Asia, and 8 percent are from other regions of the world, such as Africa and Oceania. Mexicans are the largest single group of the foreign-born and now compose 27 percent of all foreign-born. In addition to Mexico, the top nine countries of birth of the foreign-born are China, India, Korea, the Philippines, Vietnam, Cuba, the Dominican Republic, and El Salvador.

This immigration has transformed the major ethnic-racial groups in America. In 1970, 88 percent of the U.S. population was white, 11 percent was black, and less than 1 percent consisted of American Indians, Asians, and Hawaiians. Hispanics, who are counted differently in the census and can be of any race, were only 5 percent of the total 1970 U.S. population. By 2000, the effects of immigration were readily apparent in the demographics of the country—75 percent of the population was white, 12 percent black, 4 percent Asian, and 13 percent Hispanic. American Indians increased in number over the thirty years (through new people claiming or discovering their Indian heritage) but still were less than 1 percent of the population.

In addition to changing the relative numbers of different races and ethnic groups in the United States, immigration has also changed the generational distribution within American race and ethnic categories. Asians are the most impacted by immigration. Only 12 percent of Asians are third-generation or higher, 61 percent are foreign-born, and 27 percent are second-generation. As Suro and Passel point out, in the mid-twentieth century, the Latino population in the United States was dominated by the 3+ generation—it was primarily a group distant from immigrants who could be considered a native minority.[5] It was primarily composed of Mexican Americans and Puerto Ricans. By 2000 the majority (68 percent) of Latinos are first- or second-generation—but one-third are third-generation or higher. In addition to long-time Mexican Americans and Puerto Ricans, the Latino group includes immigrants and their children with origins in the Caribbean and Central and South America. Indeed, only blacks and American Indians in 2000 are a majority non-migrant stock. Even blacks— the group whose experience most racial policies in the United States are designed to address—are now 10.2 percent first- or second-generation, as African Americans have been joined by groups such as Nigerians, Haitians, West Indians, and Cape Verdeans. In their generational distribution, they are quite similar to non-Hispanic whites, who are also about 10 percent first- or second-generation.

Immigration has not only affected racial diversity in the United States but also increased class and religious diversity. Immigrants are over-represented among those with low education. According to the census, among people aged twenty-five and over, 85 percent of native-born Americans have a high school diploma or higher, while among immigrants only 67 percent do. The foreign-born are especially over-represented among those with extremely low levels of education. Approximately 7 percent of the foreign-born have less than five years of schooling, 15 percent have between five and eight years, and another 10.8 percent have between nine and eleven years. In terms of employment, immigrants are concentrated among low-wage workers. While immigrants are one in nine U.S. residents, they are one in five low-wage workers (defined as those who earned less than twice the minimum wage in 2001). Thus the fortunes of low-wage workers in American society disproportionately affect immigrants and their families.

Immigration also adds to the country's religious diversity. Between 75 percent to 80 percent of Americans are Christian, and 5 percent report a non-Christian religion. Among new immigrants, there is more religious diversity. Two-thirds of new immigrants are Christian, the majority being Catholic. Twenty percent report a non-Christian faith, and one in six reports no religious identity at all. In contrast to Western Europe, the United States has received very little Muslim immigration. Muslims in the

United States total about three million people, less than 1 percent of the total population.[6]

In 1903, W. E. B. Du Bois foretold that "the problem of the Twentieth Century is the problem of the color line."[7] More than a hundred years later, Du Bois's characterization of the main division in American society still holds true, with perhaps the qualification that the color line is now more complex and more far-reaching than "color" alone.[8] Yet, despite the changing meanings and divisions of race and racial boundaries, the historical practice of depicting and organizing American society along racial lines still persists. The centrality of race in American society today is reflected in the ways in which diverse immigrant populations are accommodated in the United States. As immigrants assimilate to American society, they also incorporate the American racial lens. For example, ethnographic research on West Indians reveals that black immigrants are often surprised when they encounter American racialization. Their newly acquired status as "black" in the United States can be shocking because in their countries of origin, West Indian immigrants (and others in their community) may not necessarily have considered themselves as black.[9] Indeed, Patterson shows that in many regions of the world where black and Hispanic immigrants emigrate from, categories of race are much more fluid.[10]

Since the civil rights movement, the United States has developed two main race-based policies that attempt to address inequalities—nondiscrimination and affirmative action. They are described here.

Nondiscrimination

The Civil Rights Act of 1964 was aimed at dismantling institutionalized discrimination against African Americans. The Civil Rights Act (and later, the 1965 Voting Rights Act) was the result of the hard-fought struggles of the civil rights movement. Its main purpose was to address the problem of racial discrimination against African Americans. According to John David Skrentny:

> Despite the inclusion of sex, religion, and national origin, the early discussion of other ethnic minorities by Truman's Civil Rights Committee, and the

presumably broad meaning of the prohibition on racial discrimination . . .
American citizens and political elites saw Title VII [which covers antidiscrimination in employment] and the entire Civil Rights Act of 1964 as being a law for African Americans.[11]

It was only later that antidiscrimination policies were expanded to cover other racial and ethnic minorities such as Hispanics, Asians, and Native Americans, as well as women and people with disabilities.[12] Since the Civil Rights Act also includes national origin as a protected characteristic, immigrants can obtain antidiscrimination protection on the basis of other protected characteristics (e.g., gender, race, ethnicity, disability status, etc.) irrespective of their noncitizen status. Thus immigrants and citizens who have one or more of these protected characteristics have legal protection against discrimination in many spheres of public and private life, ranging from voting rights, injunction relief against discrimination in places of public accommodation, desegregation of public facilities, desegregation of public education, nondiscrimination in federally assisted programs, and equal employment opportunity. In the case of immigrant accommodation, we focus on education and employment.

Title VII of the Civil Rights Act of 1964 bars discrimination in employment based on race, color, religion, sex, or national origin and prevents employer retaliation against employees who take action against discriminating businesses. The law applies to employers with at least fifteen employees, employment agencies, and unions. Title VII also created the Equal Employment Opportunity Commission (EEOC), which is responsible for enforcing antidiscrimination in employment by monitoring private employers and investigating individual allegations of employment discrimination. Title IV of the 1964 Civil Rights Act regulates the assignment of students to public schools (at all levels ranging from elementary to post-secondary institutions) and within such schools without regard to their race, color, religion, or national origin. Thus, racial and ethnic immigrants and their children are, theoretically, protected against relegation to racially segregated, inferior schools (U.S. Department of Justice, 2005).

Antidiscrimination policies enjoy considerable support from the American people. They gel well with the American ideology of equal opportunity and do not contradict notions of meritocracy. But antidiscrimination laws allow only for the redress of individual injustices after injustices have already been incurred and not necessarily for the prevention of them.[13] Furthermore, since discrimination against a person on the basis of any of the specified characteristics is illegal, both racial and ethnic minorities and whites can seek protection under antidiscrimination laws. In contrast, affirmative action, a more controversial race-based policy that has garnered much political protest on both sides of the political spectrum, is aimed at preventing exclusion from occurring in the first place by ensuring that protected minority groups are included in various spheres of economic, educational, and political life.

Affirmative Action

Similar to the various antidiscrimination laws that came out of the 1964 Civil Rights Act, affirmative action policies owed their existence to the black civil rights movement and were initially intended to redress the injustices incurred against the descendants of African-American slaves.[14] As I shall illustrate later in the essay, this initial logic of the policies challenges immigrants' claims to affirmative action benefits. The volume of immigrants who could potentially benefit from affirmative action policies is enormous. Hugh Davis Graham noted that in the year 2000, "16 million [out] of the 24.6 million foreign-born residents were non-citizens, yet they remained eligible for minority preferences under many affirmative action programs."[15] Immigrants who are noncitizens or who have yet to naturalize can claim affirmative action benefits on the sole basis of positioning themselves into membership in one of the protected minority groups.

In its simplest and least contested form, affirmative action policies are almost indistinguishable from antidiscrimination policies. This type of regulation is referred to as "soft" affirmative action. It entails activities such as outreach to protected minority communities, career advancement training, and fair assessments for promotions. On the other end of the spectrum is what scholars call "hard" affirmative action policies, which are usually implemented as preferential treatment or *compensatory* affirmative action. The most extreme and controversial form of affirmative action is quotas. But despite public perception that affirmative action always translates into quotas, they are actually rarely enacted.[16]

Affirmative action in education, employment, and federal contractors/ small businesses is covered by different regulations, executive orders, and statutes. They also differ in implementation. For example, not all employers are required to enact affirmative action policies. In the private sector, only large companies with substantial government contracts must practice af-firmative action.[17] The bulk of affirmative action regulations in education, particularly higher education, have been for the most part voluntary. As-sessment of exclusion is usually based on proportional representation, that is, whether a minority group is represented in schools or companies in pro-portion to its numbers in the general population.[18]

Affirmative action policies have enabled racial and ethnic minorities, many of whom are immigrants, to make remarkable strides in education, particularly post-secondary education. In a review of the impact of affirma-tive action in higher education, Shannon Harper and Barbara Reskin show that, contrary to opponents' claims that affirmative action harms minority students by placing them in competition with better-prepared white students, thereby increasing minority dropout rates, minorities who attend more se-lective schools actually have higher graduation rates than their counterparts at less selective schools.[19] Furthermore, minority retention rates were higher at schools that practiced hard affirmative action (as opposed to schools that implemented softer forms of affirmative action). More revealing, however, is the decline in minority student applications at public universities in states, such as California and Washington, where voter referenda ended affirmative action in public employment and education.[20] The empirical evidence indi-cates that affirmative action has been instrumental in ensuring immigrants' inclusion in American society.

Yet, the success of the aforementioned race-based public policies has also undermined the monoracial and monoethnic classification schemes that form the basis of these laws. In the absence of immigrant-specific inte-gration policies, the U.S. government has relied on affirmative action and antidiscrimination laws as well as other public policies intended to rem-edy racial discrimination against African Americans. But increasingly, the correlation between racial and ethnic categories and social disadvantage or exclusion has grown weaker.[21] The case of Asians aptly illustrates this weakened connection between race and social exclusion. Although Asians (and Pacific Islanders) have protected minority group status and qualify for affirmative action benefits, not all Asian ethnic groups are socioeco-nomically disadvantaged enough to justify preferential treatment. For ex-ample, East Asian groups such as the Chinese, Koreans, and Japanese have incomes and educational levels that are similar to whites. South Asians, namely Indians, have incomes that surpass those of whites.[22]

High intermarriage rates between Hispanics and whites and Asians and whites have also led to a substantial multiracial population who refuse to self-identify as monoracial or monoethnic. The census recognized these changes by allowing respondents to check more than one race in the 2000 census for the first time. Seven million people, or 2.4 percent of the population, said they identified with two or more races. While only a relatively small percentage of Americans did identify with more than one race in the census, the entire federal statistical reporting system needed to change to accommodate the potential of multiracial reporting. Thus the 2000 census results by race both in printed form and electronically reflect great complexity. Statistics are reported now for the six major single race categories—white, black, Asian, American Indian, Native Hawaiian, and other Pacific Islander—and "some other race." These are then reported for each possible multiple combination, including the six single race categories, the fifteen unique biracial combinations, the twenty unique three-way combinations, the fifteen unique four-race combinations, the six five-way combinations, and the one possible six-way combination—thus yielding sixty-three unique racial categories. Since Hispanic is measured separately by the census and Hispanic people can be of any race, the sixty-three race combinations are also reported by whether the individual is Hispanic or non-Hispanic, yielding 126 unique racial/Hispanic categories. A number of commentators have wondered how long a statistical system based on such complexity can function for important political purposes such as congressional redistricting. How long before the difference in how one counts multiracial black-white people tips the balance in a given district in a way that affects how lines are drawn?[23]

The number of people choosing to identify with more than one race is bound to increase as interracial marriage has been increasing a great deal. In 1970 less than 1 percent of all couples in the United States were from different races. By 2000, 5 percent of couples in the United States were from different races. Intermarriage rates are generally shaped by group size, with smaller groups having higher out-marriage rates than larger ones. For Asians and Hispanics, the foreign-born have lower intermarriage rates than the American-born; for whites and blacks, the foreign-born are more likely to out-marry. Among American Indians, a very small group, 57 percent, has out-married. Among Asians the out-marriage rate is

16 percent, among blacks 7 percent, and among whites 3 percent. But among U.S.-born Asian women, 44 percent have a non-Asian spouse; among U.S.-born Asian men, 32 percent have a non-Asian spouse. Among U.S.-born Hispanic women, 31 percent have a non-Hispanic husband; among U.S.-born Hispanic men, 29 percent have a non-Hispanic wife.

These intermarriage patterns are growing, and yet the current system for allocating social benefits ignores this diversity. In fact, for purposes of affirmative action programs and for enforcement of the Voting Rights Act, the government top-codes multi-race and multi-ethnic self-identification on the census and forces them into monoracial and monoethnic categories.[24] The Office of Management and Budget issued guidelines for allocating mixed minority and white-race individuals to the minority race, thereby inflating the statistics for both (1) proportional representation estimates and (2) projections of the number of minorities that could potentially be eligible for affirmative action benefits. The growth of the multiracial population and the logical result of growing intermarriage mean that the boundaries between groups are becoming more permeable and harder to define. This has legal implications for all kinds of antidiscrimination laws. If people can be counted as both white and black and discrimination in voting, for instance, is measured by whether the voting population matches the underlying demographics, how does one determine the base number for the denominator? And how much legitimacy can a system based on so many different permutations of multiple-race reporting have in determining access to special treatment in hiring and promotions?[25] Intermarriage has reached rates that are unprecedented in American history, and this is a very good thing. Yet the resulting ambiguity about the boundaries and meanings of our standard racial groups means that this success story of American diversity is undermining the bedrock of the system of laws and policies we have in place for protecting and ensuring that diversity. Political scientist Kenneth Prewitt, who served as director of the U.S. Census during the 2000 enumeration, has written that "when the history of that census is written the issues surrounding sampling and other aspects of measurement theory will be a footnote . . . to the real story of this count: multiracial identity. With Question 8: What is this person's race? Mark one or more, we turned a corner about how we think about race in this country."[26]

FUTURE CHALLENGES

The United States is heralded as an example of enduring stability and unity amid great population diversity along racial, ethnic, religious, language, and other boundaries. Scholars such as Peter Schuck attribute the success of America's diversity management to codified laws that regulate the distribution of scarce societal goods to diverse groups of people.[27] Policies such as affirmative action are one avenue through which racial and ethnic minority immigrants can partake in the American Dream. But this pathway to inclusion in American society is contingent on continued public support for affirmative action. As the situation currently stands, public support is waning. The expansion of affirmative action to include seemingly arbitrary racial and ethnic minority groups who may not necessarily have a history of injustice inflicted against them raises questions about affirmative action's legitimacy. The opposition to conferring affirmative action benefits on other racial and ethnic groups—including immigrants—stems mainly from the public understanding that, at its inception, affirmative action was supposed to remedy only the issue of African American exclusion.

By allowing voluntary immigrants (i.e., noncitizen, racial, and ethnic minorities) to take advantage of affirmative action benefits, the government may in effect be further undermining the intentions of affirmative action by ignoring the continued exclusion of African Americans now that black representation in employment and education is on the rise (albeit partly due to the high participation rates of foreign-born blacks).[28] Indeed, a front page article in the summer of 2004 in the *New York Times* was entitled "Top Colleges Take More Blacks, but Which Ones?" The article reported on the deep consternation among black alumni from Harvard University who discussed the fact that a majority—perhaps as much as two-thirds of the "black" students at Harvard—are first- or second-generation immigrants or the children of interracial couples. The question debated at a meeting held on the subject was whether "African-American students whose families have been in America for generations were being left behind."[29] This is not an issue for just one university; a study by Douglas Massey and Camille Charles found that 41 percent of "black" students at twenty-eight selective colleges and universities nationwide were of immigrant stock or multiracial.[30]

Recent empirical studies of the young adult children of immigrants in the United States find that they are doing better in terms of educational attainment and labor market achievements than native-born Americans of the same racial backgrounds. In the New York Second Generation Study, we surveyed a large group of young adults in New York City whose parents had come from Asia, Latin America, the Caribbean, and Russia.[31] We found impressive educational and occupational mobility. While most of the immigrant parents had "immigrant jobs"—working in low-level service and manufacturing jobs, their adult children all resembled other New Yorkers at the same age much more than their parents did. And they all had high school and college graduation rates higher than native New Yorkers of the same racial backgrounds. Dominicans had higher educational attainment than Puerto Ricans; West Indians had higher attainment than native blacks; and Chinese had higher attainment than any other group by far. In national studies, these patterns of social mobility hold for many groups, including Mexican Americans.[32] An emerging consensus in the research on the second generation reaches an optimistic conclusion—immigrant parents' sacrifices are paying off, with significant socioeconomic integration among their children. And despite the urgent fears of many Americans about the place of English as our national language, all the research shows rapid language assimilation—the second generation is overwhelmingly fluent in English, and the third generation speaks only English.

This success of the second generation of non-white immigrants may in part be due to diversity policies in education and corporate America that include them based on their non-white status. But diversity policies can do only so much in ensuring the long-run integration of non-white immigrants and their children. A much more important factor is the structure of the American economy and policies that ensure that social mobility on a large scale remains an open possibility for those at the bottom of the income distribution.

I would suggest that specific race-based policies such as affirmative action, while important, may have only marginal effects on the actual long-run successful outcomes of immigrants and their descendants. Current immigrants to the United States are over-represented among the less educated and the working poor. Policies developed in the last decade have not been designed to ease their integration into American society but rather to further restrict their access to the welfare provisions that remain for poor Americans. As Christian Joppke and Ewa Morawska point out, the traditional view of immigrant incorporation is that there is a covenant between the immigrant and American society, whose sustained openness is exchanged against requesting immigrants to be self-sufficient.[33] Historically the United States has been so successful in accommodating immigrants because of the relative openness of its labor market and the social mobility achieved by immigrants and their descendants.

In recent decades, the relative openness of America's higher education system has also played a role. The large network of community colleges, the availability of GED degrees to older students, and the large number of "second chances" the educational system provides have been an important source of opportunity and economic and social integration for first and second generations. This has been a largely unrecognized feature of American public policy, but it stands in sharp contrast to the often rigid educational systems in Western European countries. Cultural acceptance and full integration of immigrants followed behind this sometimes brutal but over the long run rather successful incorporation into the labor market for the descendants of immigrants.

But European immigrants in the twentieth century entered an economy that began a long-run expansion after the Depression. This rising tide lifted the immigrants and their children and made good on the implicit bargain offered to immigrants—an open economy with the possibility of real social mobility for a majority of the newcomers and their descendants. The cost of giving up past allegiances and becoming part of an American mainstream was worth it, given the payoff. But since the 1970s, income inequality has been growing, and the fortunes of those at the bottom of the educational distribution have been declining, not growing.

Immigrants are concentrated in the categories of workers who have seen their economic fortunes decline over time in the last few decades. Income inequality has grown rapidly among families between 1973 and 2001. As Sheldon Danziger and Peter Gottschalk conclude, "Inflation adjusted annual earnings of male high school dropouts were 23 percent lower in 2002 than in 1975, and earnings for male high school graduates were 13 percent lower."[34] Economists have been debating the causes of this rise in income inequality, but most agree that immigration itself, especially illegal immigration, played a part by increasing the supply (and thus lowering the price) of unskilled labor. In addition, most labor economists point to the rise in international trade and loss of manufacturing jobs to offshore sites, the decline in unionization, and the falling real value in the federally mandated minimum wage. The consensus is that there has been a sharp rise in the returns to education in the labor market—leading to diminished prospects for those with extremely low educations, who are disproportionately immigrants.[35]

The premium put on education in the current hourglass economy, with many low-wage, dead-end jobs and few jobs in between those and the higher-paid jobs requiring at least a college education, means that immigrants and their children are facing a difficult future. This may upset the link between economic mobility and cultural incorporation that has worked so well for Americans in the past. If the United States does not provide the kinds of opportunities for the children of immigrants that characterized past immigrant generations, then we may lose the incentive for cultural assimilation that causes individual immigrants to insert themselves into the American economy and culture. This is a challenge to the Americanization of immigrants and their children that is far greater than the usual issues framed in these types of discussions—issues such as dual citizenship, transnationalism, linguistic or religious diversity. It is also a challenge best met through economic policy changes and investments in education and social welfare for poor Americans regardless of their race or immigration status. Diversity management may just be a giant distraction from the bigger issue facing Americans—keeping opportunity for advancement available for the poor and the working class. And framing the issues around incorporating immigrants and their children in racial terms, as Winant does, also misses the inclusionary potential of economic and social mobility of first- and second-generation immigrants.

I also think that diversity policies are a poor substitute for racial justice policies. The legacy of slavery is with us both in the cumulative disadvantages suffered by African Americans, leading to less wealth, less physical health, ongoing residential segregation, and other ills, as well as in the continuing racism and discrimination that they experience at the hands of whites and other groups in the United States. Winant and I agree that the legal equalities for blacks that were instituted as a result of the civil rights movement have not led to substantive racial equality. The improvements in the position of African Americans vis-à-vis whites since the civil rights movement have been slow and fitful, and at this pace there is no way real equality will appear in the decades to come, absent a major intervention. Lyndon Johnson famously discussed affirmative action as a policy that recognizes that in a race it is not fair if one runner is in shackles while the other is free—that affirmative action is about making up for past injustices and creating a fair race. It is now possible to guarantee diversity without changing the class distribution of native-born African Americans—the presence of middle-class and immigrant blacks in the top schools, corporations, and legislatures in the country will make the upper echelons of American society diverse, but may not change the fortunes of native-born African Americans at all. Unlike immigrants, who are a selected group, poor native-born African Americans, because of ongoing racism and discrimination, cannot compete fairly with other groups. This racial injustice is different from the problems experienced by immigrants and other non-white groups, and it is not only an economic problem solved by opportunities for social mobility for those at the bottom of the social hierarchy. It is a uniquely American problem, forged in slavery and its aftermath, and it needs targeted attention to both race and class simultaneously. Creative new policies are needed that target low-skilled, native-born African Americans, such as those who were briefly in the national spotlight after Hurricane Katrina in New Orleans, and then all but disappeared from the nation's view afterward. Without the development of new policies targeted at this group, one safe prediction about future racial and ethnic inequality is that it will continue to be an entrenched and shameful scar on our national soul.

NOTES

Introduction: Poverty and Inequality in a New World

1. Tom W. Smith, Peter Marsden, Michael Hout, and Jibum Kim, *General Social Surveys, 1972–2010* [machine-readable data file]/Principal Investigator, Tom W. Smith; Co-Principal Investigator, Peter V. Marsden; Co-Principal Investigator, Michael Hout; sponsored by the National Science Foundation.

2. See, e.g., Leslie McCall and Lane Kenworthy, "Americans' Social Policy Preferences in the Era of Rising Inequality," *Perspectives on Politics* 7 (2009).

3. David B. Grusky and Emily Ryo, "Did Katrina Recalibrate Attitudes Toward Poverty and Inequality? A Test of the 'Dirty Little Secret' Hypothesis," *Du Bois Review* 3, no. 1 (2006).

4. David B. Grusky, Bruce Western, and Christopher Wimer, *The Great Recession* (New York: Russell Sage Foundation, 2011).

5. Lane Kenworthy and Lindsay Owens, "The Surprisingly Weak Effect of Recessions on Public Opinion," in *The Great Recession*, ed. David B. Grusky, Bruce Western, and Christopher Wimer.

6. Robert Reich, Christopher Wimer, Shazad Mohamed, and Sharada Jambulapati, "Has the Great Recession Made Americans Stingier?" in *The Great Recession*, ed. David B. Grusky, Bruce Western, and Christopher Wimer.

7. Emmanuel Saez, "Striking It Richer," *Pathways*, Winter 2008.

8. For a discussion of the "Obama effect" on inequality, see David Grusky and Christopher Wimer, eds., "The Obama Effect," *Pathways*, Spring 2010.

9. Arthur M. Okun, *Equality and Efficiency: The Big Tradeoff* (Washington, DC: Brookings Institution Press, 1975).

10. Pamela Stone, "Getting to Equal: Progress, Pitfalls, and Policy Solutions on the Road to Gender Parity in the Workplace," *Pathways*, Spring 2009.

11. Barbara Reskin, "Rethinking Employment Discrimination and Its Remedies," in *Social Stratification: Class, Race, and Gender in Sociological Perspective*, ed. David B. Grusky (Boulder, CO: Westview Press, 2008).

12. Maria Charles and David B. Grusky, "Egalitarianism and Gender Inequality," in *The Inequality Reader*, ed. David B. Grusky and Szonja Szelényi (Boulder, CO: Westview Press, 2011).

13. Marianne Bertrand and Sendhil Mullainathan, "Are Emily and Greg More Employable than Lakisha and Jamal? A Field Experiment on Labor Market Discrimination," in *Social Stratification: Class, Race, and Gender in Sociological Perspective*, ed. David B. Grusky.

Rich and Poor in the World Community

1. Sections of this essay have also appeared in Peter Singer, *One World* (New Haven: Yale University Press, 2002). For a more recent statement of my views on this topic, see Peter Singer, *The Life You Can Save* (New York: Random House, 2009), and visit www.thelifeyoucansave.com.

2. Peter K. Unger, *Living High and Letting Die: Our Illusion of Innocence* (Oxford: Oxford University Press, 1996), 135–36.

3. UNICEF Press Release, September 15, 2011, http://www.unicef.org /media/media_59795.html.

4. Peter Singer, *The Life You Can Save*, 85–89.

5. R. M. Hare, *Freedom and Reason* (Oxford: Oxford University Press, 1963).

6. William Godwin, *Enquiry Concerning Political Justice* (London: G. G. and J. Robinson, 1798), 127–28.

7. Samuel Parr, *A Special Sermon, Preached at Christ Church, upon Easter Tuesday, April 15, 1800* (London: J. Mawman, 1801), 4.

8. Nel Noddings, *Caring: A Feminine Approach to Ethics & Moral Education* (Berkeley: University of California Press, 1984), 86.

9. William Godwin, *Memoirs of Mary Wollstonecraft* (London: Constable and Co. Limited, 1928), 58.

10. Henry Sidgwick, *The Methods of Ethics* (London: Macmillan and Co., 7th ed., 1907), 246.

11. Bernard Williams, *Moral Luck* (Cambridge: Cambridge University Press, 1981), 18.

12. Michael Walzer, *Spheres of Justice: A Defense of Pluralism and Equality* (New York: Basic Books, 1983), 41.

13. Eamonn Callan, *Creating Citizens: Political Education and Liberal Democracy* (Oxford: Oxford University Press, 1997), 96.

14. Walter Feinberg, *Common Schools/Uncommon Identities: National Unity and Cultural Difference* (New Haven, CT: Yale University Press, 2000), 119.

15. Robert E. Goodin, *Utilitarianism as a Public Philosophy* (Cambridge: Cambridge University Press, 1995), 286.

16. Ibid.

17. Christopher Wellman, "Relational Facts in Liberal Political Theory: Is There Magic in the Pronoun 'My'?," *Ethics* 110 (2000): 545–59.

18. Karl Marx, *Wage-Labor & Capital* (Chicago: Charles H. Kerr, 1986), 40.

19. Sidgwick, *Methods*, 246.

20. Organization for Economic Cooperation and Development, "Development Aid Reaches Historic High in 2010," www.oecd.org/document /35/0,3746,en_2649_34447_47515235_1_1_1_1,00.html, and for the figures on aid to individual countries, see Organization for Economic Cooperation and Development, "Aid by Donor," www.oecd.org/dataoecd/42/30/44285539.gif, last accessed October 25, 2011.

21. Organization for Economic Cooperation and Development, *Statistics on Resource Flows to Developing Countries*, Table 11, "Non-ODA Financial Flows to Developing Countries in 2009," available at www.oecd.org/document/9/0, 3746,en_2649_34447_1893129_1_1_1_1,00.html. This table shows U.S. non-government organizations' net flow amounted to 0.12 percent of GNI. Adding this to official development assistance, which in both 2009 and 2010 amounted to 0.21 percent of GNI, yields a total of 0.33 percent.

Global Needs and Special Relationships

1. See Peter Singer, "Famine, Affluence and Morality," *Philosophy & Public Affairs* 1 (1973): 235.

2. Ibid., 241.

3. Ibid. In explaining the force of the "ought," Singer notes that it is meant to single out a dictate of moral duty, "not an act that it would be good to do, but not wrong not to do."

4. Some might disagree, claiming that such a choice does worsen my life, but only insignificantly. There is no need to pursue the disagreement here. A reader who takes this view of minor frustrations should simply recalibrate my discussion, treating "significant risk of worsening one's life" as short for "significant risk of significantly worsening one's life" and so forth.

5. See Peter Singer, *One World* (New Haven, CT: Yale University Press, 2002), 154–67.

6. Samuel Scheffler explores the connection between the proper valuing of special relationships and special concern in his influential article, "Relationships and Responsibilities," *Philosophy & Public Affairs* 26 (1997).

7. His most detailed discussion is *What We Owe to Each Other* (Cambridge, MA: Harvard University Press, 1998).

8. Philip Pettit and Robert Goodin emphasize the coordinative benefits of norms allocating special responsibilities in "The Possibility of Special Duties," *Canadian Journal of Philosophy* 16 (1986). However, they are not concerned with the moral status of closeness, and employ a rule-consequentialist framework that would yield Singer's radical conclusion in current global circumstances.

9. See Center on Philanthropy at Indiana University, *Giving USA 2008* (Indianapolis: AAFRC Trust for Philanthropy, 2008), 212f.

10. For simplicity's sake, I will treat the relationship binding compatriots as identical with fellow-citizenship. In fact, citizens of a country can be tied, as compatriots, to noncitizens, on the basis of co-residence and appropriate commitments. My arguments for duties of special concern for compatriots will suggest the general shape of these commitments, but I lack the space to develop a more precise account.

11. See World Bank, *World Development Indicators 2009* (Washington: World Bank, 2009), table 2.22. The World Bank counted countries as "low income" if per capita annual Gross National Income, converted to U.S. dollars at foreign exchange rates, was no more than $935. A fifth of the world's people lived in these countries. A half lived in "lower middle income" countries, for which the cutoff was $3,705. Five percent of them die before the age of five. In the high-income elite, where 16 percent of the world's people live, the below-five death rate is .7 percent.

12. In this essay, I can offer only a quick and partial sketch, with several controversial elements, of transnational relationships that generate demanding transnational responsibilities. I present a fuller account in *Globalizing Justice: The Ethics of Poverty and Power* (Oxford: Oxford University Press, 2010), chapters 3 through 8.

13. See Paul Collier and David Dollar, *Globalization, Growth, and Poverty* (Washington: World Bank, 2002), 44.

14. A threat by Carla Hills, the most important U.S. negotiator, who had declared that she would open other countries' markets with a crowbar, if need be. See Jarrod Wiener, *Making Rules in the Uruguay Round of the GATT* (Aldershot: Dartmouth Publishing Co., 1995), 186.

15. Secretary of State James Baker; see Ernest Preeg, *Traders in a Brave New World* (Chicago: University of Chicago Press, 1995), 80.

16. See OECD, *Agricultural Policies in the OECD at a Glance* (Paris: OECD, 2006), 19; UNCTAD, *The Least Developed Countries Report 2006* (Geneva: UNCTAD, 2006), Annex: Basic Data on the Least Developed Countries, table 1.

17. See United Nations Development Programme, *Human Development Report 2005* (New York: United Nations, 2005), 127.

18. See World Bank, *World Development Indicators 2009*, table 1.1. In assessing differences in global economic power, incomes outside the United States are, in general, best converted to dollars at foreign exchange rates. In contrast, in comparing material standards of living, the right rate is so-called "purchasing power parity," in which the dollar value of goods and services elsewhere is what it would cost to purchase them in the United States. Inequalities measured by

this standard are less, though still severe, because of the cheapness of goods and services that are locally generated and consumed in developing countries, relative to internationally traded goods and services.

(Some) Inequality Is Good for You

1. Arthur Okun, *Equality and Efficiency: The Big Trade-Off* (Washington, DC: Brookings Institution, 1975).

2. http://en.wikipedia.org/wiki/Henry_George.

3. Alfie Cohen, *Punished by Rewards: The Trouble with Gold Stars, Incentive Plans, A's, Praise, and Other Bribes* (Boston, MA: Houghton Mifflin, 1993).

4. Output should be defined as output net of the disutility of work.

5. Benny Moldovanu and Aner Sela, "The Optimal Allocation of Prizes in Contests," *American Economic Review* 91:3 (2001). See also Derek Clark and Christian Riis, "Competition over More than One Prize," *The American Economic Review* 88:1 (March 1998); and Sergio Parreiras and Anna Rubinchik, "Contests with Many Heterogeneous Agents," CORE Discussion Paper (2006).

6. Edward P. Lazear and Sherwin Rosen, "Rank-Order Tournaments as Optimum Labor Contracts," *Journal of Political Economy* 89:5 (October 1981).

7. http://en.wikipedia.org/wiki/Kuznets_curve.

8. Klaus Deininger and Lyn Squire, "New Ways of Looking at Old Issues: Inequality and Growth," *Journal of Development Economics* 57 (1998); and Robert J. Barro, "Inequality and Growth in a Panel of Countries," *Journal of Economic Growth* 5:1 (March 2000).

9. Ruth-Aïda Nahum, "Income Inequality and Growth: A Panel Study of Swedish Counties 1960–2000," Uppsala University Working Paper 2005:8 (March).

10. Kristin J. Forbes, "A Reassessment of the Relationship Between Inequality and Growth," *American Economic Review* 90:4 (September 2000); and Abhijit V. Banerjee and Esther Duflo, "Inequality and Growth: What Can the Data Say?," *Journal of Economic Growth* 8:3 (September 2003).

11. Ugo Panizza, "Income Inequality and Economic Growth: Evidence from American Data," *Journal of Economic Growth* 7:1 (2002).

12. Richard B. Freeman and Alexander M. Gelber, "Prize Structure and Information in Tournaments: Experimental Evidence," *American Economic Journal: Applied Economics* 2:1 (January 2010).

13. For a theoretical model that assumes a fixed prize purse and examines the optimal allocation of the prize money among several prizes, see Vijay Krishna and John Morgan, "The Winner-Take-All Principle in Small Tournaments," *Advances in Applied Microeconomics* 7 (1998).

14. Christine Harbring and Bernd Irlenbusch, "An Experimental Study on Tournament Design," *Labour Economics* 10 (2003).

15. Haig Nalbantian and Andrew Schotter, "Productivity Under Group Incentives: An Experimental Study," *American Economic Review* 87:3 (June 1997).

16. Wieland Müller and Andrew Schotter, "Workaholics and Dropouts in Organizations," *Journal of the European Economic Association* 8:4 (June 2010).

17. Charles Noussair and Jonathon Silver, "Behavior in All-Pay Auctions with Incomplete Information," *Games and Economic Behavior* 55 (2006); and Yasar Barut, Dan Kovenock, and Charles Noussair, "A Comparison of Multiple-Unit All-Pay and Winner-Pay Auctions Under Incomplete Information," *International Economic Review* 43 (2002).

18. Muriel Niederle and Lise Vesterlund, "Do Women Shy Away from Competition? Do Men Compete Too Much?," *Quarterly Journal of Economics* 122:3 (2007).

19. Cohen, *Punished by Rewards.*

20. Dan Ariely, Uri Gneezy, George Loewenstein, and Nina Mazar, "Large Stakes and Big Mistakes," *Review of Economic Studies* 76 (2009).

21. William F. Sharpe, *Investors and Markets: Portfolio Choices, Asset Prices, and Investment Advice* (Princeton, NJ: Princeton University Press, 2007).

22. Economic Policy Institute, Data Zone, "Hourly Wage Decile Cutoffs for Workers, 1973–2005" (2005 dollars) (available at http://www.epi.org/page /-/old/datazone/06/wagecuts_all.pdf) shows the 90/10 ratio of hourly wages rising from 1979 to 1987, then drifting slowly upward. The differential of college graduates over high school graduates drops from 1973 to 1979 and then rises (see http://www.epi.org/datazone/06/college_premium.pdf). For evidence on the effects of the recession on income inequality, see Timothy M. Smeeding, Jeffrey P. Thompson, Asaf Levanon, and Esra Burak, "Income, Inequality, and Poverty over the Early Stages of the Great Recession," in *The Great Recession*, ed. David B. Grusky, Bruce Western, and Chris Wimer (New York: Russell Sage Foundation, 2011).

23. Tabulated from Economic Policy Institute, Data Zone, "Real Hourly Wage for All by Education, 1973–2005" (2005 dollars).

24. The 262 to 1 estimate is from Economic Policy Institute (http://www .epinet.org/content.cfm/webfeatures_snapshots_20060621). The 431 to 1 pay is from United for a Fair Economy (http://www.faireconomy.org/files/Executive _Excess_2005.pdf). Also see the news report at http://money.cnn.com/2005/08/26 /news/economy/ceo_pay/; and see Jeffrey M. Stonecash, "Inequality and the American Public: Results of the Third Annual Maxwell School Survey, Conducted September–October, 2006," Campbell Public Affairs Institute, Maxwell School of Citizenship & Public Affairs, Working Paper 2006-1, revised January 2007.

Inequality and Economic Growth in Comparative Perspective

1. This hypothetical illustration is taken from Lane Kenworthy, "Do Social-Welfare Policies Reduce Poverty?," *Social Forces* 77 (1999).

2. Arthur Okun, *Equality and Efficiency: The Big Tradeoff* (Washington, DC: Brookings Institution, 1975).

3. Ibid., 4.

4. Ibid., 2.

5. Ibid., 4.

6. Cf. Alberto Alesina and Dani Rodrik, "Distributive Politics and Economic Growth," *Quarterly Journal of Economics* 109 (1994); Torsten Persson and Guido Tabellini, "Is Inequality Harmful for Economic Growth?," *American Economic Review* 84 (1994).

7. 2004 was the last year for which I had data on GDP per capita when I created these exhibits. I have not updated the exhibits because I do not want to engage in a discussion of economic performance during the Great Recession that began in 2007. Note also that GDP per capita is here measured at "purchasing power parities," a statistical procedure that takes into account cross-national differences in the cost of living.

8. The exception is that the French figure refers to net (after-tax) earnings. Note that the earliest available observations of 90-10 wage ratios for Canada, New Zealand, Norway, and Belgium refer to 1998–99. Removing these countries does not alter the overall picture.

9. OECD, National Accounts, http://stats.oecd.org/index.aspx?r=345004.

10. Following conventional practice in studies of income distribution, an equivalence scale based on the square root of the number of persons in each household was used to generate the Gini coefficients reported in Exhibits 2–3. The calculations were done by Lane Kenworthy as part of a joint project (Lane Kenworthy and Jonas Pontusson, "Rising Inequality and the Politics of Redistribution in Affluent Countries," *Perspectives on Politics* 3 (2006); see also Lane Kenworthy, *Egalitarian Capitalism?* (New York: Russell Sage, 2004)).

11. Alesina and Rodrik, "Distributive Politics and Economic Growth," Persson and Tabellini, "Is Inequality Harmful for Economic Growth?"

12. E.g., Michael Wallerstein, "Wage-Setting Institutions and Pay Inequality in Advanced Industrial Societies," *American Journal of Political Science* 43 (1999); David Rueda and Jonas Pontusson, "Wage Inequality and Varieties of Capitalism," *World Politics* 52 (2000); and Francine Blau and Lawrence Kahn, *At Home and Abroad: U.S. Labor Market Performance in International Perspective* (New York: Russell Sage, 2002).

13. Persson and Tabellini, "Is Inequality Harmful for Economic Growth?," 617. It should be noted that Alesina and Rodrik's and Persson and Tabellini's models also predict that countries with more inegalitarian distributions of

market income should be characterized by more redistributive government. The question of how inequality affects the politics of redistribution lies beyond the concerns of this essay. Suffice it to say that the association between inequality and redistribution is by no means as straightforward as Alesina and Rodrik and Persson and Tabellini seem to assume (see Kenworthy and Pontusson 2006 for an introductory discussion).

14. The measures of redistribution presented in Exhibits 4 and 5 are absolute changes in Gini coefficients as we move from gross market income to disposable income (Exhibit 4) or net market income to disposable income (Exhibit 5). I prefer these measures over percentage changes because they are unaffected by levels of market inequality, but the positive association between redistribution and growth shown in these exhibits emerges even more clearly with percentage changes on the horizontal axes.

15. For the subset of countries included in Exhibits 4 and 5, public social spending is rather closely correlated with total redistribution (r = .73) and redistribution via transfers (r = .73). See Alberto Alesina and Edward Glaeser, *Fighting Poverty in the U.S. and Europe* (Oxford: Oxford University Press, 2004), for a prominent example of using social spending as a proxy for redistribution.

16. Anders Björklund and Richard Freeman, "Mot optimal ojämlikhet?," in *Att reformer välfärdsstaten*, ed. Richard Freeman, Birgitta Swedenborg, and Robert Topel (Stockholm: SNS Förlag, 2006), 43. My translation. Note that while Björklund and Freeman claim to be making an argument about the relationship between inequality and efficiency, this formulation pertains to how inequality affects incentives to work (i.e., total supply, not quality of labor).

17. Cf. Robert Frank and Philip Cook, *The Winner-Take-All Society* (New York: Penguin, 1996).

18. Regressing economic growth over the period 1980–2000 on a larger set of independent variables, Lane Kenworthy in *Egalitarian Capitalism?* (New York: Russell Sage, 2004), ch. 4, reports consistently negative but insignificant coefficients for inequality of disposable income among working-age households.

19. See also Jonas Pontusson, *Inequality and Prosperity: Social Europe vs. Liberal America* (Ithaca: Cornell University Press, 2006), 209–10.

20. Likewise, there is no reason to believe that including more recent years would render the comparison more favorable to the more unequal countries. Not only Ireland but also Britain and the United States experienced larger GDP contractions than France, Germany, and Sweden in 2008–09 (see OECD, National Accounts, http://stats.oecd.org/index.aspx?r=345004).

21. Henry Chiu, "Income Inequality, Human Capital Accumulation and Economic Performance," *Economic Journal* 108 (1998).

22. Chiu, "Income Inequality," 45.

23. See, e.g., Gøsta Esping-Andersen, *Why We Need a New Welfare State* (Oxford: Oxford University Press, 2002), ch. 2.

24. As commonly noted, active labor market measures designed to ease the transition of workers from less efficient to more efficient firms and sectors were also a key component of the Rehn-Meidner model. See Jonas Pontusson, *The Limits of Social Democracy: Investment Politics in Sweden* (Ithaca, NY: Cornell University Press, 1992), on the theory and practice of solidaristic wage bargaining in Sweden.

25. Peter Katzenstein, *Small States in World Markets* (Ithaca: Cornell University Press, 1985).

26. See Karen S. Cook and Karen A. Hegtvedt, "Distributive Justice, Equity, and Equality," *Annual Review of Sociology* 9 (1983).

27. George Akerlof and Janet Yellen, "The Fair Wage-Effort Hypothesis and Unemployment," *Quarterly Journal of Economics* 105 (1990).

28. Okun, *Equality and Efficiency*, 46.

29. Björklund and Freeman, "Mot optimal ojämlikhet?," 49.

30. Cf. James Galbraith, *Created Unequal* (New York: Free Press, 1998).

31. See, e.g., Robert Cole, *Japanese Blue Collar* (Berkeley: University of California Press, 1973).

32. Björklund and Freeman, "Mot optimal ojämlikhet?," 44–45.

Rising Inequality and American Politics

1. These empirical claims are somewhat controversial because how much of an increase in income inequality depends both on the data sets used to make calculations and the measures employed. The former issue turns on whether to use census information, survey data, or data from IRS. The latter issue concerns whether changes are best captured by measures sensitive to the distribution of income as a whole (such as the Gini coefficient) or measures that focus on the share of income received by the top or bottom segments of the population. Obviously any attempt to reduce a multidimensional concept to a single number is bound to be misleading from some point of view; so there is no "right" answer to the question. The only way to choose sensibly is to be guided by the questions—in this case, normative questions—that one is attempting to address. In this essay, I am mostly concerned with the share of income earned by those at the very top of the distribution, and this leads me to rely on IRS-based data reported by Thomas Piketty and Emmanuel Saez (e.g., Wojciech Kopczuk, Emmanuel Saez, and Jae Song, "Earnings Inequality and Mobility in the United States: Evidence from Social Security Data Since 1937," *Quarterly Journal of Economics* (February 2010); Emmanuel Saez and Thomas Piketty, "The Evolution of Top Incomes: A Historical and International Perspective," *American Economic Review*, Papers and Proceedings, 96, no. 2 (2006)). For evidence on the effects of the recession on income inequality, see Timothy M. Smeeding, Jeffrey P. Thompson, Asaf Levanon, and Esra Burak, "Income, Inequality, and Poverty over the Early Stages of the Great Recession," in *The Great Recession*, ed. David B. Grusky, Bruce Western, and Chris Wimer (New York: Russell Sage Foundation, 2011).

2. Polybius later developed a theory of the "constitution" of republican Rome that saw its institutions as configured to balance or equilibrate class interests. Polybius differed from Aristotle in thinking that those institutions were born of class warfare and struggle and were not really designed for the purposes they turned out to serve.

3. Jacob Hacker, *Winner-Take-All-Politics: How Washington Made the Rich Richer—and Turned Its Back on the Middle Class* (New York: Simon and Schuster, 2010).

4. Simon Kuznets, "Economic Growth and Income Inequality," *American Economic Review* 45 (1955).

5. The empirical evidence on this issue is as disputed as the inferences that various writers have reached. A recent attempt to estimate the shape of the growth-inequality curve nonparametrically (i.e., without imposing a specific functional form) discovered great diversity among developed and developing countries, with some countries displaying the Kuznets U shape, others exhibiting an inverted U, and others revealing no curvature at all. The United States is, it should be said, exceptional in the recent rapid increase in inequality, followed distantly by the U.K. and China. See Garth Frazer, "Inequality and Development Across and Within Countries," Joseph L. Rotman School of Management, University of Toronto, Working Paper #06-02 (2006). Also see Anthony B. Atkinson, Thomas Piketty, and Emmanuel Saez, "Top Incomes in the Long Run of History," *Journal of Economic Literature* 49, no. 1 (2011).

6. Arthur Alderson, Jason Beckfield, and Francois Neilsen, "Exactly How Has Income Inequality Changed? Patterns of Distributional Change in Core Societies," Luxembourg Income Study Working Paper Series #422, May 2005.

7. Thomas Piketty and Emmanuel Saez, "Income Inequality in the United States, 1913–1998," *Quarterly Journal of Economics* 118 (2003).

8. Smeeding, using the Luxembourg Income Study, reports increases over the past quarter century in the United States, the U.K., the Netherlands, Belgium, Germany, and Norway. There has been a decline in France, and the results in Canada and Italy are mixed (though each exhibits some increase in the 1990s). Timothy Smeeding, "Public Policy, Economic Inequality, and Poverty: The United States in Comparative Perspective," *Social Science Quarterly* 86 (2005). The United States exhibits the most extreme increase and started with a fairly high base of inequality in the 1970s too. The U.S. trends are also observed by Piketty and Saez, "Income Inequality in the United States, 1913–1998," using IRS data and in other studies employing different data sets.

9. This is merely a descriptive statement. There are powerful arguments for each of these policies that point to effects other than increasing inequality. Usually these arguments focus on the desirability of generating appropriate incentives either for the economic health of the economy or for those people who do not, at the moment, participate in it fully.

10. K. Moene and M. Wallerstein, "Inequality, Social Insurance and Redistribution," *American Political Science Review* 95, no. 4 (2001): 859–74.

11. This is a controversial claim, as some argue that the relationship is contingent on political factors. See Geoffrey Garrett, *Partisan Politics in the Global Economy* (Cambridge: Cambridge University Press, 1998).

12. This argument has recently been made by Jacob Hacker.

13. Thomas Frank, the popular writer, and Yale economist John Roemer have produced arguments of this kind. Frank thinks that middle- and lower-income voters are somehow induced to vote against their own interests. Roemer argues that voters may be voting their real preferences, but that the options available are limited to candidates/parties that do not favor redistributive policies.

14. Recent estimates of the Kuznets curve suggest that the issue is even more complex than this. See Frazer, "Inequality and Development Across and Within Countries."

15. See, for example, Roland Benabou, "Inequality and Growth," in *NBER Economics Annual 1996*, ed. Ben Bernanke and Julio Rotemberg (Cambridge, MA: MIT Press, 1996).

16. For an argument that polarization is mostly confined to the political elites, see Morris Fiorina, *Culture War? The Myth of a Polarized America* (London: Longman, 2004).

17. John E. Roemer, "The Democratic Political Economy of Progressive Income Taxation," *Econometrica* 67 (1999).

18. See especially Martin Gilens, "Inequality and Democratic Responsiveness," *Public Opinion Quarterly* 69, no. 5: 778–96.

19. Larry Bartels, *Unequal Democracy: The Political Economy of the New Gilded Age* (Princeton, NJ: Princeton University Press, 2010).

Unequal Democracy in America: The Long View

1. For other influential examples, see Paul Krugman, *The Conscience of a Liberal* (New York: W. W. Norton, 2007); and Larry Bartels, *Unequal Democracy* (Princeton, NJ: Princeton University Press, 2008). Jacob Hacker and Paul Pierso's recent work, *Winner-Take-All Politics: How Washington Made the Rich Richer—and Turned Its Back on the Middle Class* (New York: Simon and Schuster, 2010), however, makes a similar historical point to the one here.

2. Thomas Piketty and Emmanuel Saez, "Income and Wage Inequality in the United States, 1913–2002," in Anthony Atkinson and Thomas Piketty, eds., *Top Incomes over the 20th Century* (New York: Oxford University Press, 2007), 141–225. For the comparative long-term evidence, see Anthony Atkinson, Thomas Piketty, and Emanuel Saez, "Top Incomes in the Long Run of History," *Journal of Economic Literature* 49 (2011): 3–71.

3. Clem Brooks and Jeff Manza, *Why Welfare States Persist* (Chicago: University of Chicago Press, 2007), chap. 1.

4. See Jacob Hacker, *The Divided Welfare State* (New York: Cambridge University Press, 2002); Irwin Garfinkel, Lee Rainwater, and Timothy Smeeding, *Wealth and Welfare States: Is America a Laggard or a Leader?* (New York: Russell Sage Foundation Press, 2010).

5. See U.S. Department of Labor, http://www.dol.gov/whd/minwage/chart .htm.

6. For an outstanding account of these debates, see Alexander Keyssar, *The Right to Vote* (New York: Basic Books, 2000), ch. 1. For an extended meditation on the visions of democracy embedded in the Constitution, see Robert Dahl, *How Democratic Is the American Constitution?* (New Haven, CT: Yale University Press, 2003).

7. Federal legislation following the Florida 2000 debacle has further codified federal control over state election laws. Under the Help Americans Vote Act of 2002 (HAVA), the states are now required to actually count all ballots, maintain accurate lists of eligible voters, and allow contested ballots to be cast and reviewed later if an election is sufficiently close for it to matter.

8. International Institute for Democracy and Electoral Assistance (IDEA), *Voter Turnout from 1945 to 1997: A Global Report* (Stockholm: IDEA, 1997); see also Richard Freeman, "What, Me Vote?," in Kathryn Neckerman, ed., *Social Inequality* (New York: Russell Sage Foundation Press, 2004), 703–28.

9. Arend Lijphart, "Unequal Participation: Democracy's Unresolved Dilemma," *American Political Science Review* 91 (1997); Jeff Manza and Clem Brooks, *Social Cleavages and Political Change: Voter Alignments and U.S. Party Coalitions* (New York: Oxford University Press, 1999), ch. 7; and Freeman, "What, Me Vote?"

10. Lipjhart, "Unequal Participation," 2–3.

11. G. Bingham Powell, "American Voter Turnout in Comparative Perspective," *American Political Science Review* 80 (1986); Frances Fox Piven and Richard Cloward, *Why Americans Still Don't Vote* (New York: New Press, 2000).

12. Ruy Teixeira, *The Disappearing American Voter* (Washington, DC: Brookings Institute, 1992), 122.

13. Mark Franklin, "Electoral Participation," in Laurence LeDuc, Richard G. Niemi, and Pippa Norris, eds., *Comparing Democracies: Elections and Voting in Global Perspective* (Thousand Oaks, CA: Sage Publications, 1996).

14. However, Freeman, "What, Me Vote?," 715–16, notes one little-known example that implies the impact may be even greater. He compares the extraordinary differences in turnout between Puerto Ricans voting in American national elections in Puerto Rico (where the vote is held on either Sunday or a national holiday and produces turnout above 80 percent), versus Puerto Ricans living on the U.S. mainland (who vote without such flexibility and have turnout rates at less than half that level).

15. E.g., Steven J. Rosenstone and John Mark Hansen, *Mobilization, Participation, and Democracy in America* (New York: Macmillan, 1993); Jan Leighley, *Strength in Numbers? The Political Mobilization of Racial and Ethnic Minorities* (Princeton, NJ: Princeton University Press, 2001); Donald Green and Alan Gerber, *Get Out the Vote: How to Increase Voter Turnout* (Washington, DC: Brookings Institute Press, 2004).

16. See Sidney Verba, Norman Nie, and Jae-On Kim, *Participation and Political Equality: A Seven-Nation Comparison* (Chicago: University of Chicago Press, 1987); Powell, "American Voter Turnout"; Benjamin Radcliff and Patricia Davis, "Labor Organization and Electoral Participation in Industrial Democracies," *American Journal of Political Science* 44 (2000): 132–44.

17. Leighley, *Strength in Numbers?*

18. V. O. Key, *Southern Politics in State and Nation* (Cambridge, MA: Harvard University Press, 1964 [1949]), 527.

19. Sidney Verba, Kay Lehman Scholzman, and Henry Brady, *Voice and Equality* (Cambridge, MA: Harvard University Press, 1995).

20. Kim Voss, *The Making of American Exceptionalism* (Ithaca, NY: Cornell University Press, 1994).

21. William Forbath, *Law and the Shaping of the American Labor Movement* (Cambridge, MA: Harvard University Press, 1991); Steve Fraser, *Labor Will Rule: Sidney Hillman and the Rise of American Labor* (Ithaca, NY: Cornell University Press, 1993); Nelson Lichtenstein, *State of the Union: A Century of American Labor* (Princeton, NJ: Princeton University Press, 2003).

22. See, e.g., Steven J. Rosenstone, Roy L. Behr, and Edward H. Lazarus, *Third Parties in America*, 2nd ed. (Princeton, NJ: Princeton University Press, 1996); Michael Kazin, *The Populist Persuasion* (Ithaca, NY: Cornell University Press, 1998); Micah Sifry, *Spoiling for a Fight: Third-Party Politics in America* (New York: Routledge, 2003).

23. Rosenstone, Behr, and Lazarus, *Third Parties in America*. The most important of these party efforts were those of the populists at the end of the nineteenth century, socialists and communist parties in the first half of the twentieth century, Midwestern Progressive and farmer-labor parties in the 1930s, and in the recent era of increased third-party activism a plethora of efforts by libertarians, Ross Perot's Reform Party, the Green Party, the short-lived New Party, and others (for an overview, see Sifry, *Spoiling for a Fight*).

24. See, e.g., Melvyn Dubofsky, *The State and Labor in Modern America* (Chapel Hill: University of North Carolina Press, 1994); and Taylor Dark, *The Unions and the Democrats: An Enduring Alliance* (Ithaca, NY: Cornell University Press, 1999).

25. See Michael Brown, *Race, Money, and the American Welfare State* (New York: Cambridge University Press, 1999). To be sure, Southern Democrats historically were strongly supportive of social spending programs that could be controlled by state governments; it is incorrect to view them as "conservatives" in

the conventional sense. See, e.g., Keith Poole and Howard Rosenthal, *Congress: A Political-Economic History of Roll-Call Voting* (New York: Oxford University Press, 1997).

26. Werner Sombart, *Why Is There No Socialism in the United States?* (White Plains, NY: M. E. Sharpe, 1976); see also Jerome Karabel, "The Failure of American Socialism Reconsidered," in Ralph Miliband and John Saville, eds., *The Socialist Register 1979* (London: Merlin Press, 1979), 204–27.

27. Alexander Hicks, *Social Democracy and Welfare Capitalism* (Ithaca, NY: Cornell University Press, 1999); Evelyne Huber and John Stephens, *Development and Crisis of the Welfare State* (Chicago: University of Chicago Press, 2001); Duane Swank, *Global Capital, Political Institutions, and Policy Change in Developed Welfare States* (New York: Cambridge University Press, 2002).

28. Brooks and Manza, *Why Welfare States Persist*, ch. 1.

29. E.g., John Zaller, *The Nature and Origins of Mass Opinion* (New York: Cambridge University Press, 1992).

30. Jill Quadagno, *The Color of Welfare* (New York: Oxford University Press, 1994).

31. See, e.g., Morton Horwitz, *The Transformation of American Law, 1870–1960: The Crisis of Legal Orthodoxy* (New York: Oxford University Press, 1992).

32. Robert Lieberman, *Shifting the Color Line* (Princeton, NJ: Princeton University Press, 1998); Jill Quadagno, *The Color of Welfare*.

33. On labor policy, see Joel Rogers, "Divide and Conquer: Further 'Reflections on the Distinctive Character of American Labor Laws,'" *University of Wisconsin Law Review 1990* (1990): 1–147; on the frustration of national health insurance, see Colin Gordon, *Dead on Arrival: The Politics of Health Care in Twentieth-Century America* (Princeton, NJ: Princeton University Press, 2004); on the New Deal, see Edwin Amenta, *Bold Relief* (Princeton, NJ: Princeton University Press, 1998); on the Great Society, see Quadagno, *The Color of Welfare*; on the right to vote, see Keyssar, *The Right to Vote*. This list could be extended quite considerably—the role of fragmentation and decentralized policy-making as a source of conservative strength in the American system is one of the most enduring and powerful tropes of American history.

34. The case, *Citizens United v. Federal Election Commission*, 558 U.S. 50 (2010), was decided by a 5-4 vote. It held that Congress could not lawfully limit the right of corporations to make unlimited "independent" expenditures on behalf of candidates for office. The full impact of the ruling is not yet clear, but concerns about its potential impact are high. A normally cautious President Barack Obama immediately denounced the ruling, calling it "a major victory for big oil, Wall Street banks, health insurance companies and the other powerful interests that marshal their power every day in Washington to drown out the voices of everyday Americans," and generating headlines by staring down the justices while denouncing the ruling in his 2010 State of the Union address to

Congress. A key earlier ruling was *Buckley v. Valeo*, 424 U.S. 1 (1976), which barred Congress from setting limits on "independent" expenditures on behalf of candidates or parties.

35. Louise Overacker, *Money in Elections* (New York: Macmillan, 1932).

36. See Robert K. Goidel, Donald A. Gross, and Todd G. Shields, *Money Matters: Consequences of Campaign Finance Reform in U.S. House Elections* (New York: Rowman and Littlefield, 1999). The most recent attempt at reform, the 2002 legislation known as the Bipartisan Campaign Reform Act or McCain-Feingold (after its congressional sponsors), establishes a financing structure in which in each two-year election cycle individuals may contribute up to $2,100 (now $2,300) to any candidate, $10,000 to a political action committee (PAC), and $28,500 to national parties, and up to $108,200 total. PACs are allowed to contribute up to $5,000 each election to a candidate, $5,000 to other PACs, and $15,000 to national parties. McCain-Feingold eliminated unregulated so-called "soft money" contributions, but still permits unlimited spending for "issue advocacy" under a provision known as section 527. It has been gutted by a variety of federal court rulings, most notoriously the *Citizens United* ruling cited in note 34, so that independent campaigns on behalf of candidates are also still permitted.

37. See Thomas Ferguson, *Golden Rule* (Chicago: University of Chicago Press, 1995); and Mark A. Smith, *American Business and Political Power* (Chicago: University of Chicago Press, 2000).

38. Stephen Ansolabehere and Alan Gerber, "The Mismeasure of Campaign Spending: Evidence from the 1990 U.S. House Elections," *Journal of Politics* 56 (1994): 1115.

39. There are a couple of common issues that recur. Most notably, there are linked questions about simultaneity bias and assumptions about the endogenity of money in the political process. For instance, statistical studies that treat campaign contributions as an exogenous variable tend to ignore the possibility that PACs give legislators money *because* these legislators vote in a particular way. Such models are unable to distinguish between these two scenarios. The most sophisticated attempts to model the role of money at any stage of the political process attempt to build in parameters for capturing processes that may shape *both* the amounts of money received and their impact, but analytical difficulties continue.

40. My colleagues and I have developed a broader summary of the data and evidence elsewhere; see Jeff Manza, Clem Brooks, and Michael Sauder, "Money, Participation, and Votes: Social Cleavages and Electoral Politics," in Thomas Janoski et al., eds., *Handbook of Political Sociology* (New York: Cambridge University Press, 2004), 201–26.

41. "Guide to the Money in U.S. Elections," Center for Responsive Politics, http://opensecrets.org/, accessed May 15, 2007.

42. For an overview of this literature, see Manza et al., "Money, Participation, and Votes."

43. See Stephen Ansolabehere, John M. de Figueiredo, and James M. Snyder, "Why Is There So Little Money in U.S. Politics?," *Journal of Economic Perspectives* 17 (2003).

44. Dan Clawson, Alan Neustadtl, and Mark Weller, *Dollars and Votes* (Philadelphia: Temple University Press, 1998).

45. Clawson and his colleagues (ibid.) provide a compelling analysis of the case of the Clean Air Act amendments of 1990, a nearly 900-page piece of legislation filled with exemptions for individual companies that partially, though not completely, offset the overall goals of the legislation. See Dan Clawson, Alan Neustadtl, and Mark Weller, *Money Talks: How Business Campaign Contributions Subvert Democracy* (Philadelphia: Temple University Press, 1998).

46. For an exception, see Claude Fischer and Michael Hout, *Century of Difference: How America Changed in the Past 100 Years* (New York: Russell Sage Foundation Press, 2006), ch. 6.

47. Simon Johnson and James Kwak, *13 Bankers: The Wall Street Takeover and the Next Financial Meltdown* (New York: Pantheon, 2010), 61–64.

48. Michael Hout, "More Universalism and Less Structural Mobility: The American Occupational Structure in the 1980s," *American Journal of Sociology* 93 (1988): 1358–1400.

49. Claudia Golden and Lawrence Katz, *The Race Between Technology and Education* (Cambridge, MA: Harvard University Press, 2010).

50. Krugman, *Conscience of a Liberal*, 3.

51. John Skrentny, *The Minority Rights Revolution* (Cambridge, MA: Harvard University Press, 2004); Brian Steensland, *The Failed Welfare Revolution: America's Struggle over Guaranteed Income Policy* (Princeton, NJ: Princeton University Press, 2007).

52. See Gerald Davis, *Managed by the Markets* (New York: Oxford University Press, 2009), for an overview.

53. Johnson and Kwak, *13 Bankers*, ch. 3; see also Neil Fligstein and Adam Goldstein, "The Anatomy of the Mortgage Securitization Crisis," *Research in the Sociology of Organizations* 30A: 29–70.

54. Thomas Phillipon and Ariell Reshef, "Wages and Human Capital in the U.S. Financial Industry, 1909–2006" (Unpublished ms., Stern School of Business, New York University, 2008).

55. Jeff Manza, "The Right to Vote," in Jeff Manza and Michael Sauder, eds., *Inequality and Society* (New York: Norton, 2009), 846–56.

56. See, e.g., Jan Leighley and Jonathan Nagler, "The Voters Remain the Same: Socioeconomic Class Bias in Turnout, 1964–1988," *American Political Science Review* 86 (1992); and Michael Hout, Clem Brooks, and Jeff Manza, "The Democratic Class Struggle in the United States, 1948–1992," *American Sociological Review* 60 (1995): 805–28.

57. Freeman, "What, Me Vote?"; Leighley and Nagler, "The Voters Remain the Same."

58. Note, however, that companies cannot give directly in their own name; firm-level political action committees are financed through donations from corporate executives. Firms may give to association committees representing a number of different businesses in, say, a single industry or to the Chamber of Commerce. Direct firm investment takes the form of paying for ever more elaborate lobbying operations separate from (though indirectly linked to) campaign contributions.

59. Eric Klinenberg, *Fighting for Air* (New York: Metropolitan Books, 2006).

60. Hacker and Pierson, *Winner-Take-All Politics*.

61. Andrew Rich, *Think Tanks, Public Policy, and the Politics of Expertise* (New York: Cambridge University Press, 2004); G. William Domhoff, *Who Rules America?* (New York: McGraw-Hill, 2004).

62. John Kingdon, *Agenda, Alternatives, and Public Policies* (New York: Longman, 1995).

63. See Rich, *Think Tanks*, for a recent summary.

64. The absence of competing and similarly endowed policy organizations promoting progressive ideas has remained something of a mystery. Foundations supporting programs aimed at helping the poor and progressive civic activism have resources that far exceed those of conservative foundations supporting right-wing think tanks and policy organizations. But these organizations have not invested in ideas to nearly the same degree as the leading conservative foundations. For details, see Domhoff, *Who Rules America?*, ch. 4.

65. Cf. Sean Wilentz, *The Age of Reagan, 1974–2008* (New York: Harper, 2008).

66. Jacob Hacker and Paul Pierson, *Off Center* (New York: Oxford University Press, 2005).

67. Bartels, *Unequal Democracy*, chap. 3; Nolan McCarty, Keith Poole, and Howard Rosenthal, *Polarized America* (Cambridge, MA: MIT Press, 2006).

68. Clem Brooks and David Brady, "Income, Economic Voting, and Long-Term Political Change in the U.S., 1952–1996," *Social Forces* 77 (1999):

69. McCarty, Poole, and Rosenthal, *Polarized America*; Bartels, *Unequal Democracy*.

70. See David Grusky and Jesper Sorensen, "Can Class Analysis Be Salvaged?," *American Journal of Sociology* 103 (1998).

71. Hout, Brooks, and Manza, "The Democratic Class Struggle in the United States"; see also Manza and Brooks, *Social Cleavages and Political Change*, ch. 3.

72. Michael Hout and Benjamin Moody, "The Realignment of U.S. Presidential Voting, 1948–2004," in David B. Grusky, ed., *Social Stratification* (Stanford: Stanford University Press, 2006), 945–54.

73. Thomas Frank, *What's the Matter with Kansas?* (New York: Metropolitan Books, 2004).

74. Manza and Brooks, *Social Cleavages and Political Change*, ch. 3.

75. Bartels, in *Unequal Democracy*, ch. 3, challenges Frank's evidence of shifting class voting, in relation to either income groups or educational level. Bartels shows that neither voters with low education or low income have moved toward the Republicans as Frank claims.

76. Jeff Manza and Clem Brooks, "Classes and Politics," in Annette Lareau and Dalton Conley, eds., *Social Class: How Does It Work?* (New York: Russell Sage Foundation Press), 201–31.

77. Jeff Manza and Clem Brooks, *Social Cleavages and Political Change: U.S. Party Coalitions Since the 1960s* (New York: Oxford University Press, 1999), chap. 7.

78. Bartels, *Unequal Democracy*; and Nathan Kelley, *The Politics of Income Inequality* (New York: Cambridge University Press, 2009).

79. See Manza and Brooks, *Social Cleavages and Political Change*; and Clem Brooks and Jeff Manza, "A Great Divide? Religion and Political Change in U.S. National Elections, 1972–2000," *Sociological Quarterly* 45 (2004): 421–50.

80. See Jeff Manza and Clem Brooks, "The Changing Political Fortunes of Mainline Protestants," in Robert Wuthnow and John Evans, eds., *The Quiet Hand of God: The Public Role of Mainline Protestantism* (Berkeley: University of California Press, 2002), 159–80.

81. See, e.g., Brooks and Manza, *Why Welfare States Persist*.

82. Jeff Manza, Jennifer Heerwig, and Brian McCabe, "Political Trends 1972–2006: What Impact Did the Republican Resurgence Have on Mass Opinion?," forthcoming in Peter Marsden, ed., *Social Trends in the United States, 1972–2006* (Princeton, NJ: Princeton University Press, 2012).

83. For an overview of the upsurge, see Michael Goldfield, "Worker Insurgency, Radical Organization, and New Deal Labor Legislation," *American Political Science Review* 83 (1989): 1257–82.

84. David S. Meyer and Sidney Tarrow, eds., *The Social Movement Society* (Lanham, MD: Rowman and Littlefield, 1997).

85. As I write these lines, the Occupy Wall Street movement that began in the fall of 2011 continues to maintain an active presence in lower Manhattan and elsewhere around the United States. OWS explicitly challenges rising inequality and the political regime that supports it. Whether the movement will grow into a potent political force, or is the beginning of a new wave of social movement challenges, is at this writing unclear.

86. Cf. Manza and Brooks, *Social Cleavages and Political Change*, ch. 5.

A Human Capital Account of the Gender Pay Gap

1. This essay emanates from a debate between me and Fran Blau that took place at Cornell University, March 7, 2003. That debate stimulated my article "How the Life-Cycle Human-Capital Model Explains Why the Gender Wage Gap Narrowed," published in Francine Blau, Mary Brinton, and David Grusky, *The*

Declining Significance of Gender? (New York: Russell Sage Foundation, 2006). This essay is an update and extension. My special thanks to Francine Blau and David Grusky for their stimulating discussions and valuable comments.

2. Betsy Morris, "Trophy Husbands," *Fortune*, October 14, 2002.

3. Ibid., 80.

4. For example, see The Shriver Report, available at http://awomansnation .com/execSum.php.

5. The film *Kramer vs. Kramer*, directed by Robert Benton (1979) and starring Dustin Hoffman and Meryl Streep, illustrates how divorce causes a particular husband's household responsibilities to change so much that he is forced to take a job with fewer responsibilities.

6. The classic film *Manhanagar* (The Big City), by Satyajit Ray (1963), describes such an example for India, but the story could have taken place in many other countries, including the United States.

7. For a recent analysis of societal discrimination and its effects on labor force participation, see M. Cunningham, "Influences of Gender Ideology and Housework Allocation on Women's Employment over the Life Course," *Social Science Research* 37 (2007).

8. Morris, "Trophy Husbands," 80.

9. For further discussion of this deceleration, see Francine Blau and Lawrence Kahn, "The US Gender Pay Gap in the 1990s: Slowing Convergence," NBER Working Paper No. 10853 (2004), and Pamela Stone, "Getting to Equal: Progress, Pitfalls, and Policy Solutions on the Road to Gender Parity in the Workplace," *Pathways* (Spring 2009).

10. This data set is described at www.bls.gov/nls/home.htm.

11. Carole Miller, "Actual Experience, Potential Experience or Age, and Labor Force Participation by Married Women," *Atlantic Economic Journal* 21, no. 4 (1993).

12. Moon-Kak Kim and Solomon Polachek, "Panel Estimates of the Gender Earnings Gap: Individual Specific Intercept and Individual Specific Slope Models," *Journal of Econometrics* 61, no. 1 (1994).

13. Wayne Simpson, "Intermittent Work Activities and Earnings," *Applied Economics* 32, no. 14 (2000).

14. "Workplace Flexibility Is Still a Women's Advancement Issue," Catalyst, http://64.233.167.104/u/Catalyst?q=cache:BGumQKH8saEJ:www .catalystwomen.org/bo okstore/files/view/Workplace%2520Flexibility%2520Is% 2520Still%2520a%2520Wome n%27s%2520Advancement%2520Issue.pdf+mba +and+men+and+women&hl=en&ie=UTF-8.

15. Susan Harkness and Jane Waldfogel, "The Family Gap in Pay: Evidence from Seven Industrialized Countries," in *Research in Labor Economics, Volume 22: Worker Well-Being and Public Policy*, ed. S. Polachek (2003).

16. Jacob Mincer, "Investments in Human Capital and Personal Income Distribution," *Journal of Political Economy* 66, no. 5 (1958), and *Schooling, Experience and Earnings* (New York: Columbia University Press, 1974).

17. Yoram Ben-Porath, "The Production of Human Capital over the Lifecycle," *Journal of Political Economy* 75 (1967).

18. There are some other more intangible benefits, like how one conducts him/herself in everyday life, as well as social benefits such as reduced crime, lower unemployment, and greater economic growth. Some of these intangible benefits are addressed in Robert Michael, "Education on Non-Market Production," *Journal of Political Economy* 81 (1973), as well as in Dora Polachek and Solomon Polachek, "An Indirect Test of Children's Influence on Efficiencies in Parental Consumer Behavior," *Journal of Consumer Affairs* 23, no. 1 (1989). Such social and familial benefits might be one reason why some cultures value more highly educated wives even though these cultures advocate wives being in the home rather than the workplace. I don't deal with these social benefits in this essay.

19. See Elisabeth Landes, "Sex-Differences in Wages and Employment: A Test of the Specific Capital Hypothesis," *Economic Inquiry* 15, no. 4 (1977).

20. This phenomenon is also true over the life cycle. Studies that examine life-cycle earning within families show that the husband–wife wage gap is largest during the childbearing years (e.g., Solomon Polachek, "Potential Biases in Measuring Male-Female Discrimination," *Journal of Human Resources* 10, no. 2 (1975)).

21. The present value of a human capital investment such as training is the discounted value of the increased wages one receives over the remainder of one's work-life. In mathematical terms, this is $\sum_{i=1}^{R} \dfrac{\Delta y}{(1+r)^i}$, where R is the number of years one expects to stay on the job reaping returns from the investment, ΔY is the extra earnings the human R capital yields, and r is the discount rate. In continuous time, the present value is $\int_{0}^{R} \Delta Y e^{-rt}\, dt$. The present value of any given investment diminishes as one gets older because R is smaller for older individuals.

22. Edward Lazear and Sherwin Rosen, "Rank-Order Tournaments as Optimum Labor Contracts," *Journal of Political Economy* 89, no. 5 (1981).

23. Solomon Polachek, "Differences in Expected Post-School Investment as a Determinant of Market Wage Differentials," *International Economic Review* 16 (1975); Yoram Weiss and Reuben Gronau, "Expected Interruptions in Labor Force Participation and Sex Related Differences in Earnings Growth," *Review of Economic Studies* 48, no. 4 (1981).

24. Jacob Mincer and Solomon Polachek, "Family Investments in Human Capital," *Journal of Political Economy* 82 (1974).

25. Obtained from the University of Chicago Economics 350 website: http://lily.src.uchicago.edu/econ350/mincer_graphs.pdf.

26. Blau and Kahn, "The US Gender Pay Gap in the 1990s."

27. Harkness and Waldfogel, "The Family Gap in Pay."

28. Polachek, "Potential Biases in Measuring Male-Female Discrimination."

29. Ibid.

30. Michael J. Greenacre and Jörg Blasius, eds., *Correspondence Analysis in the Social Sciences: Recent Developments and Applications* (London and San Diego, CA: Academic Press, 1994); see also Shelley J. Correll, Stephen Benard, and In Paik, "Getting a Job: Is There a Motherhood Penalty?," *American Journal of Sociology* 112 (2007).

31. Phillip Nelson and Solomon Polachek, "Discerning Discrimination: Does Interviewing Firms Make a Difference?," *Eastern Economic Journal* 21, no. 3 (1995). James J. Heckman and Peter Siegelman, "The Urban Institute Audit Studies: Their Methods and Findings," in *Clear and Convincing Evidence: Measurement of Discrimination in America* (Washington, DC: Urban Institute Press, 1993), and Heckman, "Detecting Discrimination," *Journal of Economic Perspectives* 12, no. 2 (1998), raise other, more technical pitfalls of the approach.

32. Jennifer M. Mellor and Elizabeth A. Paulin, "The Effects of Gender and Race on Salary Growth: The Role of Occupational Structure in a Service Sector Firm," *Eastern Economic Journal* 21, no. 3 (1995); David Neumark, "Sex Discrimination in Restaurant Hiring: An Audit Study," *Quarterly Journal of Economics* 111, no. 3 (1996).

33. Marianne Bertrand and Sendhil Mullainathan, "Are Emily and Greg More Employable than Lakisha and Jamal? A Field Experiment on Labor Market Discrimination," *American Economic Review* 94, no. 4 (2004).

34. The 1992 U.S. Bureau of Census *Characteristics of Business Owners* Survey indicates a smaller proportion of businesses owned by women (especially among older women, where discrimination is likely to be greatest) and fewer women employed in female-owned businesses. See http://www.census.gov/csd /cbo/1992/www/cbo9201.htm.

35. Barbara Bergmann, "Occupational Segregation, Wages, and Profits When Employers Discriminate by Race or Sex," *Eastern Economic Review* 1, no. 1–2 (1974), was probably the first to popularize occupational segregation models.

36. The theory was developed by Masatoshi Kuratani, "A Theory of Training, Earnings and Employment in Japan" (PhD diss., Columbia University, 1973), and repeated in Masanori Hashimoto, "Specific Human Capital as a Shared Investment," *American Economic Review* 71 (1981).

37. James Smith and Finis Welch, "Affirmative Action and the Labor Market," *Journal of Labor Economics* 2 (1984).

38. Ibid., 273, indicates that in 1970 only 340 Title VII cases were filed in federal courts, whereas in 1981, 6,250 cases were filed. One should note (as an anonymous referee pointed out) that a number of these cases refer to race discrimination.

39. Solomon Polachek and John Robst, "Trends in the Male-Female Wage Gap: The 1980s Compared to the 1970s," *Southern Economic Journal* 67, no. 4 (2001).

40. Harry Holzer and David Neumark, "Assessing Affirmative Action," *Journal of Economic Literature* 38, no. 3 (2000): 558.

41. Harish Jain, Peter Sloane, and Frank Horwitz, *Employment Equity and Affirmative Action: An International Comparison* (New York and London: M. E. Sharpe, 2003), 214.

42. Francine Blau, Marianne Ferber, and Anne Winkler, *The Economics of Women, Men and Work* (Upper Saddle River, NJ: Prentice-Hall, 2002), 242.

43. Ibid., 243.

44. Polachek, "Potential Biases in Measuring Male-Female Discrimination."

45. Sanders Korenman and David Neumark, "Marriage, Motherhood, and Wages," *Journal of Human Resources* 27, no. 2 (1992).

46. Jane Waldfogel, "Understanding the 'Family Gap' in Pay for Women with Children," *Journal of Economic Perspectives* 12, no. 1 (1998).

47. Michelle Budig and Paula England, "The Wage Penalty for Motherhood," *American Sociological Review* 66, no. 2 (2001).

48. Charles Baum, "The Effect of Work Interruptions on Women's Wages," *Labour* 16, no. 1 (2002): 2.

49. Mark Berger et al., "Children, Non-Discriminatory Provision of Fringe Benefits, and Household Labor Market Decisions," *Research in Labor Economics* 22 (2003): 309.

50. Heather Joshi, Pierella Paci, and Jane Waldfogel, "The Wages of Motherhood: Better or Worse," *Cambridge Journal of Economics* 23, no. 5 (1999). Not adjusting more directly for labor market expectations could account for why childless women earn less than childless men. See Claudia Goldin and Solomon Polachek, "Residual Differences by Sex: Perspectives on the Gender Gap in Earnings," *American Economic Review* 77 (1987).

51. E.g., Polachek, "Potential Biases in Measuring Male-Female Discrimination"; Richard J. Butler, "Estimating Wage Discrimination in the Labor Market," *Journal of Human Resources* 17, no. 4 (1982); F. L. Jones, "On Decomposing the Gender Wage Gap: A Critical Comment on Blinder's Decomposition," *Journal of Human Resources* 18, no. 1 (1983); George Borjas, *Labor Economics* (New York: McGraw Hill, 2005), 377.

52. E.g., Polachek, "Differences in Expected Post-School Investment"; Goldin and Polachek, "Residual Differences by Sex"; and Charng Kao, Solomon Polachek, and Phanindra Wunnava, "Male-Female Wage Differentials in Taiwan," *Economic Development and Cultural Change* 42, no. 2 (1994).

53. These patterns are illustrated in Mincer and Polachek, "Family Investments in Human Capital."

54. Ibid.

55. Elaine Sorensen, "Continuous Female Workers: How Different Are They from Other Women?," *Eastern Economic Journal* 19, no. 1 (1993).

56. Actually, it is more like one and a half years according to Kim and Polachek, "Panel Estimates of Male-Female Earnings Functions."

57. This is a prediction of the human capital model. See Polachek, "Differences in Expected Post-School Investment," and Weiss and Gronau, "Expected Interruptions in Labor Force Participation."

58. Alternatively, one could ask what men would earn if they had discontinuous labor force participation rather than full-time participation. Each approach gives a different answer because female earnings function parameters differ from male earnings function parameters. Ronald Oaxaca and Michael Ransom recently became aware of this problem and as a result suggested a weighted average technique to combine the answers to both questions. But in reality, this weighted average approach is essentially comparable to estimating a gender dummy categorical variable in a wage regression using *both* male and female data. It turns out that this dummy categorical approach is the same as that used in the original initial empirical wage discrimination studies, such as Victor Fuchs, "Differences in Hourly Earning Between Men and Women," *Monthly Labor Review* 94 (1971).

59. Studies without work history information (e.g., Ronald Oaxaca, "Male-Female Wage Differentials in Urban Labor Markets," *International Economic Review* 14, no. 3 (1973)) aggregate e_1 and H (i.e., $e = e_1 + H$). This biases downward the e_1 coefficient, thereby leading to even lower projected female earnings than D. This erroneous specification severely overestimates discrimination. See Mincer and Polachek, "Family Investments in Human Capital."

60. I expositied this bias in terms of how to appropriately account for expected lifetime labor force participation. However, the arguments are more general. This generalization can be elucidated mathematically. Typically DK is estimated from a regression model. Female earnings B are estimated from earnings function $y = f_F(x_F)$, where $y = \ln y$, and x is a vector of worker characteristics including e_1, H, and e_2, as well as other worker attributes such as industry, occupation, race, union status, and more. The F subscript in f indicates that the earnings function is estimated with data on females. Male values for x are denoted by x_M. Female values are denoted as x_F. The value $y_F = f_F(x_M)$ equals projected female earnings, had women male characteristics (e.g., zero H). It is comparable to D in Exhibit 12. Male earnings (K) are estimated by $y_M = f_M(x_M)$. The difference D – K represents discrimination—the gap in earnings between what males make and what females should make if they had male characteristics. This measure is often called the "Blinder-Oaxaca" decomposition because Alan Blinder ("Wage Discrimination: Reduced Form and Structural Estimates," *Journal of Human Resources* 8, no. 4 (1973)) and Ronald Oaxaca ("Male-Female Wage Differentials in Urban Labor Markets") were the first to apply this type of decomposition to gender differences in wages. However, the problem is that this decomposition approach is marred by bias. To see the problem, note that the measure assumes that discrimination is defined by differences in male and female earnings functions because $K - D = y_M - y_F = f_M(x_M) - f_F(x_M)$. This means that male–female differences in characteristics (i.e., $x_M - x_F$) are deemed legitimate reasons for gender earnings differences, whereas male–female differences in earnings structure (i.e., $f_M - f_F$) constitute discrimination. But, there are two major biases. First, discrimination is overestimated if f_M differs from f_F for legitimate reasons. As mentioned, human capital theory predicts f_M to be steeper

270 Notes to A Human Capital Account of the Gender Pay Gap

than f_F when female lifetime work expectations are less than male lifetime work expectations. Second, discrimination is underestimated when x_M and x_F differ because of discrimination. As will be discussed, one can easily argue that women work less than men do because society dictates that they are burdened with home responsibilities.

61. These biases are pointed out in a number of papers (e.g., Polachek, "Potential Biases in Measuring Male-Female Discrimination," Butler, "Estimating Wage Discrimination," and Jones, "On Decomposing the Gender Wage Gap") and are even in an undergraduate labor economics textbook (Borjas, *Labor Economics*).

62. This is obtained as follows: 0.20/0.40 = 50% and 0.25/0.40 = 62.5%.

63. For example, see Polachek, "Differences in Expected Post-School Investment," Goldin and Polachek, "Residual Differences by Sex," and Kao, Polachek, and Wunnava, "Male-Female Wage Differentials in Taiwan."

64. Barry Chiswick et al., "The Effect of Occupation on Race and Sex Differences in Hourly Earnings," *Review of Public Use* 3, no. 7 (1975).

65. Donald Treiman and Heidi Hartmann, eds., *Women, Work and Wages: Equal Pay for Equal Value* (Washington, DC: National Academy Press, 1981). Trond Peterson and Laurie Morgan ("Separate and Unequal: Occupation-Establishment Sex Segregation and the Gender Wage Gap," *American Journal of Sociology* 101, no. 2 (1995)) argue that occupational segregation explains as much as 64 percent of the gender wage gap. However, this study is not comparable to others because it restricts itself to two narrow samples (one a sixteen-industry study and the other a study of ten professional and administrative occupations), rather than an economy-wide investigation as in other studies. But more importantly, the study appears to contain computational idiosyncrasies. For example, it finds women earn 5.3 percent *more* than men in the hospital industry. Yet, the study claims that occupation explains 178.7 percent of this industry's gender wage *gap*. Surely occupational segregation might be important in this industry, especially if it includes physicians. But according to the table there is no wage gap; women earn more than men!

66. In "Occupational Self-Selection: A Human Capital Approach to Sex Differences in Occupational Structure," *Review of Economics and Statistics* 63, no. 1 (1981), I show how lifetime human capital accumulation helps determine occupational choice. Although there has been some debate about the model's validity, the latest evidence seems to corroborate its predictions. See John Robst and Jennifer VanGilder, "Atrophy Rates in Male and Female Occupations," *Economics Letters* 9, no. 3 (2000).

67. George Johnson and Gary Solon, "Estimates of the Direct Effects of Comparable Worth Policy," *American Economic Review* 76, no. 5 (1986).

68. Paula England, "The Failure of Human Capital Theory to Explain Occupational Segregation," *Journal of Human Resources* 17 (1982). Also see my rebuttal in "Occupational Segregation: A Defense of Human Capital Predictions," *Journal of Human Resources* 20, no. 3 (1985), and "Occupational

Segregation and the Gender Wage Gap," *Population Research and Policy Review* 6, no. 1 (1987).

69. Victor Fuchs, "Differences in Hourly Earning Between Men and Women."

70. David Macpherson and Barry Hirsch, "Wages and Gender Composition: Why Do Women's Jobs Pay Less?," *Journal of Labor Economics* 13 (1995).

71. Silke Aisenbrey and Hannah Brückner, "Occupational Aspirations, Gender Segregation, and the Gender Gap in Wages," *European Sociological Review* 42 (2008).

72. Claudia Goldin, *Understanding the Gender Gap: An Economic History of American Women* (Oxford: Oxford University Press, 1990).

73. June O'Neill, "The Gender Gap in Wages, Circa 2000," *American Economic Review* 93, no. 2 (2003).

74. Based on CPS Outgoing Rotation Groups, O'Neill, ibid., finds that the gender wage ratio is 0.792 in 1994, 0.788 in 1995, 0.795 in 1996, 0.796 in 1997, 0.793 in 1998, 0.789 in 1999, 0.793 in 2000, and 0.798 in 2001.

75. Polachek and Robst, "Trends in the Male-Female Wage Gap."

76. According to Francine Blau, Marianne Ferber, and Anne Winkler, the average annual increase in labor force participation was .7 percentage points for the 1980s and .8 percentage points for the 1970s, but declined to .3 percentage points in the 1990s. See Blau, Ferber, and Winkler, *The Economics of Women, Men and Work*, Chapter 4, footnote 4.

77. Polachek and Robst, "Trends in the Male-Female Wage Gap."

78. Francine Blau and Lawrence Kahn, "Swimming Upstream: Trends in the Gender Wage Differential in the 1980s," *Journal of Labor Economics* 15 (1997).

79. June O'Neill, "The Gender Gap in Wages."

80. Those countries with no reported hourly wages have annual earnings. These data could have been used to compute earnings variance. But in order to be consistent with the computations done for the United States, I limited the analysis to countries reporting hourly earnings.

81. Blau and Kahn, "The US Gender Pay Gap in the 1990s"; Casey Mulligan and Yona Rubenstein, "Selection, Investment, and Women's Relative Wages Since 1975," NBER Working Paper No. 11159 (2005).

82. See Stone, "Getting to Equal."

The Sources of the Gender Pay Gap

1. U.S. Department of Labor, Bureau of Labor Statistics, "2011 Employment & Earnings Online," available at http://www.bls.gov/opub/ee/2011/cps/annual .htm; and Francine D. Blau, Marianne A. Ferber, and Anne E. Winkler, *The Economics of Women, Men, and Work*, 6th ed. (Upper Saddle River, NJ: Pearson/Prentice-Hall, 2010), 142.

2. Jacob Mincer and Solomon Polachek, "Family Investments in Human Capital: Earnings of Women," *Journal of Political Economy* 82 (March/April 1974, pt. 2).

3. Gary S. Becker, "Human Capital, Effort, and the Sexual Division of Labor," *Journal of Labor Economics* 3 (January 1985 Supp.). A number of studies have found that additional hours spent in housework by workers are associated with lower wages, all else equal (e.g., Joni Hersh and Leslie Stratton, "Housework, Fixed Effects and Wages of Married Workers," *Journal of Human Resources* 32 (Spring 1997)), although, using self-reports of effort levels, Denise D. Bielby and William T. Bielby ("She Works Hard for the Money: Household Responsibilities and the Allocation of Work Effort," *American Journal of Sociology* 93 (March 1988)) do not find that women put in less effort. See also, Mick Cunningham, "Influences of Gender Ideology and Housework Allocation on Women's Employment over the Life Course," *Social Science Research* 37 (2007), for an analysis of the effects of housework on women's labor force participation over the life course.

4. While firms may perceive that women are more likely to quit than men, the preponderance of the economic evidence on this question finds that, controlling for qualifications and pay, women are no more likely to quit their jobs than men (e.g., Francine D. Blau and Lawrence M. Kahn, "Race and Sex Differences in Quits by Young Workers," *Industrial & Labor Relations Review* 34 (July 1981); Michael Ransom and Ronald L. Oaxaca, "Intrafirm Mobility and Sex Differences in Pay," *Industrial and Labor Relations Review* 58 (January 2005)). However, gender differences in quitting do still indirectly contribute to the gender pay gap because women are more likely than men to quit their jobs to exit the labor force; this intermittency contributes to the gender pay gap. See, for example, J. L. Hotchkiss and M. Melinda Pitts, "The Role of Labor Market Intermittency in Explaining Gender Wage Differentials," *American Economic Review* 97 (2007).

5. See, for example, Barbara F. Reskin, "The Proximate Causes of Employment Discrimination," *Contemporary Sociology* 29 (March 2000); and Marianne Bertrand, Dolly Chugh, and Sendhil Mullainathan, "Implicit Discrimination," *American Economic Review* 95 (May 2005).

6. As discussed ahead, Gary S. Becker, *The Economics of Discrimination*, 2nd ed. (Chicago: University of Chicago Press, 1971; 1st ed. 1957), played an extremely important role in shaping economists' analyses of discrimination. For a more detailed discussion of the various models, see Blau, Ferber, and Winkler, *The Economics of Women, Men, and Work*.

7. Gary S. Becker, *The Economics of Discrimination*.

8. Ronald G. Ehrenberg and Robert S. Smith, *Modern Labor Economics: Theory and Public Policy*, 11th ed. (New York: Pearson/Addison Wesley, 2011).

9. Two recently proposed models of discrimination suggest alternative motivations for male employees to discriminate against female coworkers than the personal prejudices assumed in the Becker model, particularly for resisting the introduction of women into traditionally male occupations. In one, occupations are associated with societal notions of "male" and "female," leading men to

resist the entry of women due to the loss in male identity (or sense of self) that this would entail; see George A. Akerlof and Rachel E. Kranton, "Economics and Identity," *Quarterly Journal of Economics* 115 (August 2000). In the second, the entry of women would reduce the prestige of the occupation, based on perceptions that women are, on average, less productive; see Claudia Goldin, "A Pollution Theory of Discrimination: Male and Female Differences in Occupations and Earnings," National Bureau of Economic Research Working Paper 8985 (June 2002).

10. Dan A. Black, "Discrimination in an Equilibrium Search Model," *Journal of Labor Economics* 13 (April 1995). See also Janice F. Madden, *The Economics of Sex Discrimination* (Lexington, MA: Lexington Books, 1973), one of the first analyses of the impact of monopsony on the gender wage gap.

11. A problem with the monopsony explanation, however, is that it requires that women's labor supply to the *firm* be less sensitive to wages than men's. Yet, women's labor supply to the *market* tends to more sensitive than men's; see, e.g., Francine D. Blau and Lawrence M. Kahn, "Changes in the Labor Supply Behavior of Married Women: 1980–2000," *Journal of Labor Economics* 25 (July 2007). While proponents of the monopsony view do suggest plausible reasons why women's mobility at the firm level may be reduced, these may or may not be sufficient to outweigh women's greater overall wage elasticity of labor supply to the market. After reviewing results from three studies of the quit behavior of men and women, Lawrence Kahn and I find no evidence that men's labor supply is more sensitive to wages than women's at the firm level; see, Francine D. Blau and Lawrence M. Kahn, "Institutions and Laws in the Labor Market," in *Handbook of Labor Economics*, ed. Orley Ashenfelter and David Card (The Netherlands: Elsevier Science, 1999). However, some recent evidence is emerging that is more consistent with a role for monopsony; see, for example, Michael R. Ransom and Ronald L. Oaxaca, "New Market Power Models and Sex Differences in Pay," *Journal of Labor Economics* 28 (April 2010).

12. Models of statistical discrimination have also considered the situation in which female workers' productivity or behavior is less reliably predicted than that of male workers; this can also result in gender differences in outcomes.

13. Dennis J. Aigner and Glen G. Cain, "Statistical Theories of Discrimination in Labor Markets," *Industrial and Labor Relations Review* 30 (1977).

14. For an interesting exploration of these issues, see Stefania Albanesi and Claudia Olivetti, "Home Production, Market Production and the Gender Wage Gap: Incentives and Expectations," *Review of Economic Dynamics* 12 (January 2009).

15. Chinhui Juhn, Kevin M. Murphy, and Brooks Pierce, "Accounting for the Slowdown in Black-White Wage Convergence," in *Workers and Their Wages*, ed. Marvin Kosters (Washington, DC: AEI Press, 1991).

16. Francine D. Blau and Lawrence M. Kahn, "Wage Structure and Gender Earnings Differentials: An International Comparison," *Economica* 63 (1996,

Supp.); "Gender Differences in Pay," *Journal of Economic Perspectives* 14 (Fall 2000); and "The US Gender Pay Gap in the 1990s: Slowing Convergence," *Industrial and Labor Relations Review* 60 (October 2006).

17. E.g., Bruce Weinberg, "Computer Use and the Demand for Female Workers," *Industrial and Labor Relations Review* 53 (January 2000).

18. See Lex Borghans, Bas ter Weel, and Bruce A. Weinberg, "People People: Social Capital and the Labor-Market Outcomes of Underrepresented Groups," National Bureau of Economic Research Work Paper No. 11985 (January 2006).

19. Francine D. Blau and Lawrence M. Kahn, "The US Gender Pay Gap in the 1990s"; for a summary of this literature, see Joseph G. Altonji and Rebecca M. Blank, "Race and Gender in the Labor Market," in *Handbook of Labor Economics*, ed. Orley Ashenfelter and David Card (The Netherlands: Elsevier Science, 1999).

20. Note that because PSID wage data are not available for 1999, the two periods are of slightly unequal length. In Blau and Kahn, "The US Gender Pay Gap in the 1990s," we calculate decade-equivalent changes for the 1980s and the 1990s, and this does not change the conclusions that I describe in the text here.

21. Ibid.

22. Ibid.

23. Ibid. Shifts in labor force composition due to the pattern of labor force entries and exits also appear to have played a role. We find that, controlling for measured human capital, female labor force entrants were less skilled during the 1990s than during the 1980s, perhaps as a result of the entry of many relatively low-skilled, female single-family heads in the latter decade. Indeed, our results suggest that differences between the two periods in such shifts in labor force composition explain as much as 25 percent of the apparent slowdown in convergence in the unexplained gender wage gap in the 1990s (see Francine D. Blau and Lawrence M. Kahn, "The US Gender Pay Gap in the 1990s"). See also Casey B. Mulligan and Yona Rubinstein, "Selection, Investment, and Women's Relative Wages Since 1975," *Quarterly Journal of Economics* 123 (August 2008), who give a larger role to selection in explaining the trends over 1975–2001.

24. Blau, Ferber, and Winkler, *The Economics of Women, Men, and Work*.

25. Mary C. Noonan, Mary E. Corcoran, and Paul Courant, "Pay Differences Among the Highly Trained: Cohort Differences in the Sex Gap in Lawyers' Earnings," *Social Forces* 84 (December 2005).

26. Catherine J. Weinberger, "Race and Gender Wage Gaps in the Market for Recent College Graduates," *Industrial Relations* 37 (January 1998). See also Dan A. Black, Amelia M. Haviland, Seth G. Sanders, and Lowell J. Taylor, "Gender Wage Disparities Among the Highly Educated," *Journal of Human Resources* 43 (Summer 2008), who report broadly similar results for white and black women, although mixed evidence for Hispanic and Asian women (all relative to white, non-Hispanic men).

27. David M. Neumark, "Sex Discrimination in Restaurant Hiring: An Audit Study," *Quarterly Journal of Economics* 111 (August 1996).

28. Claudia Goldin and Cecilia Rouse, "Orchestrating Impartiality: The Impact of 'Blind' Auditions on Female Musicians," *American Economic Review* 90 (September 2000).

29. A third study, again based on a hiring audit, showed that employers discriminated against mothers but not fathers; see, Shelley J. Correll, Stephen Benard, and In Paik, "Getting a Job: Is There a Motherhood Penalty?," *American Journal of Sociology* 112 (March 2007).

30. Gary S. Becker, *The Economics of Discrimination.*

31. Judith K. Hellerstein, David Neumark, and Kenneth Troske, "Market Forces and Sex Discrimination," *Journal of Human Resources* 37 (Spring 2002).

32. Sandra E. Black and Philip E. Strahan, "The Division of Spoils: Rent-Sharing and Discrimination in a Regulated Industry," *American Economic Review* 91 (September 2001).

33. Sandra E. Black and Elizabeth Brainerd, "The Impact of Globalization on Gender Discrimination," *Industrial & Labor Relations Review* 57 (July 2004).

34. Claudia Goldin, *Understanding the Gender Gap* (New York: Oxford University Press, 1990).

35. "Sex Suit Costs Morgan Stanley $54M," July 12, 2004, http://www.cbsnews.com/stories/2004/07/12/national/main628907.shtml?tag=mncol;lst;1 and Patrick McGeehan, "Discrimination on Wall St.? Run the Numbers and Weep," *New York Times*, July 14, 2004, Section C, pp. 1, 7.

36. Bureau of National Affairs, "American Express Financial Advisors Reach $31 Million Agreement on Sex Bias Charges," *Employment Discrimination Report* 18, no. 9 (February 27, 2002): 251.

37. "Government to pay $508 million for sex discrimination at U.S. Information Agency," *Federal Human Resources Week* 6 (2000): 47.

38. Ronette King, "Women Taking Action Against Many Companies," *Times-Picayune*, April 27, 1997.

39. Ransom and Oaxaca, "Intrafirm Mobility and Sex Differences in Pay."

40. Ibid., 219.

A Dream Deferred: Toward the U.S. Racial Future

1. Gunnar Myrdal, *An American Dilemma: The Negro Problem and Modern Democracy* (New York: Harper and Row, 1962 [1944]).

2. Ralph Ellison, "An American Dilemma: A Review," in *Shadow and Act* (New York: Random House, 1964).

3. Myrdal's *An American Dilemma* in this sense anticipated his later work on underdevelopment. See Gunnar Myrdal, *Economic Theory and Underdeveloped Regions* (New York: Harper and Row, 1971).

4. See Mary L. Dudziak, *Cold War Civil Rights: Race and the Image of American Democracy* (Princeton, NJ: Princeton University Press, 2000); Thomas Borstelmann, *The Cold War and the Color Line: American Race Relations in the Global Arena* (Cambridge, MA: Harvard University Press, 2002); Robin D. G. Kelley, *Race Rebels: Culture, Politics, and the Black Working Class* (New York: Free Press, 1994).

5. See, e.g., Richard D. Alba and Victor Nee, *Remaking the American Mainstream: Assimilation and Contemporary Immigration* (Cambridge, MA: Harvard University Press, 2003); Alejandro Portes and Rubén G. Rumbaut, *Immigrant America: A Portrait*, 3rd ed. (Berkeley: University of California Press, 2006); Min Zhou, "Contemporary Immigration and the Dynamics of Race and Ethnicity," in *America Becoming: Racial Trends and Their Consequences*, Volume I, ed. Neil Smelser et al., Commission on Behavioral and Social Sciences and Education, National Research Council (Washington, DC: National Academy Press, 2001).

6. Howard Winant, *The World Is a Ghetto: Race and Democracy Since World War II* (New York: Basic Books, 2001).

7. Robert C. Lieberman, *Shifting the Color Line: Race and the American Welfare State*, 2nd ed. (Cambridge, MA: Harvard University Press, 2001).

8. Marc Mauer, *Race to Incarcerate*, 2nd ed. (New York: New Press, 2006); Bruce Western, *Punishment and Inequality in America* (New York: Russell Sage Foundation, 2006); see also Angela Y. Davis, *Are Prisons Obsolete?* (New York: Seven Stories Press, 2003); Ruth Wilson Gilmore, *Golden Gulag: Prisons, Surplus, Crisis, and Opposition in Globalizing California* (Berkeley: University of California Press, 2007).

9. See Lawrence Bobo, "What Do You Call a Black Man with a Ph.D.?," in *The Inequality Reader*, ed. David B. Grusky and Szonja Szelényi, 2nd ed. (Boulder, CO: Westview Press, 2011); Thomas J. Sugrue, *Not Even Past: Barack Obama and the Burden of Race* (Princeton, NJ: Princeton University Press, 2010); David Remnick, *The Bridge: The Life and Rise of Barack Obama* (New York: Knopf, 2010); David Roediger, *How Race Survived US History: From Settlement and Slavery to the Obama Phenomenon* (New York: Verso, 2008); Clarence Lusane, *The Black History of the White House* (San Francisco: City Lights Books, 2011).

10. "State and County QuickFacts," U.S. Census Bureau, Internet report, January 12, 2007, http://quickfacts.census.gov/qfd/states/15000.html.

11. Population projections are notoriously iffy. In 2004 the U.S. Census Bureau estimated that in 2050 the proportion of the U.S. population designated as "Whites, non-Hispanic" would comprise 50.1 percent of the total U.S. population. See "Projected Population of the United States, by Race and Hispanic Origin: 2000 to 2050," Table 1A, U.S. Census Bureau, Population Division, Population Projections Branch, March 18, 2004, http://www.census.gov/ipc/www/usinterimproj/.

12. Nancy J. Weiss, *Farewell to the Party of Lincoln: Black Politics in the Age of FDR* (Princeton, NJ: Princeton University Press, 1983); Ira Katznelson, *When Affirmative Action Was White: An Untold History of Racial Inequality in Twentieth-Century America* (New York: Norton, 2005).

13. Ian Haney Lopez, *Racism on Trial: The Chicano Fight for Justice* (Cambridge, MA: Harvard University Press, 2003).

14. Robin Jacobson, *The New Nativism: Proposition 187 and the Debate over Immigration* (Minneapolis: University of Minnesota Press, 2008); Kent A. Ono and John M. Sloop, *Shifting Borders: Rhetoric, Immigration, and California's Proposition 187* (Philadelphia: Temple University Press, 2002); Dale Maharidge, *The Coming White Minority: California, Multiculturalism, and America's Future* (New York: Vintage, 1999); Daniel HoSang, *Racial Propositions: Ballot Initiatives and the Making of Postwar California* (Berkeley: University of California Press, 2010).

15. William Kandel and Emilio A. Parrado, "Hispanics in the American South and the Transformation of the Poultry Industry," in *Hispanic Places, Latino Spaces: Community and Cultural Diversity in Contemporary America*, ed. Daniel D. Arreolam (Austin: University of Texas Press, 2004); Ann V. Millard and Jorge Chapa, *Apple Pie and Enchiladas: Latino Newcomers in the Rural Midwest* (Austin: University of Texas Press, 2004).

16. Tomás R. Jiménez, "Mexican Immigrant Replenishment and the Continuing Significance of Ethnicity and Race," *American Journal of Sociology* 113 (2008); Yen Le Espiritu, *Asian American Panethnicity: Bridging Institutions and Identities* (Philadelphia: Temple University Press, 1992); Dina Okamoto, "Toward a Theory of Panethnicity: Explaining Asian American Collective Action," *American Sociological Review* 68, no. 6 (2003).

17. Roger Waldinger, "The Bounded Community: Turning Foreigners into Americans in Twenty-First Century L.A.," *Ethnic and Racial Studies* 30, no. 3 (2007).

18. John Higham, *Strangers in the Land: Patterns of American Nativism, 1860–1925*, 2nd ed. (New Brunswick, NJ: Rutgers University Press, 2002).

19. Milton Gordon, *Assimilation in American Life: The Role of Race, Religion, and National Origins* (New York: Oxford University Press, 1964).

20. Alexander Saxton, *The Rise and Fall of the White Republic: Class Politics and Mass Culture in Nineteenth-Century America*, 2nd ed. (London: Verso, 2003); Jean Pfaelzer, *Driven Out: The Forgotten War Against Chinese Americans* (New York: Random House, 2007).

21. Francisco Balderrama and Raymond Rodríguez, *Decade of Betrayal: Mexican Repatriation in the 1930s*, rev. ed. (Albuquerque: University of New Mexico Press, 2006).

22. Lest we think that assaults upon the welfare state that disproportionately affect the "life-chances" of people of color began in 2000 with the *Bush v. Gore* case that decided the presidential election of that year (when the Supreme Court

invoked the Voting Rights Act to justify suspending the Florida vote recount),
let it be remembered that the same Bill Clinton whom Toni Morrison designated
"our first black president" also fulfilled his commitment to "end welfare as we
know it" in 1996 (Toni Morrison, "Clinton as the First Black President," *New
Yorker*, October 5, 1998). His welfare program (Temporary Assistance to Needy
Families (TANF)), which replaced the previous AFDC program, forced welfare
recipients (particularly women of color) into "workfare" jobs and substantially
eroded the well-being of low-income children across a wide range of health,
housing, education, and indeed survival issues. See Peter Edelman, "Welfare and
the Politics of Race: Same Tune, New Lyrics," *Georgetown Journal on Poverty
Law & Policy* 389 (2004).

23. John Charles Boger and Gary Orfield, eds., *School Resegregation: Must
the South Turn Back?* (Chapel Hill: University of North Carolina Press, 2005);
Chungmei Lee, "Denver Public Schools: Resegregation, Latino Style" (working
paper, The Civil Rights Project, Harvard University, 2006).

24. White flight and suburbanization also greatly exacerbated the
consumption of fossil fuels in the United States, contributing to tensions in the
Middle East as demand for imported oil skyrocketed, and also increasing global
warming. Race is a much more comprehensive social dynamic than is usually
recognized.

25. James O'Connor, *The Fiscal Crisis of the State* (New Brunswick, NJ:
Transaction, 2001 [1973]).

26. Calculated from Table M, U.S. Census Bureau, Current Population
Reports, *Population Projections of the United States by Age, Sex, Race, and
Hispanic Origin: 1995 to 2050*, issued February 1996, updated April 13, 1999,
16–17.

27. Richard D. Vogel, "Harder Times: Undocumented Workers and the U.S.
Informal Economy," *Monthly Review* 58, no. 3 (2006).

28. Mitra Toossi, "A Century of Change: The U.S. Labor Force, 1950–
2050," *Monthly Labor Review* 125, no. 5 (2002).

29. Social Security privatization was also presented as benefiting blacks, a
claim that was doubtful at best. See Peter Wallsten and Tom Hamburger, "Blacks
Courted on Social Security," *Los Angeles Times*, February 28, 2005; Paul
Krugman, "Little Black Lies," *New York Times*, January 28, 2005.

30. Thanks to Joe Feagin for suggesting these points to me.

31. David Kairys, "Unexplainable on Grounds Other than Race," *American
University Law Review* 45, no. 3 (1996).

32. A substantial literature has developed on whites' "beleaguered" sense
of racial identity. See Melanie Bush, *Breaking the Code of Good Intentions:
Everyday Forms of Whiteness* (Lanham, MD: Rowman and Littlefield, 2004);
David Roediger, *Colored White: Transcending the Racial Past* (Berkeley:
University of California Press, 2002); John Hartigan, Jr., *Racial Situations: Class
Predicaments of Whiteness in Detroit* (Princeton, NJ: Princeton University Press,

1999); Steve Martinot, *The Rule of Racialization: Class, Identity, Governance* (Philadelphia: Temple University Press, 2002).

33. Samuel P. Huntington, *Who Are We: The Challenges to America's National Identity* (New York: Simon and Schuster, 2005).

34. A contemporary social science version of this nightmare scenario, in which the ghetto and barrio converge with the prison, has been proposed by Loïc Wacquant in *Punishing the Poor: The Neoliberal Government of Social Insecurity* (Durham, NC: Duke University Press, 2009). This seemingly radical critique, however, conceals a hidden conservative message: if the black and brown poor are effectively in prison *already*, whether incarcerated or "free," what political agency is available to them? Wacquant is in effect arguing that the United States (and other countries as well) are fully established racial dictatorships. The United States has passed from slavery to Jim Crow to carcerality without any significant racial democratization at all.

35. Colorblindness is an abhorrent term, a neologism twice over. First and most obviously, it is rooted in an ophthalmic condition that has no relevance to race, unless we understand race as being "about" skin color, a deep reductionism in the term's meaning. Second, the term appears in the dissent of Justice John Marshall Harlan in the 1896 *Plessy* case, where the justice's insistence that "our Constitution is colorbind," coexists blissfully with a range of support claims for eternal white superiority and supremacy (see Neil Gotanda, "A Critique of 'Our Constitution Is Colorblind,'" in *Critical Race Theory: The Key Writings That Formed the Movement*, ed. Kimberlé Crenshaw et al. (New York: New Press, 1995)). A far better term has been suggested by my colleague France Winddance Twine: "race aversion."

36. My own work on racial formation has been one of the main manifestos for this position. See Michael Omi and Howard Winant, *Racial Formation in the United States: From the 1960s to the 1990s*, 2nd ed. (New York: Routledge, 1994).

37. These lines, much trumpeted by neoconservative advocates of colorblindness, can be harnessed to that cause only if they are entirely removed from their context. One such context is the speech itself, which is all about ongoing racial injustice. The speech must also be understood in its broader sociohistorical context: Dr. King's fundamental claim that U.S. society has failed to deliver on its promise of freedom. "Instead of honoring this sacred obligation, America has given the Negro people a bad check which has come back marked 'insufficient funds.'" Noting the distortions and perversions of Dr. King's "I Have a Dream" speech, Mike Dyson once proposed a ten-year moratorium on it (Michael Eric Dyson, *I May Not Get There with You: The True Martin Luther King, Jr.* [New York: Free Press, 2001]). That moratorium has now expired.

38. Other speakers included John Lewis, Roy Wilkins, Whitney Young Jr., and A. Philip Randolph, as well as various religious figures (Protestant, Catholic, and Jewish). Josephine Baker was the only woman who spoke; she also intro-

duced Rosa Parks. Marian Anderson, Joan Baez, Bob Dylan, Mahalia Jackson, Peter, Paul, and Mary, and Josh White sang. Charlton Heston spoke as the representative of an assemblage of Hollywood celebrities in attendance, including Harry Belafonte, Marlon Brando, Diahann Carroll, Ossie Davis, Sammy Davis Jr., Lena Horne, Paul Newman, and Sidney Poitier, who read a speech by James Baldwin. Roy Wilkins announced the death in Ghana of W. E. B. Du Bois.

39. For good overview material, see Alice O'Connor, Chris Tilly, and Lawrence Bobo, ed., *Urban Inequality: Evidence from Four Cities* (New York: Russell Sage Foundation, 2001). For data on residential segregation, see Krysan et al., "Does Race Matter in Neighborhood Preferences? Results from a Video Experiment," *American Journal of Sociology* 115, no. 2 (2009); Ming Wen, Diane S. Lauderdale, and Namratha R. Kandula, "Ethnic Neighborhoods in Multi-ethnic America, 1990–2000: Ethnoburbs and a Resurgence of Ethnicity?" *Social Forces* 88, no. 1 (2009); John Iceland and Daniel H. Weinberg with Erika Steinmetz, "Racial and Ethnic Residential Segregation in the United States: 1980– 2000," *US Bureau of the Census Special Report* (Washington, DC: Government Printing Office, August 2002); Douglas S. Massey, "Residential Segregation and Neighborhood Conditions in US Metropolitan Areas," in Neil J. Smelser, William Julius Wilson, and Faith Mitchell, eds., *America Becoming: Racial Trends and Their Consequences*, vol. 1 (Washington, DC: National Academies Press, 2001); Douglas S. Massey and Nancy A. Denton, *American Apartheid: Segregation and the Making of the Underclass* (Cambridge, MA: Harvard University Press, 1993). For data on incarceration, see Mauer, *Race to Incarcerate*; Western, *Punishment and Inequality in America*. For data on educational segregation, see Salvatore Saporito and Deenesh Sohoni, "Mapping Educational Inequality: Concentrations of Poverty Among Poor and Minority Students in Public Schools," *Social Forces* 85, no. 3 (2007); Gary Orfield and John T. Yun, *Resegregation in American Schools* (Cambridge, MA: The Civil Rights Project, Harvard University, 1999). For data on workplace segregation, see Judith Hellerstein and David Neumark, "Workplace Segregation in the United States: Race, Ethnicity, and Skill," NBER Working Paper No. 11599 (2005). For data on black-white economic inequality, see Melvin L. Oliver and Thomas M. Shapiro, *Black Wealth/White Wealth: A New Perspective on Racial Inequality*, 2nd ed. (New York: Routledge, 2006). For data on racial attitudes and racial politics, see Maria Krysan, "Data Update to *Racial Attitudes in America*," an update and website to complement Howard Schuman, Charlotte Steeh, Lawrence Bobo, and Maria Krysan, *Racial Attitudes in America: Trends and Interpretations, Revised Edition* (Cambridge, MA: Harvard University Press, 1997), http://www.igpa.uillinois.edu/programs/ racial-attitudes/; Lawrence Bobo, "Racial Attitudes and Relations at the Close of the Twentieth Century," in Smelser, Wilson, and Mitchell, eds., *America Becoming: Racial Trends and Their Consequences*, vol. 1 (Washington, DC: National Academies Press, 2001).

40. Melvin L. Oliver and Thomas M. Shapiro, *Black Wealth/White Wealth: A New Perspective on Racial Inequality*, 2nd ed. (New York: Routledge, 2006). By 2010 this "wealth gap" had increased significantly, as economic recession took a heavier toll on black and brown families, and as default on debt—especially mortgage debt, but also student debt and consumer debt—accelerated rapidly. African-American and Latino families were particularly damaged by the subprime mortgage crisis; see Thomas Shapiro, Tatjana Meschede, and Laura Sullivan, "The Racial Wealth Gap Increases Fourfold" (research and policy brief, Institute on Assets and Social Policy, Brandeis University, May 2010); Mazher Ali et al., "State of the Dream 2011" (Boston: United for a Fair Economy, 2011).

41. Orfield and Yun, *Resegregation in American Schools*.

42. The Border Protection, Antiterrorism, and Illegal Immigration Control Act—HR 4437, also known as the Sensenbrenner bill—was passed by the House of Representatives in 2005 but subsequently died in the Senate. The bill was a major factor triggering immigrants' rights protests by and on behalf of the estimated twelve million undocumented immigrants currently residing in the United States (see Nicholas Confessore, "Immigration Debates Mirror Concerns in Washington," *New York Times*, March 26, 2006). Some of the objectives of the 2005 initiative are now being achieved by the Obama administration's aggressive enforcement of the "Secure Communities" program, an effort by the Immigration and Customs Enforcement division of the Department of Homeland Security to step up the deportation rate. Arizona's SB 1070 law, which empowered state officials to act as immigration enforcement officers, is now (as of mid-2011) tied up in the courts. A recent U.S. Supreme Court ruling, *Chamber of Commerce v. Whiting* (563 U.S. 09-115 [2011]), upheld the right of a state (Arizona again) to revoke the business license of an employer who hires an undocumented worker.

43. "An adolescent white male at a bar mitzvah wears a FUBU shirt while his white friend preens his perfectly braided corn rows. A black model dressed in yachting attire peddles a New England yuppie boating look in Nautica advertisements . . . White, black, and Asian students decorate their bodies with tattoos of Chinese characters and symbols. In cities and suburbs, young adults across the color line wear hip-hop clothing and listen to white rapper Eminem and black rapper Jay-Z. A north Georgia branch of the NAACP installs a white biology professor as its president. The music of Jimi Hendrix is used to sell Apple computers" (Charles A. Gallagher, "Color Blind Privilege: The Social and Political Functions of Erasing the Color Line in Post-Race America," in idem, ed., *Rethinking the Color Line: Readings in Race and Ethnicity*, 3rd ed. [New York: McGraw-Hill, 2007], 130). See also Ralph Ellison: "What is one to make of a white youngster who, with a transistor radio screaming a Stevie Wonder tune glued to his ear, shouts racial epithets at black youngsters trying to swim at a public beach?" (*Going to the Territory* [New York: Random House, 1986], 21).

44. Michael Brown et al., *White-Washing Race: The Myth of a Color-Blind Society* (Berkeley: University of California Press, 2003); Eduardo Bonilla-Silva, *Racism Without Racists: Color-Blind Racism and the Persistence of Racial Inequality in the United States*, 2nd ed. (Lanham, MD: Rowman and Littlefield, 2006).

45. The transition from racial domination to racial hegemony may be understood as the key achievement of the civil rights era in the United States. Hegemony is understood here in the Gramscian sense of rule through incorporation of opposition:

> In other words, the dominant group is coordinated concretely with the general interests of the subordinate groups, and the life of the state is conceived of as a continuous process of formation and superseding of unstable equilibria . . . between the interests of the fundamental group and those of the subordinate groups—equilibria in which the interests of the dominant group prevail, but only up to a certain point. (Antonio Gramsci, *Selections from the Prison Notebooks*, ed. Quinton Hoare and Geoffrey Nowell-Smith [New York: International Publishers, 1971], 182)

46. There are of course many forms of race-consciousness that I neglect here; these are generally rooted in pre–civil rights era frameworks: unreconstructed white supremacism; biologistic racism; "new right" race-baiters (think Lee Atwater, for example); authoritarian nationalists (see Paul Gilroy, *Against Race: Imagining Political Culture Beyond the Color Line* [Cambridge, MA: Harvard University Press, 2000]). For an earlier attempt to inventory varieties of white race-consciousness, see Howard Winant, "Behind Blue Eyes: Whiteness and Contemporary U.S. Racial Politics," *New Left Review* 225 (September/October 1997).

47. For a recent critique of "groupism," see Rogers Brubaker, *Ethnicity Without Groups* (Cambridge, MA: Harvard University Press, 2004). Brubaker quite properly insists on the sociohistorical constructedness (and hence flexibility in practice) of group identities such as ethnicity, race, and nationality. But he overreaches in his call for dispensing with such collective categories as units of analysis. Indeed, Brubaker cannot avoid employing such categorizations himself. Efforts to dispense with "groupism" are necessarily self-refuting. For a better sociological account of racial "groupism," see Herbert Blumer, "Race Prejudice as a Sense of Group Position," *Pacific Sociological Review* 1, no. 1 (Spring 1958).

48. Michael J. Rosenfeld, "Racial, Educational, and Religious Endogamy in the United States: A Comparative-Historical Perspective," *Social Forces* 87 (2008); G. Reginald Daniel, *More Than Black? Multiracial Identity and the New Racial Order* (Philadelphia: Temple University Press, 2001); David Parker and Miri Song, ed., *Rethinking "Mixed Race"* (London: Pluto, 2001).

49. These questions, raised in sketchy and preliminary fashion here, are the central concerns of Paul Gilroy's recent work (*Against Race*). While my argument differs in important ways from his, I share his critique of "unanimism," admire his profound humanism, and learn from his insistence on the ludic qualities of politics.

50. For a sampling of classic neoconservative raciology, see Mark Gerson, ed., *The Essential Neoconservative Reader* (New York: Addison-Wesley, 1996).

51. Hans Joas, *The Creativity of Action*, trans. Jeremy Gaines and Paul Keast (Chicago: University of Chicago Press, 1996).

52. On the moral significance of "the other," see Emmanuel Levinas, *Totality and Infinity: An Essay on Exteriority*, trans. Alphonso Lingis (Pittsburgh: Duquesne University Press, 1969).

53. john a. powell, "Lessons from Suffering: How Social Justice Informs Spirituality," *University of St. Thomas Law Journal* 1 (2003).

54. On this last matter, consider Condoleezza Rice:

We should never indulge in the condescending voices that allege that some people are not interested in freedom or aren't ready for freedom's responsibility. That view was wrong in 1963 in Birmingham, and it's wrong in 2004 in Baghdad. (Condoleezza Rice, "Remarks by the National Security Advisor Condoleezza Rice," Vanderbilt University Commencement Address, May 13, 2004, http://www.whitehouse.gov/news/releases/2004/05/20040517.html)

Critique seems superfluous: the spirit of Dr. King recalls his attacks on the Vietnam War as he rolls in his grave. Rice dares to invoke the racial justice campaign he led (in Rice's hometown) to justify a U.S. war of aggression against another poor—and surely non-white—nation.

55. Troy Duster, "Explaining Differential Trust of DNA Forensic Technology: Grounded Assessment or Inexplicable Paranoia?," *Journal of Law, Medicine & Ethics* 34, no. 2 (2006); "Lessons from History: Why Race and Ethnicity Have Played a Major Role in Biomedical Research," *Journal of Law, Medicine & Ethics* 34, no. 3 (2006); "Race and Reification in Science," *Science* 307, February 18, 2005.

56. Jonathan Kozol, *Savage Inequalities: Children in America's Schools* (New York: Harper, 1992).

57. Luke Cole and Sheila Foster, *From the Ground Up: Environmental Racism and the Rise of the Environmental Justice Movement* (New York: New York University Press, 2000); Robert D. Bullard, *The Quest For Environmental Justice: Human Rights and the Politics of Pollution* (San Francisco: Sierra Club Books, 2005); Kristin Shrader-Frechette, *Environmental Justice: Creating Equity, Reclaiming Democracy* (New York: Oxford University Press, 2002).

Racial and Ethnic Diversity and Public Policy

1. William Z. Ripley, "Races in the US," *Atlantic Monthly*, December 1908.

2. Henry Cabot Lodge, "Restriction of Immigration," Speech to the United States Senate, Congressional Record, March 16, 1896, p. 2819.

3. David R. Roediger, *The Wages of Whiteness: Race and the Making of the American Working Class* (London: Verso, 1999); Noel Ignatiev, *How the Irish Became White* (New York: Routledge, 1995); Matthew Frye Jacobson, *Whiteness*

of a Different Color: European Immigrants and the Alchemy of Race (Cambridge, MA: Harvard University Press, 1999); Mae M. Ngai, *Impossible Subjects: Illegal Aliens and the Making of Modern America* (Princeton, NJ: Princeton University Press, 2004); Thomas A. Guglielmo, *White on Arrival: Italians, Race, Color, and Power in Chicago, 1890–1945* (Oxford: Oxford University Press, 2003).

4. See Mary C. Waters, *Ethnic Options: Choosing Identities in America* (Berkeley: University of California Press, 1990); Richard Alba, *Ethnic Identity: The Transformation of White America* (New Haven, CT: Yale University Press, 1990); Herbert H. Gans, "The Possibility of a New Racial Hierarchy in the Twenty-First-Century United States," in *The Cultural Territories of Race: Black and White Boundaries*, ed. M. Lamont (Chicago: University of Chicago Press, 1999).

5. Roberto Suro and Jeffrey S. Passel, "The Rise of the Second Generation: Changing Patterns in Hispanic Population Growth" (Washington, DC: Pew Hispanic Center Study, 2003), 6.

6. Steven Warner, "Immigrants and the Faith They Bring," *The Christian Century*, February 10, 2004.

7. W. E. B. Du Bois, *The Souls of Black Folk: Essays and Sketches* (New York: Blue Heron Press, 1953), vii.

8. Scholars of race and ethnicity, such as Herbert Gans in "The Possibility of a New Racial Hierarchy," hypothesized that the emergent division in the twenty-first century may not be between blacks and whites but rather between blacks and non-blacks. Other scholars like Mia Tuan in *Forever Foreigners or Honorary Whites?: The Asian Ethnic Experience Today* (New Brunswick, NJ: Rutgers University Press, 1998) contend that certain racial groups such as Asians would remain "forever foreigners" and not be so easily absorbed into one side or the other of the color line.

9. Mary C. Waters, *Black Identities: West Indian Immigrant Dreams and American Realities* (Cambridge, MA: Harvard University Press, 1999).

10. Orlando Patterson, "Four Modes of Ethno-Somatic Stratification: The Experience of Blacks in Europe and the Americas," in *Ethnicity, Social Mobility, and Public Policy: Comparing the US and UK*, ed. G. C. Loury, T. Modood, and S. M. Teles (Cambridge: Cambridge University Press, 2005).

11. John David Skrentny, *The Minority Rights Revolution* (Cambridge, MA: Belknap Press of Harvard University Press, 2002), 100.

12. Skrentny, *The Minority Rights Revolution*.

13. Shannon Harper and Barbara Reskin, "Affirmative Action at School and on the Job," *Annual Review of Sociology* 31 (2005).

14. Skrentny, *The Minority Rights Revolution*.

15. Hugh Davis Graham, "Affirmative Action for Immigrants? The Unintended Consequences of Reform," in *Color Lines: Affirmative Action, Immigrants, and Civil Rights Options for America*, ed. J. D. Skrentny (Chicago: University of Chicago Press, 2001), 64.

16. Graham, "Affirmative Action for Immigrants?"

17. Harper and Reskin, "Affirmative Action at School and on the Job," 365.

18. Harper and Reskin, "Affirmative Action at School and on the Job."

19. Ibid.

20. Ibid., 363–64.

21. Peter H. Schuck, *Diversity in America: Keeping Government at a Safe Distance* (Cambridge, MA: Belknap Press of Harvard University Press, 2003).

22. Mary C. Waters and Karl Eschbach, "Immigration and Ethnic and Racial Inequality in the United States," *Annual Review of Sociology* 21 (1995).

23. Joel Perlmann and Mary C. Waters, ed., *The New Race Question: How the Census Counts Multiracial Individuals* (New York: Russell Sage Foundation, 2002).

24. Joel Perlmann and Mary C. Waters, "Intermarriage Then and Now: Race, Generation and the Changing Meaning of Marriage," in *Not Just Black and White: Historical and Contemporary Perspectives on Immigration, Race and Ethnicity in the United States*, ed. Nancy Foner and George Frederickson (New York: Russell Sage Foundation, 2004).

25. See Joshua Goldstein and Ann Morning, "Back in the Box: The Dilemma of Using Multiple Race Data for Single Race Laws," Roderick Harrison, "Inadequacies of the Multiple Response Data in the Federal Statistical System," and Kenneth Prewitt, "Race in the 2000 Census: A Turning Point," in *The New Race Question: How the Census Counts Multiracial Individuals*, ed. Joel Perlmann and Mary C. Waters (New York: Russell Sage Foundation, 2002).

26. Quoted in Jennifer Hochschild, "Multiple Racial Identifiers in the 2000 Census, and Then What?" in *The New Race Question: How the Census Counts Multiracial Individuals*, ed. Perlmann and Waters, 340.

27. Schuck, *Diversity in America*.

28. Graham, "Affirmative Action for Immigrants?"

29. Sara Rimer and Karen Arensen, "Top Colleges Take More Blacks, but Which Ones?," *New York Times*, June 24, 2004.

30. Massey et al., *The Source of the River: The Social Origins of Freshmen at America's Selective Colleges and Universities* (Princeton, NJ: Princeton University Press, 2003).

31. Kasinitz et al., *Inheriting the City: The Children of Immigrants Come of Age* (Cambridge, MA: Harvard University Press, 2008).

32. James Smith, "Assimilation Across the Latino Generations," *American Economic Review* 93, no. 2, pp. 315–319; Julie Park and Dowell Myers, "Intergenerational Mobility in the Post-1965 Immigration Era: Estimates by an Immigrant Generation Cohort Method," *Demography* 47 (May 2010): 369–92; Joel Perlmann, *Italians Then, Mexicans Now: Immigrant Origins and Second Generation Progress, 1890–2000* (New York: Russell Sage Foundation, 2005).

33. Christian Joppke and Ewa Morawska, ed., *Toward Assimilation and Citizenship: Immigrants in Liberal Nation States* (New York: Palgrave, 2003); see also Alexander Aleinikoff, "Between National and Postnational: Membership in the United States," in that volume.

34. Sheldon Danziger and Peter Gottschalk, "Diverging Fortunes: Trends in Poverty and Inequality," in *The American People: Census 2000*, ed. Reynolds Farley and John Haaga (New York: Russell Sage Foundation, 2005), 50.

35. Gabriel Lenz, "The Policy-Related Causes and Consequences of Income Inequality" (New York: Russell Sage Foundation Working Paper, 2003).

Italic page numbers indicate material in tables or figures.

STUDIES IN SOCIAL INEQUALITY